ADOBE® PHOTOSHOP® LIGHTROOM® 2

D1119325

CLASSROOM IN A BOOK®

The official training workbook from Adobe Systems

www.adobepress.com

Adobe

Lesson files . . . and so much more

The *Adobe Photoshop Lightroom 2 Classroom in a Book* CD includes the lesson files that you'll need to complete the exercises in this book, as well as other content to help you learn more about Adobe Photoshop Lightroom and use it with greater efficiency and ease. The diagram below represents the contents of the CD, which should help you locate the files you need.

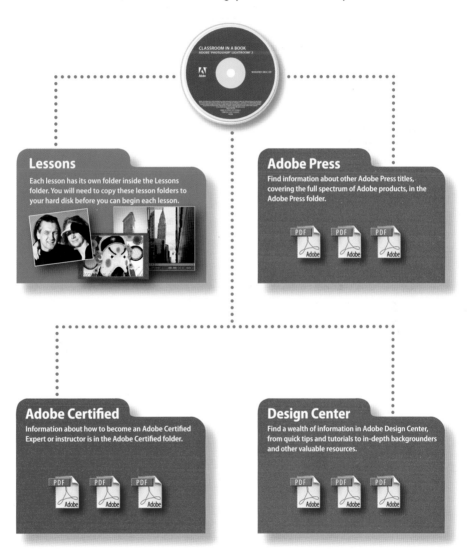

Lessons

Each lesson has its own folder inside the Lessons folder. You will need to copy these lesson folders to your hard disk before you can begin each lesson.

Adobe Press

Find information about other Adobe Press titles, covering the full spectrum of Adobe products, in the Adobe Press folder.

Adobe Certified

Information about how to become an Adobe Certified Expert or instructor is in the Adobe Certified folder.

Design Center

Find a wealth of information in Adobe Design Center, from quick tips and tutorials to in-depth backgrounders and other valuable resources.

Contents

Getting Started

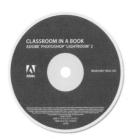

1 A Quick Tour of Photoshop Lightroom

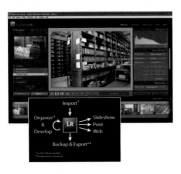

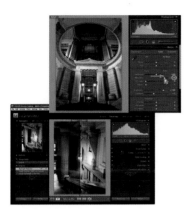

2 Introducing the Workspace

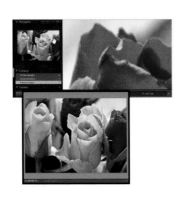

3 Importing

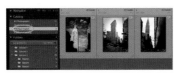

4 Reviewing

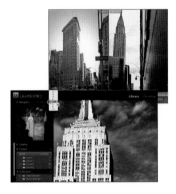

5   Organizing and Selecting

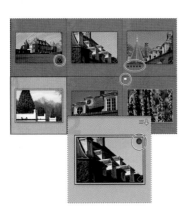

6 Developing and Editing

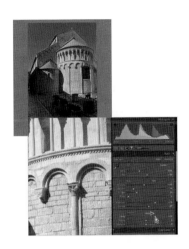

7 **Creating Slideshows**

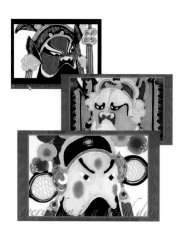

8 **Printing Images**

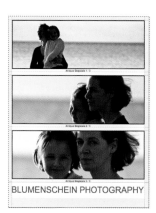

9   Publishing your Photos on the Web

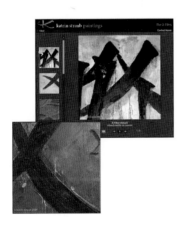

10 Creating Backups and Exporting Photos

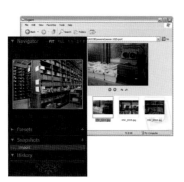

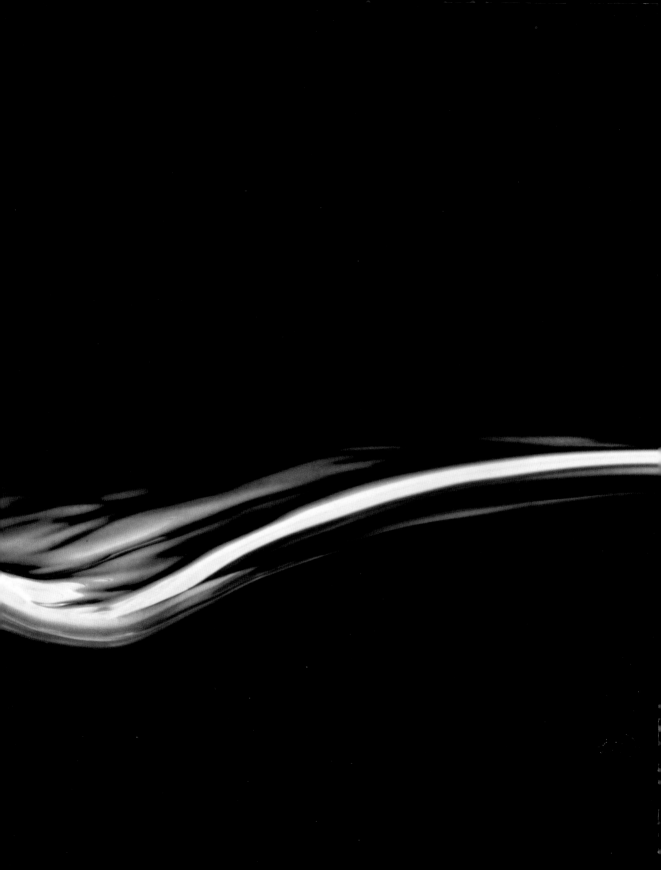

Getting Started

Adobe® Photoshop® Lightroom® delivers a complete workflow solution for the digital photographer—from importing, reviewing, organizing, and enhancing digital images to producing client presentations, web galleries, and high-quality prints. The user interface is highly intuitive and easy to learn, yet Lightroom has all the power and versatility you would expect from an Adobe application, utilizing state-of-the-art technologies to manage large volumes of digital photographs and to perform sophisticated image processing tasks. Whether you are a home user, a professional photographer, a hobbyist, or a business user, Lightroom enables you to stay in control of your growing digital photo library and to easily produce good-looking pictures and polished presentations for both web and print.

If you've used an earlier version of Lightroom, you'll find that this Classroom in a Book® will teach you advanced skills and covers the many new innovative features that Adobe Systems introduces in this version. If you're new to Lightroom, you'll learn the fundamental concepts and techniques that will help you master the application.

About Classroom in a Book

Adobe Photoshop Lightroom 2 Classroom in a Book is part of the official training series for Adobe graphics and publishing software developed by Adobe product experts. Each lesson in this book is made up of a series of self-paced projects that give you hands-on experience using Adobe Photoshop Lightroom 2.

Adobe Photoshop Lightroom 2 Classroom in a Book includes a CD attached to the inside back cover. On the CD you'll find all the image files used for the lessons in this book, along with additional learning resources.

Prerequisites

Before you begin working on the lessons in this book, make sure that you and your computer are ready.

Requirements on your computer

You'll need about 400 MB of free space on your hard disk for the lesson files and the work files that you'll create as you work through the exercises.

Required skills

The lessons in this book assume that you have a working knowledge of your computer and its operating system. Make sure that you know how to use the mouse and the standard menus and commands, and also how to open, save, and close files. Do you know how to use context menus, which open when you right-click / Control-click items? Can you scroll (vertically and horizontally) within a window to see contents that may not be visible in the displayed area?

If you need to review these basic and generic computer skills, see the documentation included with your Microsoft® Windows® or Apple® Mac® OS X software.

Installing Adobe Photoshop Lightroom

Before you begin using *Adobe Photoshop Lightroom 2 Classroom in a Book*, make sure that your system is set up correctly and that you've installed the required software and hardware. You must purchase the Adobe Photoshop Lightroom 2 software separately. For system requirements and complete instructions on installing the software, see the Adobe Photoshop Lightroom 2 Read Me file on the application CD or the Adobe Photoshop Lightroom Support Center on the web at www.adobe.com/support/photoshoplightroom.

Copying the Classroom in a Book files

The CD attached to the inside back cover of this book includes a Lessons folder containing all the image files you'll need for the lessons. You'll import these images into your Lightroom library and learn to organize them using the catalog that is central to many of the projects in this book. Keep the lesson files on your computer until you have completed all the exercises.

Note: The files on the CD are practice files, provided for your personal use in these lessons. You are not authorized to use these files commercially, or to publish or distribute them in any form without written permission from Adobe Systems, Inc. and the individual photographers who took the pictures, or other copyright holders.

Copying the Lessons files from the CD

1 Create a new folder named **LR2CIB** inside the *username*/My Documents (Windows) or *username*/Documents (Mac OS) folder on your computer.

2 Insert the *Adobe Photoshop Lightroom 2 Classroom in a Book* CD into your CD-ROM drive.

3 Locate the Lessons folder on the CD and copy it into the LR2CIB folder you created in step 1.

4 When your computer finishes copying the Lessons folder, remove the CD from your CD-ROM drive and put it away.

Creating a catalog file for working with this book

In the following steps you'll create a library folder and a catalog file before you start the lessons.

Creating a library folder

First create a folder for the files you'll create as you complete the lessons in this book.

1 Locate the LR2CIB folder you've created on your computer.

2 Within that folder, create a new folder called **LR2CIB Library**. This new folder should be located right next to the Lessons folder you've just copied from the CD.

Creating a catalog file

The first time you launch Lightroom, a catalog file named Lightroom Catalog.lrcat is automatically created on your hard disk. By default, Lightroom catalog files are located in the *username*/My Documents/My Pictures/Lightroom (Windows) or *username*/Pictures/Lightroom (Mac OS) folder. The catalog file stores information about all the photos in your library including the location of the master files, any metadata you've added in the process of organizing your images, and every adjustment or edit you've made. Most users will keep all their photos in one catalog, which can easily manage thousands of files. Some might want to create separate catalogs for different purposes, such as home photos and business photos. Although you can create multiple catalogs, you can only have one catalog open in Lightroom at a time.

You will now create a new catalog to manage the image files for the lessons in this book. This will allow you to leave the default catalog untouched while working through the lessons, and to keep your lesson files together in one easy-to-remember location.

1   Start Adobe Photoshop Lightroom 2.

2   From the Lightroom menu bar, choose File > New Catalog.

3   In the Create Folder With New Catalog dialog box, navigate to the LR2CIB Library folder inside the LR2CIB folder you've created on your hard disk.

4   Create a new catalog:

• In Windows, type **LR2CIB Library Catalog** in the File Name text box, and then click Save.

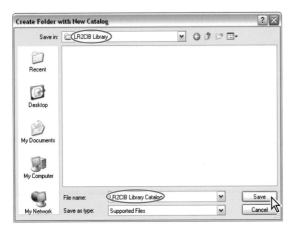

- In Mac OS, type **LR2CIB Library Catalog** in the Save As text box, and then click Create.

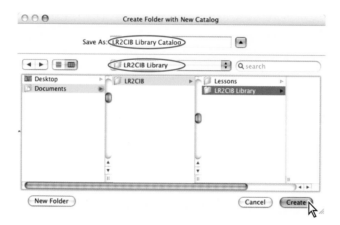

Note: *In the remainder of this book, instructions that differ for Macintosh users and those working on Windows systems are given in a compact format, such as* Ctrl+B / Command+B *for a keyboard shortcut. The Windows instructions appear first and the Macintosh instructions second. The two are separated by a backslash, which is not part of either instruction.*

Lightroom has now opened your new library catalog, which is empty as you have not yet imported any photos.

You can switch back to the default catalog (or any other previously created catalog) by choosing it from the File > Open Recent menu. Before you continue working on the lessons, make sure you have LR2CIB Library Catalog.lrcat selected—indicated by a check mark in front of the name in the File > Open Recent menu.

In order to be sure that you're always working with the right catalog as you progress through the lessons in this book, you will now set the preferences so that you will be prompted to specify the LR2CIB catalog each time you launch Lightroom. It is recommended that you keep this preference set as long as you're working through the lessons in this book.

5   Choose Edit > Preferences (Windows) / Lightroom > Preferences (Mac OS).

6   In the Preferences dialog box, click the General tab. From the Default Catalog menu, choose Prompt Me When Starting Lightroom.

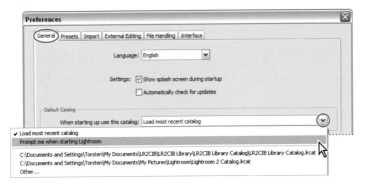

7   Click OK / the Close button (⊖) to close the Preferences dialog box.

Next time you start Lightroom the Select Catalog dialog box will appear. While working through the lessons in this book, make sure the file LR2CIB Library Catalog.lrcat is selected before clicking Continue to close the dialog box.

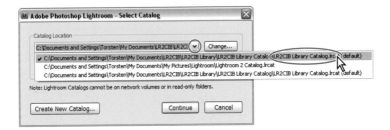

💡 *Hold down the Clrl+Alt / Control+Option keys immediately after launching Lightroom to open the Select Catalog dialog box regardless of your preference settings.*

Additional resources

Adobe Photoshop Lightroom 2 Classroom in a Book is not meant to replace documentation that comes with the program, nor is it designed to be a comprehensive reference for every feature in Adobe Photoshop Lightroom 2. For additional information about program features, refer to any of these resources:

• Adobe Photoshop Lightroom Help, which is built into the Adobe Photoshop Lightroom 2 application. You can view it by choosing Help > Lightroom Help, or by pressing the F1 key / Command+?.

• You can also choose Help > Lightroom Online for access to the support pages and links to additional learning resources on the Adobe web site (www.adobe.com). This option requires that you have Internet access.

• The Adobe Photoshop Lightroom 2 Getting Started Guide, which is included either in the box with your copy of Adobe Photoshop Lightroom, or on the installation CD for the application software in PDF format. If you don't already have the latest version of Adobe Reader, formerly called Acrobat Reader, installed on your computer, you can download a free copy from the Adobe web site (www.adobe.com/reader).

Adobe Certification

The Adobe Training and Certification Programs are designed to help Adobe customers improve and promote their product-proficiency skills. The Adobe Certified Expert (ACE) program is designed to recognize the high-level skills of expert users. Adobe Certified Training Providers (ACTP) use only Adobe Certified Experts to teach Adobe software classes. Available in either ACTP classrooms or on-site, the ACE program is the best way to master Adobe products. For Adobe Certified Training Programs information, visit the Partnering with Adobe web site at http://partners.adobe.com.

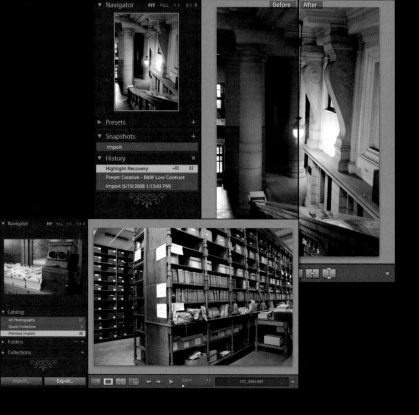

*In this lesson, you'll get an overview of how Lightroom
works. You'll familiarize yourself with the workspace,
tools, and controls and explore the Library, Slideshow,*

1 | A Quick Tour of Photoshop Lightroom

This lesson will help you understand how Lightroom works and familiarize you with the workspace. The exercises will guide you through a typical workflow: you'll import, review, and edit images, and then create a web gallery to present them.

In the process, you'll be introduced to the Lightroom workspace modules:

- The Library Module, where you'll import and review images.

- The Develop Module, where you can modify and enhance your photos.

- The Slideshow Module.

- The Print Module.

- The Web Module, where you'll create your own web page.

Further lessons in this book provide more in-depth exercises and specific details of the workspace modules, tools and features.

Understanding how Lightroom works

Working with Lightroom will be easier and more productive if you understand how Lightroom differs from other image processing applications in the way it handles digital images.

When you import a photo into your library, Lightroom does not import the image file itself but creates a new entry in the library catalog to record the file's location. When you add a flag, a keyword, or a rating to an image, or organize the photographs in your library into convenient collections, those changes and groupings are also recorded in the catalog file. Even the modifications you make to the image itself—by cropping, correcting color, or applying effects—are actually recorded only in the catalog file.

This is called non-destructive editing. Lightroom shows you a preview of the effects of your work, but the original image file remains unaltered. The edits are applied only when you export or output your image. In this respect, Lightroom works very differently from other image processing applications such as Photoshop or Photoshop Elements, which write modifications to the source file.

Managing photos in a library

To begin working with your photos you must first import them into the Lightroom library. You can import files from your computer hard disk, from external storage media, or download them directly from a digital camera or card reader. When you import images, Lightroom offers you several options to help you manage your files; you can leave them at their current locations, preserving your accustomed folder structure, copy them to a new location leaving the originals intact, or move them and delete the originals to avoid having two copies of the files. When you copy or move your files, you can choose to replicate their original folder structure, to consolidate them into a single folder, or to sort them into subfolders based on date.

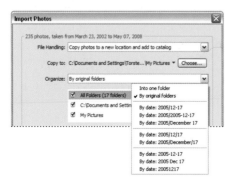

You will learn more about the options available during the import process in Lesson 3, "Importing." For now it is important to remember that the images in your library can be located anywhere on your computer hard disk—or even on external storage media—and that references to their locations are stored in the library catalog file. If you wish to rename or move an image file that you have already imported into your library, you should only do so from within Lightroom. Otherwise, Lightroom will report the renamed or moved file as missing and you will be asked to reestablish the link so that the information in the catalog file can be updated.

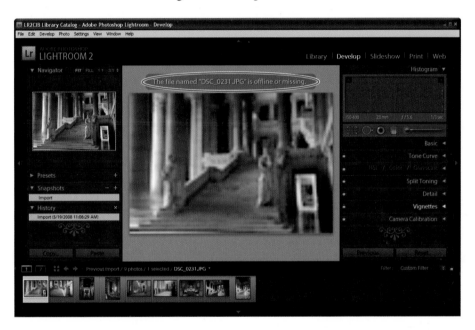

Non-destructive editing

When you make adjustments or modifications to an image in your library, such as changing the white balance or removing spots, Lightroom stores this editing information only in the library catalog file. The original image file remains unchanged. The library catalog file also stores metadata, and any keywords, flags, color code or rating you may have assigned to an image, together with information about its place in the collections you create to group your photos. Everything you do with an image in Lightroom is captured in the catalog.

There are many advantages in storing modifications separately from the image data. Did you ever save a document only to realize that you'd just overwritten an important previous version? Or realize too late that you should have cropped an image differently? If you were lucky you may have had a copy of the original file, but you still would have lost whatever other adjustments and modifications you had already made.

In Lightroom, non-destructive editing frees you to experiment with adjusting, cropping, or otherwise modifying your images. Crop an image and later change your mind—no problem! You can undo, redo, or adjust any modification you've applied without ever losing any information from the original file. You don't have to worry about degrading the image quality of a JPEG file every time you save your changes. You don't actually save changes to the image file at all; they are recorded only in the catalog.

Changes are only applied to an image during output—while it is being exported as a low resolution JPEG image to be used in a web page, as a preview image to be displayed in the Lightroom workspace, or as part of a print layout. The original image remains unchanged and only copies created as part of the rendering process will be altered according to the editing instructions captured in the catalog.

Non-destructive editing may be different from what you're used to if you've worked with other image processing applications such as Photoshop or Photoshop Elements, which store modifications in the source file itself.

Should you wish to edit an image using an external image processing application, you should always launch the process from within Lightroom. In this way, you can be sure that Lightroom will keep track of changes made to the file, and the edited copy will automatically be added to your Lightroom library. For a JPEG, TIFF, or PSD image, Lightroom gives you the option to edit the original file, or a copy of the original—either with or without your Lightroom adjustments applied. For files in any other file format, you can edit a copy, to which your Lightroom adjustments have already been applied.

> ♀ *You can specify your favorite external editor in the External Editing preferences. Otherwise, Lightroom will preselect Photoshop or Photoshop Elements by default, if you have either application installed on your computer.*

The Lightroom workspace

The Lightroom workspace is divided into panels. Although Lightroom has several workspace *modules*, the arrangement of the basic panels in each module is identical. Only the contents of the panels change from module to module, to address the specific requirements of each working mode.

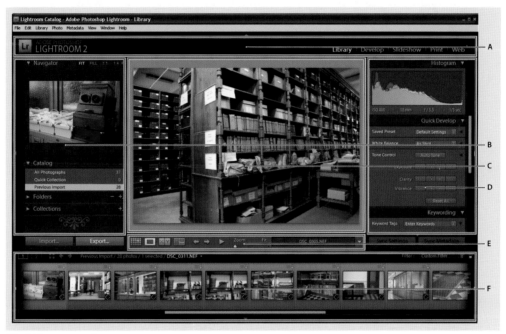

The Lightroom workspace:
A. *Top panel with Identity Plate and Module Picker.* **B**. *Left panel group.*
C. *Work area.* **D**. *Right panel group.* **E**. *Toolbar.* **F**. *Filmstrip.*

Note: *The illustration above shows the Windows version of Lightroom. On Macintosh, the arrangement is the same barring the differences in style between the two operating systems. On Windows, for example, the menu bar is normally located under the title bar of the application window, while on Mac OS the menu bar is anchored at the top of the screen.*

The top panel

The top panel displays an identity plate on the left and the Module Picker on the right. The identity plate can be customized to feature your own company name or logo and will be temporarily replaced by a progress bar whenever Lightroom is performing a background process. You use the Module Picker to move between the different workspace modules by clicking their names. The name of the currently active module is always highlighted.

The work area

At center-stage is the main preview and working area. This is where you select, review, sort, compare, and apply adjustments to your images, and where you preview the work in progress. You can increase the size of the work area by hiding any or all of the surrounding panels. The work area is the only part of the Lightroom workspace that you cannot hide from view. From module to module, the work area offers different viewing options, allowing you to see either one photo or multiple images, at a range of magnification levels.

The left and right panel groups

The content of the side panel groups changes as you switch from module to module. As a general rule, you use panels in the left group to find and select items, and panels in the right group to edit or customize settings for your selection. In the Library Module for example, you use the panels below the Navigator panel in the left group (Catalog, Folders, and Collections) to locate and select the images you want to work with, and the panels below the Histogram panel in the right panel group (Quick Develop, Keywording, Keyword List, and Metadata) to apply changes to them. In the Develop Module, you can choose from develop presets on the left, and fine-tune their settings on the right. In the Slideshow, Print and Web Modules, you can select templates on the left, and customize their appearance on the right.

The Toolbar

The tools available in the Toolbar also change as you move from module to module. You can customize the Toolbar for each module independently to suit your working habits, choosing from a variety of tools and controls for switching viewing modes, setting ratings, flags, or labels, adding text, and navigating through preview pages. You can show or hide individual controls, or hide the Toolbar altogether until needed. There are also menu commands or keyboard shortcuts for most of the commands available in the Toolbar.

The Filmstrip

The Filmstrip always displays the same set of images as the Grid view in the Library module. It can show every image in the library, the contents of a selected folder or collection, or a filtered selection based on subject, date, keywords, or a range of other criteria. You can work directly with the thumbnails in the Filmstrip or the Library module's Grid view to assign ratings, flags, or color labels, apply metadata and developing presets, and rotate, move, or delete photos. The main purpose of the Filmstrip is to keep your selected images accessible when you're using a view other than the Grid view in the Library Module, or working in one of the other modules. Using the Filmstrip, you can quickly navigate through your selected images, or move between different sets of images, whichever module you are working in.

Customizing the workspace

All of the workspace panels are highly customizable. You can open, close, resize, hide, and show panels and groups of panels, either manually or automatically. You can add or remove control elements, change the font size, background color, and more. All of these options will be covered in more detail in Lesson 2, "Introducing the Workspace."

The Lightroom modules

Lightroom has five workspace modules: Library, Develop, Slideshow, Print, and Web. Each module offers a specialized set of tools and features tailored to the different phases of your workflow: importing and organizing, adjusting and enhancing, producing presentations, and generating output for print or web. You can move effortlessly between modules to suit the task at hand. Some operations—such as creating backup copies or exporting images in various file formats—are not tied to any specific module and are always accessible via menu commands.

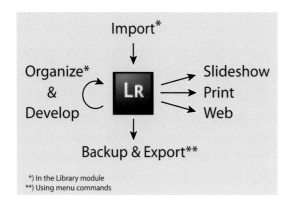

The Library module

In the Library module you can review and organize the images in your library. The work area offers several different viewing modes so you can browse, inspect, compare, or select images with ease. You can move between these viewing modes—the Grid, Loupe, Compare, and Survey views—using the controls in the Toolbar. You can customize the Toolbar for each of the viewing modes independently, choosing from a range of features, tools, and controls. Customize your Toolbar using the menu at the far right of the Toolbar.

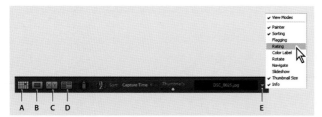

A. Grid. B. Loupe. C. Compare. D. Survey. E. Select Toolbar content menu.

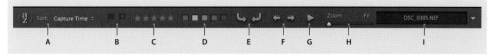

A. Sorting. B. Flagging. C. Rating. D. Color Label. E. Rotate. F. Navigate. G. Slideshow. H. Zoom. I. Info.

In the Library module, the left panel group consists of the Navigator panel and any combination of the Catalog, Folders, and Collections panels, which help you to find and organize the images in your library. The Navigator panel is always available but you can show or hide any of the other three panels as you create additional folders and collections and move your photos between them. The right panel group contains the Histogram panel, which can be collapsed but not hidden, and any combination of the Quick Develop, Keywording, Keyword List, and Metadata panels. You can use these four panels to quickly apply developing presets, make color corrections and tonal adjustments, and review or edit any keyword tags and metadata attached to an image.

To choose which panels are displayed in a panel group, right-click (Windows) / Ctrl-click (Mac OS) on any panel header in the group, and choose from the options in the context menu. Right-click (Windows) / Ctrl-click (Mac OS) the outside edge of the panel group (beyond the scrollbar) to choose options that affect the behaviour of the panel group as a whole.

The buttons below the panel groups give quick access to the Import, Export, Synchronize Settings, and Synchronize Metadata dialog boxes.

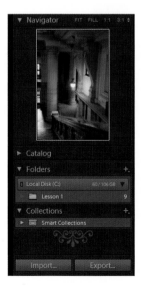

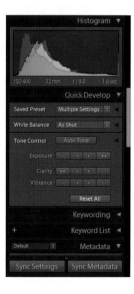

The Develop module

Although the Library module's Quick Develop panel offers some image editing options, you will work in the Develop module when you wish to make more detailed adjustments and modifications to your photos. You can correct the color or tonal scale, crop or straighten an image, remove red eye, and apply selective local adjustments—all non-destructively.

In the Develop module, the work area offers two viewing modes: a Loupe view, enabling you to see a photo at different levels of magnification, and a Before & After view (with a variety of layout options), making it easy to compare original and edited versions of the photo. You can move between these viewing modes using the controls in the Toolbar and customize the Toolbar for each view mode independently. Choose from a range of controls—Flagging, Rating, Color Label, Navigate, Slideshow, and Zoom—available in the menu at the far right of the Toolbar. Some tools are available only in one module, such as the Painter tool for applying attributes and settings directly to your images in the Library module. Others appear only in a particular viewing mode—such as the Before & After controls in the Develop module's Before/After view, which allow you to swap or copy develop settings between edited and unedited versions of a photo.

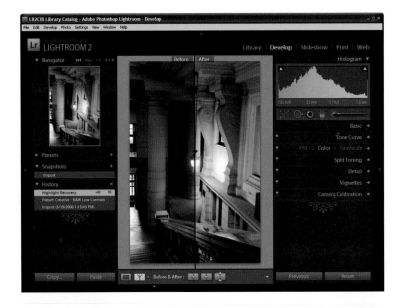

💡 *By hiding panels you're not currently using, as done with the Filmstrip in the illustration above, you'll have more space available for your working view.*

The left panel group contains the Navigator panel, which can be collapsed but not hidden, and—depending on the way you prefer to work—any combination of the Presets, Snapshots, and History panels. Develop presets are used to apply a series of develop settings with a single click. Lightroom ships with a set of default presets, and also allows you to add your own. Snapshots are development stages you have chosen to save during the editing process, and the History panel enables you to selectively undo or redo changes. The right panel group always contains the Histogram panel and an array of editing tools—the Crop Overlay, Remove Spots, Remove Red Eye, Graduated Filter, and Adjustment Brush tools—but you can select any combination of the Basic, Tone Curve, HSL / Color / Grayscale, Split Toning, Detail, Vignettes, and Camera Calibration panels. You can use these panels to fine-tune many aspects of your photos: adjust the tonal balance, create special dual tone effects, or correct lens vignetting. The buttons below the panel groups simplify the process of copying and pasting settings between photos, applying previously used settings to an image, and resetting an edited photo to its original state.

The Slideshow module

In the Slideshow module you can easily create stylish presentations from any image collection in your library.

The images in your collection are displayed in the Filmstrip, where you can choose which photos to include in your slideshow, and drag their thumbnails to change the order in which they will appear. The work area shows one image at a time in the Slide Editor view, where you can work on the slides individually, or preview your slideshow as a whole. The left panel group contains the Preview, Template Browser, and Collections panels. The Collections panel allows you to navigate between your collections or create new ones and the Template Browser offers a list of customizable slide layouts. The right panel group can contain any combination of the Options, Layout, Overlays, Backdrop, Titles, and Playback panels. You can use the Options, Layout, Overlays, and Backdrop controls to customize your slide: to specify the way text or ratings appear, choose a background, or change the layout. You can save your customized settings as a new template. The Playback panel offers options for adding a soundtrack, and controls for fades and timing and the Titles panel lets you add start and end screens. In the Toolbar below the Slide Editor view you'll find playback controls for the slideshow preview and tools for rotating or adding text to your slides. Buttons below the left panel group make it simple to export a single slide or the whole presentation.

The Print module

The Print module's many layout tools provide everything you'll need to quickly prepare any selection of images from your library for printing.

The photos in your collection are displayed in the Filmstrip, where you can drag their thumbnails to change their placement in the layout, and make your selection for printing. The work area—the Print Editor view—shows your print layout, which may include only one image, one image repeated, or multiple images. The left panel group contains the Preview panel, the Template Browser, and the Collections panel. You can use the Collections panel to navigate between your collections or to create new ones, and the Template Browser to choose from a list of customizable print layout templates. The right panel group contains the Layout Engine panel and a suite of other panels that varies a little with your choice of layout engine. You use the Image Settings, Layout, Rulers, Grid & Guides, Cells, and Overlay panels to customize your print layout. If you wish, you can save your settings as a custom template. The Print Job panel has settings for print resolution, color management and other output options. The Toolbar below the Print Editor view contains controls for navigating through multiple-page print previews and buttons below the panel groups make it simple to access page setup and print settings.

The Web module

In The Web module you can build, preview, and export or upload your own website to showcase your photos. As in the Slideshow and Print modules, you can select and arrange images from your collections using the Filmstrip. The panels in the left panel group are also the same as those in the Slideshow and Print modules, except that, in the Web module, the Template Browser contains web gallery templates. The work area—the Gallery Editor view—shows a working preview of your web gallery. The panels in the right hand group are used to access settings and controls that enable you to customize the gallery templates, add text, and manage output. The Toolbar below the Gallery Editor view offers controls for navigating through multiple-page galleries and buttons below the panel groups make it easy to preview your work in a web browser and export or upload your presentation.

A typical workflow

These are the basics of the Lightroom workflow:

- Import digital images into your library.

- Organize and sort your photos using keywords, flags, and ratings, and group them in image collections.

- Adjust and enhance your images: correct, retouch or apply effects. Optionally, use an external image editor for additional pixel-based editing.

- Present your photos in a slide show or web gallery, or output them for print.

- Export pictures and presentations as e-mail attachments, or create backups on CD or DVD ROM.

Importing photos

You can import photos into your Lightroom library from your hard disk, your camera, a memory card reader, or other storage media. During the import process you can choose from many options to help you manage and organize your files. For the purposes of this Quick Tour we will ignore most of these advanced options. Lesson 3, "Importing," will go into more details.

Before you begin, make sure that you have correctly copied the Lessons folder from the CD in the back of this book onto your computer's hard disk and created the LR2CIB Library Catalog file. See "Copying the Classroom in a Book files" and "Creating a catalog file for working with this book" on page 3.

1   Start Lightroom.

2   In the Adobe Photoshop Lightroom - Select Catalog dialog box, make sure the file LR2CIB Library Catalog.lrcat is selected under Catalog Location, and then click Continue.

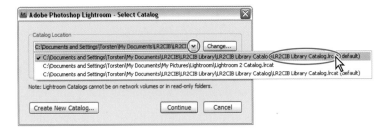

3   If the Back Up Catalog dialog box appears, click Skip Now.

4   Lightroom will open in the screen mode and workspace module that were active when you last quit. If necessary, click Library in the Module Picker to switch to the Library module.

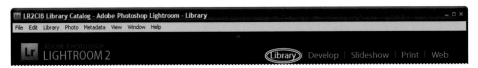

💡 *If you can't see the Module Picker, choose Window > Panels > Show Module Picker, or press the F5 key.*

Note: *In Mac OS some function keys are assigned to specific operating system functions by default. If pressing a function key in Lightroom does not work as expected, either press the fn key (not available on all keyboard layouts) together with the respective function key, or change the keyboard behavior in the system preferences.*

5   Choose File > Import Photos From Disk.

6   In the Import Photos Or Lightroom Catalog dialog box, navigate to the Lessons folder you copied into the LR2CIB folder on your hard disk. Select the Lesson 1 folder, and then click Import All Photos In Selected Folder (Windows) / Choose (Mac OS). *(See illustrations on the next page.)*

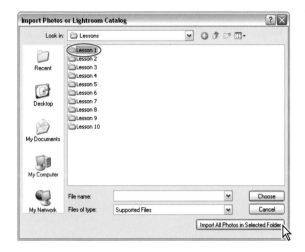

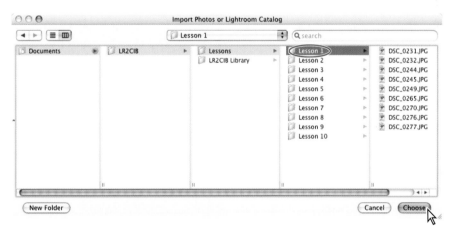

7 In the Import Photos dialog box, make sure the Show Preview option in the lower left corner of the dialog box is activated. In the Preview pane, you will see thumbnail images of the photos you're about to import. Use the slider below the preview area to change the thumbnail size. To add or remove a photo from the selection to be imported, click the box in the upper left corner of the thumbnail image. For this exercise, leave all of the photos selected.

8 Choose Add Photos To Catalog Without Moving from the File Handling menu. Choose None from both the Develop Settings menu and the Metadata menu. Type **Lesson 1** in the Keywords text box, and choose Minimal from the Initial Previews menu. Make sure your settings are exactly as shown in the illustration on the next page, and then click Import.

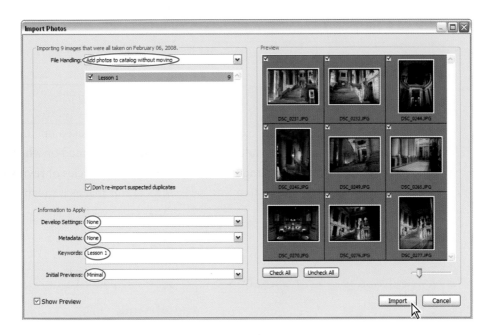

Congratulations! You've just imported the first photos into your library. You can see thumbnails of your photos in the Grid view of the Library module and in the Filmstrip.

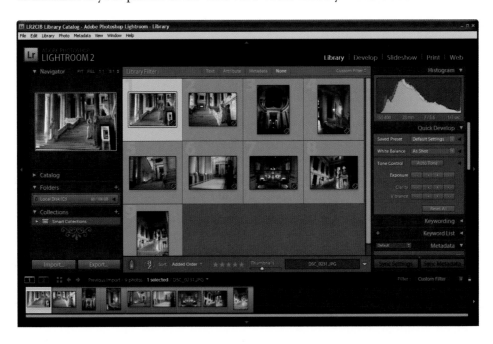

Reviewing and organizing

When you work with a library containing many images, you need to be able to find exactly what you're looking for quickly. Lightroom delivers numerous tools to make finding and organizing your files intuitive and enjoyable. You've already started structuring your catalog by applying the keyword tag "Lesson 1" to the images you imported. Keyword tags enable you to find or group image files based on any description you associate with them, independent of how they are named or where they are stored. You should make it a working habit to go through a few cycles of reviewing and organizing your files each time you import new images. This makes it much easier to retrieve the photos you want when you need to work with them.

Working while watching a slideshow

As a convenient way to review the images you've just imported, sit back and enjoy an impromptu slideshow:

1 In the Library module, make sure the Grid view is displaying the thumbnail images from the previous import, and then choose Window > Impromptu Slideshow, or press Ctrl+Enter / Command+Return. This will play a slideshow in full-screen mode using the settings current in the Slideshow module. The slideshow will repeat until you return to the Library module by pressing the Esc key.

2 While the slideshow is playing, press the spacebar to pause and resume playback. Press the left arrow key to return to the previous image or the right arrow key to advance to the next image.

You can assign star ratings to rank your photos. The more you like a photo the more stars you give it. You can then use search filters to sort your images on this basis.

3 To quickly assign a rating to the currently displayed image in your slideshow, press a number between 1 (for 1 star) and 5 (for 5 stars) on your keyboard. To remove the rating, press 0. You can only attach one rating to each photo; assigning a new rating will replace the old one.

Rating stars are displayed under the thumbnail images in all of the Library module views and in the Filmstrip as shown in the illustration below.

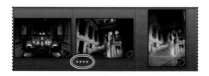

About keyword tags

Keyword tags are labels (such as "Architecture" or "New York") that you attach to your images to make them easy to find and organize. There's no need to painstakingly sort your photos into subject-specific folders or rename files according to their content; simply assign one or more keyword tags to each image and you can easily retrieve it by searching the images in your library with the Metadata and Text filters located in the Filter bar across the top of the work area.

You can create keyword tags for photographic categories, subjects, places, or events; use keyword tags to organize your photos by content, occasion, or even mood.

Attach multiple keyword tags to a photo to make retrieving it even easier; you can quickly find all the images you've tagged with the keyword Architecture, and then narrow the selection to those that are also tagged New York—regardless of how the photos are named or where they are stored.

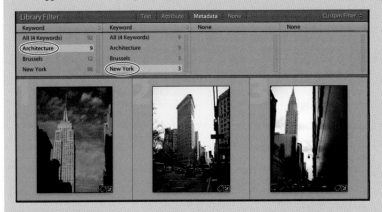

For more detailed information on using keyword tags, see Lesson 5, "Organizing and Selecting."

Another way to sort your images is to flag them.

4 Press the P key on your keyboard to flag the current image in the slideshow as a pick (⚑), press the X key to flag it as a reject (⚑), or press the U key to remove any flags.

You have the option to display flags—and other information—beside the thumbnail images in the Library views (as shown in the illustration below) and under the thumbnails in the Filmstrip. Images that are flagged as rejects are grayed out.

Use color labels to mark photos for specific purposes or projects. You might use a red label for images you intend to crop, green for those that need color correction, or blue to identify photos you wish to use in a particular presentation.

> 💡 *To help you remember what meaning you've attached to each color, you can assign your own names to the color labels by choosing Metadata > Color Label Set > Edit. In fact, you can create several presets, each with a different set of names for the color labels, and switch between them as needed. For example, you could customize one set for working in the Library module and another for the Develop module.*

5 To assign a color label to the current image in your slideshow, use the number keys. Press 6 on your keyboard to assign a red color label (■), 7 for yellow (■), 8 for green (■), or 9 for blue (■). There's no keyboard shortcut to assign a purple color label (■). To remove a color label simply press the same number again.

In the Grid View of the Library module and in the Filmstrip, a photo with a color label will be framed in that color when selected, and has a tinted background when unselected. If you prefer, you can change the view options so that the color label will appear only under the thumbnail image in the Grid view (as shown in the illustration below). You'll learn about customizing view options and how to assign ratings, flags, and color labels—using both menu commands and the controls in the Toolbar—in Lesson 5, "Organizing and Selecting."

6   Press the Esc key to stop the slideshow and return to the Grid view in the Library module.

In the Library module, you can filter your images by text and metadata content, and refine your search by specifying a star rating, flag status, or color label, so that only those photos you wish to work with are displayed in the Grid view and the Filmstrip.

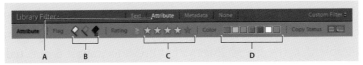

The Filter bar above the Grid view:
*A. Turn Attribute filters on or off. **B**. Filter by flag status. **C**. Filter by star rating. **D**. Filter by color label.*

7   If the Filter bar above the work area is not already open, open it by choosing View > Show Filter Bar. Click the Attribute filter. Click the third star, and choose Rating Is Greater Than Or Equal To from the Rating menu. Lightroom will now display only the photos with at least a 3 star rating.

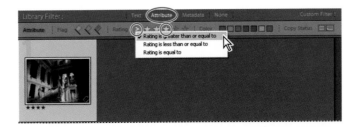

When working with only a few images, as you are in this example, rating, flagging, and filtering seems unnecessary, but as your library grows to contain hundreds or even thousands of photos you will find these tools invaluable.

The goal of this step in your workflow is to ready your images for processing in the Develop, Slideshow, Print, and Web modules.

Creating a collection

When you've reviewed and sorted your library, narrowed your search using keywords, and filtered out unwanted images, you can group the remaining photos as a *collection*, so that you can easily retrieve the same selection at any time. To group your photos in a collection you can choose between three options:

- The Quick Collection, a temporary holding collection where you can assemble a selection of images.

- A Collection, a more permanent grouping of photos that can be organized in the Collections panel.

- A Smart Collection, a selection filtered according to whatever rules you specify.

1 If the star rating filter is still active in the Grid view, clear this setting by choosing Library > Filter by Rating > Reset this Filter, or simply click None in the Filter bar above the Grid view to disable all active filters. Ensure that Previous Import is selected in the Catalog panel; the Grid view and the Filmstrip should display all nine images.

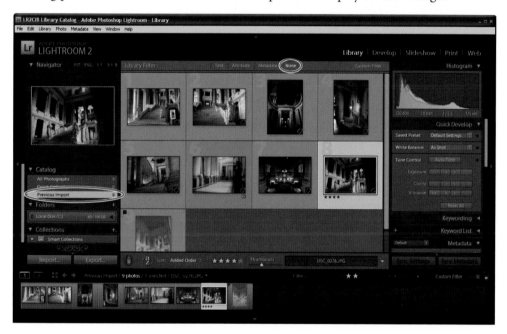

If you select a folder in one of the panels in the left group, the Grid view and the Filmstrip display the images in that folder. Right now, you have the Previous Import folder in the Catalog panel selected. The next time you import photos, the Previous Import folder will contain those new images. In this case, you would still be able to retrieve the current selection of images by choosing the Lesson 1 folder in the Folders panel, but what if you need to retrieve a group of photos that are not all located in the same folder, or if you want only a selection of all the images in one folder? Simply create a collection. You'll now save the group of 9 images from the Previous Import folder as a new collection. You will be able to retrieve your images at any time; your new collection will be listed in the Collections panel.

> *Folders in the Collections panel can be nested. For example, you could create a Portfolio folder, and then create subfolders named Portraits, Landscape, Product shots, Black &White, etc. Each time you import an outstanding image, add it to one of these collections to slowly build up your portfolio.*

2   Choose Edit > Select All.

Note: Selected images are highlighted in the Grid view and the Filmstrip by a thin white border—or it may be colored to denote a color label—and a lighter background color. If more than one photo is selected, the active photo is indicated by and even lighter background. Some commands affect only the active photo while others affect all selected photos.

3   With all nine photos highlighted in the Grid view and the Filmstrip, choose Library > New Collection. In the Create Collection dialog box, enter **My First Collection** in the Name box and select None from the Set menu. Under Collection Options, activate Include Selected Photos and disable Make New Virtual Copies. Then, click Create.

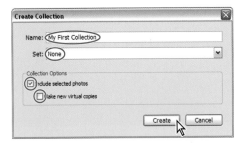

4   In the Collections panel, note the new entry named My First Collection, containing 9 images.

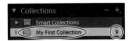

Rearranging and deleting images in a collection

Now that you have grouped the images in a collection you can do things with them in the Grid view and the Filmstrip that you couldn't do before, such as rearranging their order and removing them from the working view without deleting them from the catalog.

1 If My First Collection is not already selected in the Collections panel, click it now.

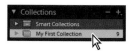

Although nothing has changed in the Grid view—because for the moment the My First Collection folder contains the same images as the Previous Import folder—you're now working with a collection, where you are free to rearrange the order of your images.

2 Choose Edit > Select None. If necessary, scroll down in the Grid view and Ctrl-click / Command-click to select the last two images. Drag the selected images towards the top of the view. As you drag, the view will automatically scroll up as necessary. Drag your selection between the second and third photos and drop it when the vertical black insertion line appears. The selected photos snap to their new position in the Grid view and the Filmstrip.

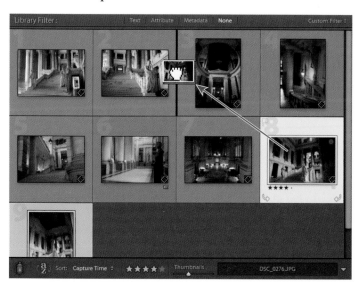

3   Choose Edit > Select None. Right-click / Control-click the fourth image in the Grid view and choose Remove From Collection from the context menu. In the Collections panel you can see that My First Collection now contains only 8 images.

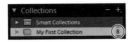

Although you have removed the photo from the collection, it hasn't been deleted from your catalog. The Previous Import folder and the All Photographs folder in the Catalog panel still contain all nine images. A collection contains only links or references to the original files; deleting the reference does not affect the original file.

You can include a single image in any number of collections—each collection will then contain its own reference to the same file.

Note: If you apply a modification to a photo in a collection, the modification will be visible in each folder and collection that references the same image. This is because Lightroom stores only one entry for each image file in its library catalog, and a record of modifications is associated with that entry; any collection including that image refers to the same catalog entry, and therefore displays the modified photo. Although the original image file still remains untouched, its catalog entry has changed. Should you wish to edit the same image differently in two collections, you need to make a virtual copy—an additional catalog entry—for the second collection. You will learn how to do this in Lesson 6, "Developing and Editing."

For more information on collections, please refer to "Using collections to organize images" in Lesson 5.

Comparing photos side by side

Often you'll have two or more similar photos you'd like to compare side by side. Lightroom features a Compare view for exactly this purpose.

1   If you have any images selected in the Grid view, choose Edit > Select None.

2   In the Toolbar click Compare View (■■). Alternately, choose View > Compare, or press C on your keyboard. The work area switches to the Compare view.

3   In the Filmstrip, click the first photo to add it to the left pane in the Compare view. Click the second photo, to add it to the right pane. *(See illustration on the next page.)*

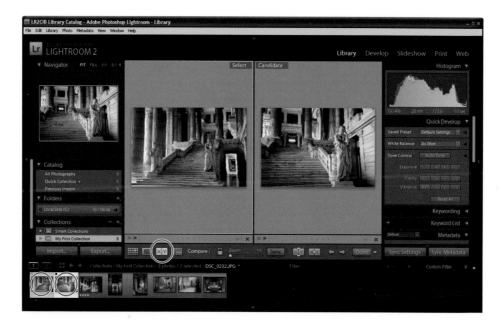

4 To quickly hide the side panel groups, so that your photos can be displayed at a larger size in the Compare view, press the Tab key on your keyboard.

5 Click the Candidate pane to select it, then press the right arrow key on your keyboard to select the next candidate photo from the Filmstrip.

6 If you prefer the Candidate photo to the current Select photo, click the Make Select button (▣) in the Toolbar. You can then continue to use the arrow keys to compare the new Select photo with other candidates.

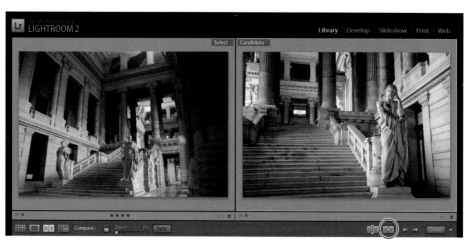

7   When you've made your choice, click Done at the right end of the Toolbar. The Select image will appear in the Loupe view.

8   Press the Tab key on your keyboard to show the hidden side panel groups.

Comparing several photos

To compare and select from several photos use the Survey view. You can view all the candidate images at the same time and narrow your selection one by one, until only the best photo remains.

1   Choose Edit > Select None. In the Filmstrip, Ctrl-click / Command-click three or four images that you'd like to compare, and then click Survey view (■■) in the Toolbar.

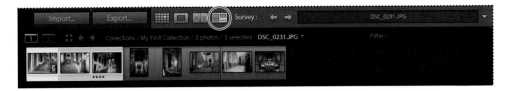

💡 *You can also use the menu command View > Survey, or simply press N on the keyboard to switch to Survey view.*

Note: *Sometimes Lightroom may need a few seconds to update the image display. You'll see a notification such as* Rendering Larger Preview *in the lower part of the image. Don't make any judgments about the image quality until the image update is complete.*

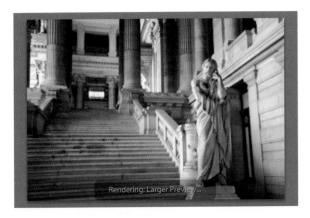

The Survey view will display all the selected images. The more images you select the smaller the individual thumbnail images in the Survey view. As you eliminate candidates the remaining photos are progressively resized. Eliminating a photo from Survey view does not remove it from the collection.

In Survey view, there is always one photo selected, or active, as indicated by a thin white border. To activate a different photo, click its thumbnail. In the right panel group you will find additional information about the active photo, from a histogram to information—in the Metadata panel—about which lens or ISO settings were used.

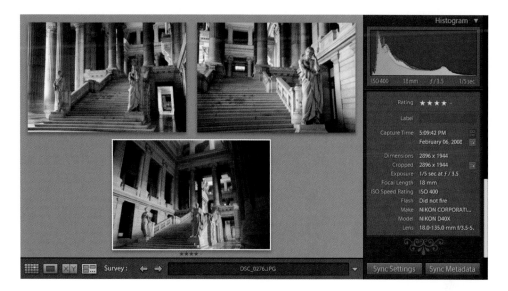

2　Drag a thumbnail to reposition it in the Survey view. The other images will automatically move to accommodate your changes.

3　As you move the pointer over each of the thumbnails, notice the Deselect Photo icon (✖) in the lower right corner. Click this icon to remove a photo from the Survey view.

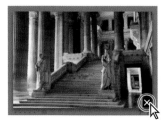

💡 *If you eliminated a photo accidentally, choose Edit > Undo to add it back to the selection. To add a photo to the selection in the Survey view, Ctrl-click / Command-click its thumbnail in the Filmstrip.*

💡 *While working with images in the Compare view or the Survey view, you can use menu commands and the controls in the Toolbar to assign star ratings, flags, and color labels. If necessary, use the Toolbar Content menu to show the controls in the Toolbar.*

4   Eliminate photos from the Survey view until you've narrowed your selection to one photo, and then press E on your keyboard to switch to Loupe view.

Developing and Editing

Now that you've selected the photos you wish to work with, you can use the comprehensive set of tools and features in Lightroom to correct and enhance your images. The Quick Develop panel in the right panel group enables you to do some quick, but effective, adjustments without even having to leave the Library module. Additional adjustment tools as well as a more convenient editing environment are available in the Develop module.

Using Quick Develop in the Library module

The Quick Develop panel offers simple controls for making basic adjustments to color and tone and a choice of develop settings presets. In the following example you will brighten up a dark image using the Auto Tone button.

1   If you are not already in the Loupe view from the previous exercise, press E on your keyboard to switch to it now.

2   If the Filmstrip is not visible, choose Window > Panels > Show Filmstrip. In the Filmstrip, select the file DSC_0244.JPG. You can see the name of a file in the tooltip window that appears when you place the pointer over a thumbnail, and in the status bar of the Filmstrip when the image is selected.

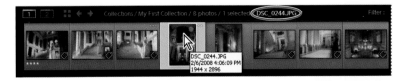

As you can see from both the image preview in the Loupe view, and the Histogram panel (in the right panel group) this photo is much too dark. You'll fix that in the next few steps.

3   To make room for a larger preview of this photo in portrait format, you can hide the Filmstrip by pressing the F6 key or choosing Window > Panels > Hide Filmstrip.

4   In the Quick Develop panel, click the Auto Tone button and you'll notice an immediate improvement in the image.

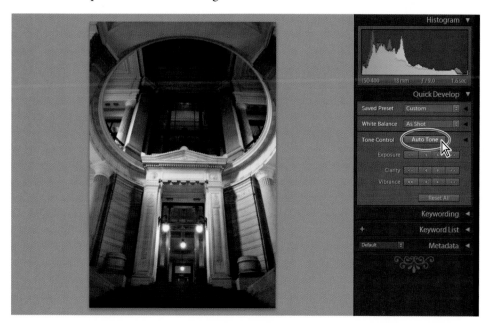

5   (Optional) Click the triangle to the right of the Auto Tone button to reveal more controls for fine-tuning the tonal balance. Experiment with the settings for Exposure, Recovery, Fill Light, Blacks, Brightness, and Contrast.

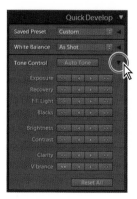

6   Click the Reset All button in the lower right corner of the Quick Develop panel.

Working in the Develop module

The controls in the Quick Develop panel let you change settings but don't indicate absolute values for the adjustments you make to your images. In our example there is no way to tell which parameters were changed by Auto Tone to improve the photo, or how much they were changed. For that level of control, and a more comprehensive editing environment, you need to move to the Develop module.

1   Switch to the Develop module now by doing one of the following:

- Click Develop in the Module Picker.
- Choose Window > Develop.
- Press Ctrl+Alt+2 / Command+Option+2.

2   Click the Auto button in the Tone adjustment settings in the Basic panel—the equivalent of clicking Auto Tone in the Quick Develop panel. Notice that for this image clicking Auto Tone increases Brightness by a fair amount, decreases Contrast slightly, and nudges Blacks up by 1 unit. Applying Auto Tone to another photo will produce different adjustment values. Note that the Auto button is now disabled for this image— the automatic adjustments needed in this photo have already been made.

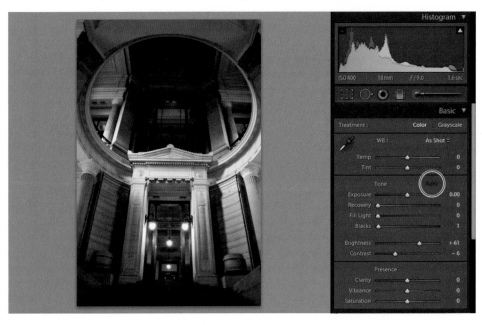

3   In the Toolbar (View > Show Toolbar), make sure the View Modes controls are selected in the Toolbar Content menu. From the menu beside the Before/After button select Before/After Left/Right.

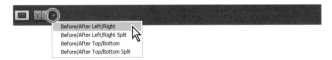

4   Press the F7 key to hide the left panel group and make more space in the work area for the two images side by side.

Auto Tone did a great job lightening the image, but you can improve it even more by making further adjustments manually.

5   Drag the Brightness slider to about +100. Or, click on the number beside the slider, type **100**, and then press Enter on your keyboard. Now increase Contrast to +7.

Your adjustments have improved the image considerably but in some places the white marble of the portal has become too light and detail has been lost. Using the Recovery slider you can tone down these clipped highlights while only slightly changing the brightness of the image as a whole.

6   Drag the Recovery slider to the right until you see the detail reappear in the marble above the portal. We used a value of 88.

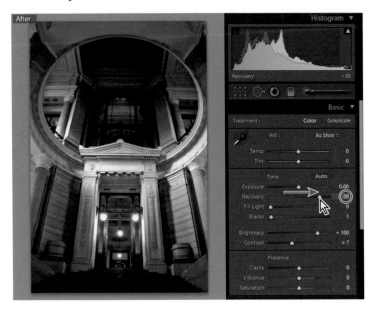

Rather than experimenting with every slider in the right panel group, you can try some of the Develop module presets to quickly apply different combinations of settings and achieve a wide range of effects. Use the Lightroom develop presets as a starting point, and then create your own.

7 Move your pointer close to the left edge of the Lightroom window. The left panel group should appear and remain visible until you move the pointer away.

Note: If the left panel group doesn't appear and disappear automatically, press the F7 key to manually show and hide it; you'll learn how to customize the behavior of the panel groups in Lesson 2, "Introducing the Workspace."

8 If necessary, expand the Presets panel and the Lightroom Presets folder within that panel. Move the pointer slowly down the list of presets in the Lightroom Presets folder. The Navigator panel displays a preview of how each preset would affect your image. Click General - Punch. The General - Punch preset adds depth and improves the perceived sharpness of the photo by increasing Clarity and Vibrance, leaving your Tone settings unchanged.

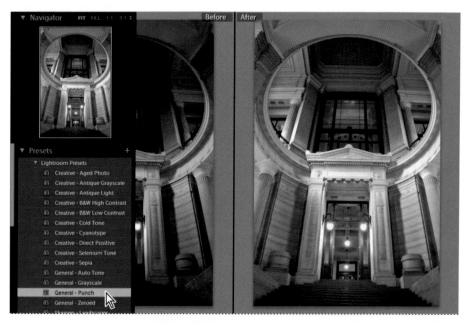

By comparing the Before and After images, you can see how dramatically you've improved the picture with just a few clicks. There's much more to learn about the tools and features in the Develop module, but we'll leave that for later. For now you'll straighten this image, and then crop it.

Using the Crop Overlay tool

1   Press D on your keyboard to activate the Loupe view in the Develop module, and press the F7 key to show the left panel group again.

2   Click the Crop Overlay Tool button (■), loacted below the Histogram panel. The Crop Overlay Tool enables you to both crop and straighten your image.

3   Additional controls are now available below the Crop Overlay Tool button. Click to select the Straighten tool (●). The pointer changes to a cross-hair, and the spirit level icon of the Straighten tool follows your movement across the preview.

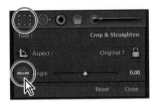

4   Look for a line in the image that should be either true horizontal or vertical. For this image we'll use the vertical axis that runs through the center of the portal and the hanging lights. Starting at the apex of the portal, drag downward with the Straighten tool, and align the white plumb line with the lights. Release, and the image is rotated so that your plumb line is vertical. The Straighten tool returns to its tool well in the Crop Overlay Tool controls.

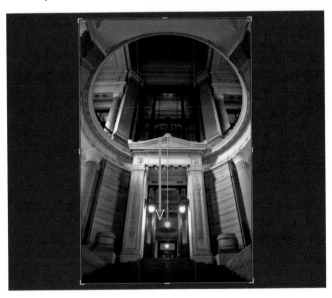

The image is now straight, but needs to be cropped slightly so that the round opening above the portal is centered in the frame. To crop an image you can either use the Crop Frame tool, located above the Straighten tool, or simply drag the handles of the cropping rectangle that is already overlaid on your image.

5   If Original is not already selected, choose it from the cropping Aspect menu to maintain the original aspect ratio of the image when you crop it. Don't pick up the Crop Frame tool for this exercise—you'll use the handles of the cropping rectangle to crop this image.

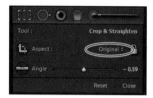

6   Drag the left handle of the cropping rectangle slightly to the right so that the oval opening in the image sits centered in the picture frame.

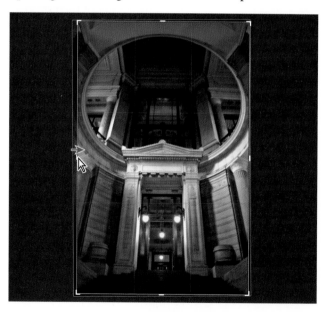

💡 *You can crop the image by dragging any of the six handles on the cropping rectangle, or by dragging the image itself to change its position in the cropping rectangle.*

7 (Optional) While you are in the process of cropping your image, press L on your keyboard (Window > Lights Out > Lights Dim) to dim everything around the cropping rectangle. Press L again to darken the workspace altogether (Lights Off). Now press L a third time to return to normal Light Mode (Lights On). Choose a different grid overlay from the View > Crop Guide Overlay menu, or turn the grid off altogether by choosing View > Tool Overlay > Never Show.

8 When you're done, exit the Crop Overlay mode by clicking the Close button in the lower right corner of the panel with the crop tool controls.

Using Fill Light

This following short exercise will complete the Develop module section of this lesson. Lesson 6, "Developing and Editing," will cover the Develop module in much more detail.

In a previous exercise you adjusted the Recovery control to darken highlights. For this exercise you will use the Fill Light feature to lighten areas that are too dark.

1 Press F6 to show the Filmstrip. Click the image DSC_0265.JPG, to display it in the Loupe view.

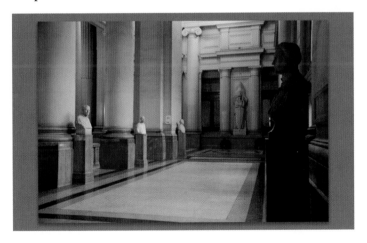

The statue on the right is much too dark, but you may be surprised how much detail is still available in the image data and how easily it can be retrieved and enhanced by yet another powerful Lightroom feature.

2　In the Basic panel, drag the Fill Light slider to the right until you see the lost detail reappear in the marble on the side of the statue. We used a value of 70.

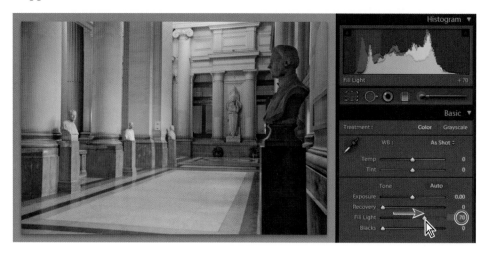

Note: You'll get even better results using the tools in the Develop module when working with Raw images.

Sharing your work

Now that you've enhanced and edited your photos, the next step is to present them to your client, share them with your friends and family, or display them for the world to see on your website. In Lightroom, it takes only seconds to create sophisticated slideshows, customize layouts for printing photos—singly, in multiples, or as contact sheets—or generate web photo galleries ready to be uploaded directly to your web server from within Lightroom.

In this lesson you will use the images from your collection to create a web gallery, with just a few clicks. Lesson 7, "Creating Slideshows," Lesson 8, "Printing Images," and Lesson 9, "Publishing your Photos on the Web" will cover, in much more detail, many Lightroom features and options that make it simple to create stylish presentations, layouts, and galleries, to showcase your photos.

Whether you are working on a slideshow, a print layout, or a web presentation, the workflow follows the same basic steps. You start with the creation of an image collection, move to the relevant Lightroom module to apply a layout template and customize its settings, preview your work, and then generate the appropriate output—export your slideshow in PDF format, print your photo layouts, or upload a web page.

Exploring the Web module

You should create a new collection for each presentation. Your layouts and settings will be saved with the collection so you can return at any time to refine or add to your work or to tweak the output settings. For this exercise you'll use the collection you created earlier in this lesson.

1 Click Web in the Module Picker to switch to the Web module.

2 In the left panel group, scroll down, if necessary, to see the Collections panel. Ensure that the collection My First Collection is selected in the list.

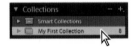

💡 *As you create more collections, you can manage them in the Collections panel. Group related collections—all those assembled for presentations made to a particular client, for example—as nested subfolders.*

3 From the Use menu in the Toolbar, choose All Filmstrip Photos.

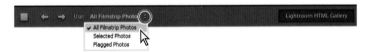

4 Press the F6 key to hide the Filmstrip.

The Gallery Editor view shows a preview of how your images will look in a web gallery. You can now choose a new gallery template, and quickly customize the design and layout.

5 In the left panel group, scroll up, if necessary, so that you can see the Template Browser panel. Move the pointer slowly down the list of gallery templates in the Lightroom Templates folder. The Navigator panel displays a preview of each layout. Click a template in the browser to see your photos previewed in that layout in the Gallery Editor view. For this exercise, choose the template named "HTML gallery (default)."

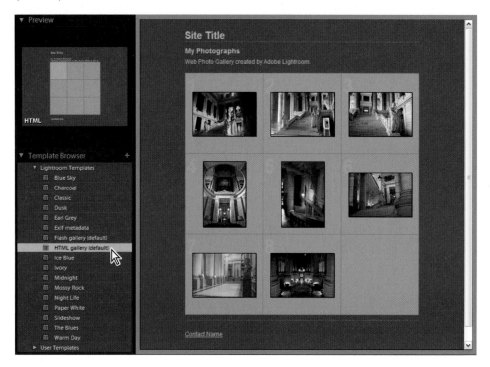

6 The preview in the Gallery Editor view functions exactly as your published web gallery will. Click a thumbnail to see a larger version of the image. Click the Previous and Next buttons to navigate through the collection. Click the Index button to return to the first page.

You can customize the text that appears on the HTML pages, and the design of your gallery, using the various panels in the right panel group. You will examine these in more detail in Lesson 9, "Publishing your Photos on the Web."

As well as the templates available in the Template Browser, you can also select from website templates developed by Airtight Interactive. These templates are not located in the Template Browser; you'll find them in the Engine panel at the top of the right panel group.

7　In the Engine panel, choose the Airtight PostcardViewer template. An animated intro scatters your images across the screen as if they were postcards.

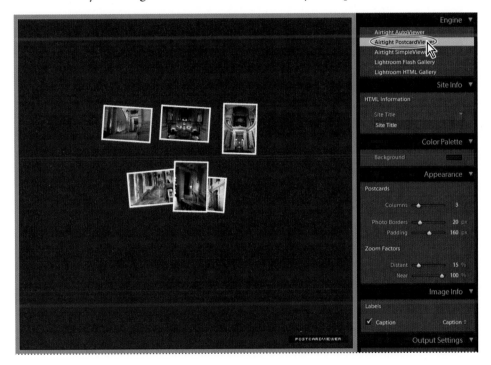

8　Click a postcard for a closer look. Use the arrow keys to navigate through the images. Press the spacebar on your keyboard to return to the index page.

Previewing in a browser

The Airtight galleries work not only in Lightroom but also in your regular web browser.

1　Choose Web > Preview In Browser.

Lightroom will generate the necessary files in a temporary location on your hard disk and then launch your default web browser to display the website. You can watch the progress bar on the left side of the top panel in the Lightroom workspace.

2   The Airtight PostcardViewer requires that Adobe Flash is installed on your system. If your web browser displays a notification as shown in the illustration below, do the following:

•   If you don't yet have Adobe Flash, click Get Adobe Flash and follow the installation instructions.

•   Click the link Click To View Gallery.

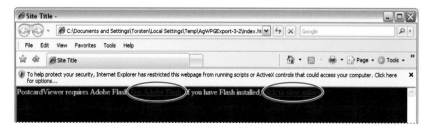

3   Depending on the security settings on your computer, you might also see a notification concerning running scripts or ActiveX controls. Click that notification, and a menu will appear—choose Allow Blocked Content. Finally, click Yes in the Security Warning dialog box.

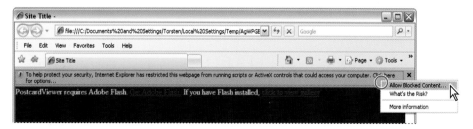

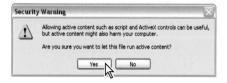

Your browser will play the scattering postcards animation, and present your gallery just as you saw it previewed in Lightroom.

4   Click a thumbnail to see a larger version of the photo. Use the arrow keys to navigate to the previous, or next postcard, or to the picture above or below the current view.

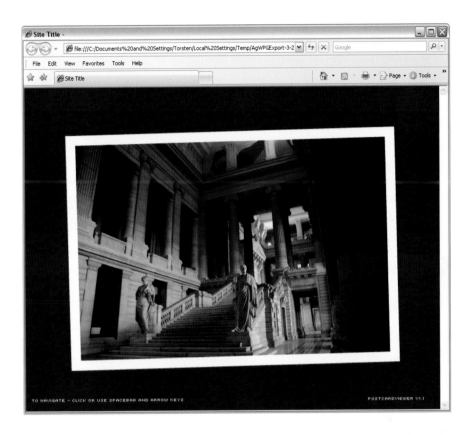

5 Click the zoomed image or press the spacebar on your keyboard to return to the index page.

6 When you're done previewing your website, close the page in your web browser and return to Lightroom.

7 (Optional) Experiment with customizing the settings for this website using the panels in the right group. You can change the title displayed in your browser's title bar in the Site Info panel, choose a different background color in the Color Palette panel, change the number of columns for the index page in the Appearance panel, or adjust the size of the large images in the Output Settings panel. Be sure to review your changes not only in the Lightroom preview, but also in your web browser.

The final step is to upload the site to a web server. You can enter the necessary information in the Upload Settings panel, and upload the site from within Lightroom. For more details, see Lesson 9, "Publishing your Photos on the Web."

Getting Help

Help is available from several sources, each one useful to you in different circumstances:

Help in the application: The complete documentation for Adobe Photoshop Lightroom is available from the Help menu, in the form of HTML content that displays in your default web browser. This documentation provides quick access to summarized information on common tasks and concepts, and can be especially useful if you are new to Lightroom or if you are not connected to the Internet.

Note: You do not need to be connected to the Internet to view Help in Lightroom. However, with an active Internet connection, you can click the "LiveDocs" link on any page in Lightroom's Help to access the most up-to-date information.

LiveDocs Help on the Web: LiveDocs Help provides the most comprehensive and up-to-date documentation on Lightroom. It is the recommended choice, if you have an active Internet connection.

Help PDF: Help is also available as a PDF document, optimized for printing; download the PDF document at: www.adobe.com/go/learn_lightroom_helppdf_en.

Note: The Help PDF file is several MB in size, and may take a considerable time to download if you are using a slow Internet connection.

Navigating Help in the application

1   Choose Help > Lightroom Help, or press the F1 key / Command+?. If you are not currently connected to the internet, your default web browser will open to the front page of Adobe Photoshop Lightroom Help documentation that was installed on your computer with the Lightroom application.

Note: When connected to the Internet, you default web browser will open the LiveDocs Help on the Web page.

2   Choose a topic from the table of contents. Click the plus sign (+) to the left of any topic heading to see a list of sub-topics.

3   Click a sub-topic to see it's content displayed on the right. *(See illustration on the next page.)*

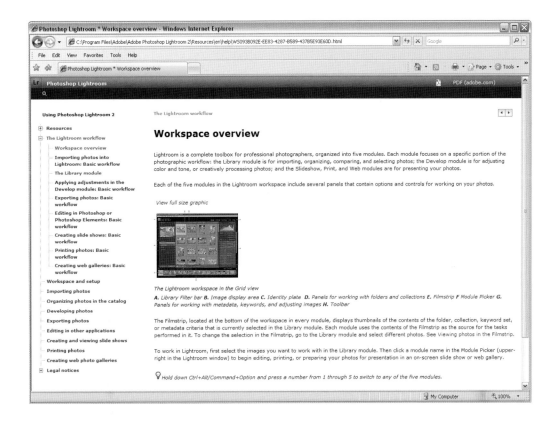

Accessing LiveDocs Help on the Web

LiveDocs Help on the Web contains the most up-to-date Help documentation for Lightroom. You can access them even if Lightroom is not currently running.

1 To access LiveDocs Help for Lightroom—part of the Adobe Help Resource Center—navigate to the Adobe Help Resource Center at www.adobe.com/support/documentation, select Lightroom from the list of products, and then click Go.

2   On the Lightroom resources page, click the LiveDocs link.

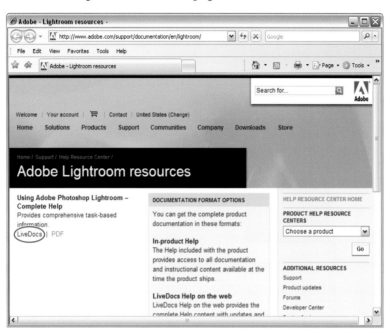

3   To switch to LiveDocs Help for a different product, select another product from the list under Browse, and then click Go.

4   To search for a particular topic in the Help documentation, enter a search term in the Search text box on the left side of the page, and then click Search. If necessary, narrow your search by selecting a category from the list on the LiveDocs Search Results page, and then click Go.

Search tips

Adobe Help Search searches the entire Help text for topics that contain all the words typed in the Search box. These tips can help you improve your search results in Help:

• Make sure that the search terms are spelled correctly.

• If a search term doesn't yield results, try using a synonym, such as "photo" instead of "picture."

Congratulations! You've reached the end of the first lesson. You've imported images, reviewed and organized your library, edited and enhanced photos, and created a web gallery. The following lessons will cover each of these subjects in far greater detail. But before you move on to the next lesson, be sure to review the lesson you've just completed by working through the questions and answers on the next page.

Review

▶ **Review questions**

1   What is non-destructive editing?

2   List the steps in a typical Lightroom workflow.

3   How can you increase the viewing area without resizing the application window?

4   What advantage is there to grouping images in a collection, rather than grouping them by a shared keyword tag?

5   Why is it recommended to create a special collection for each slideshow, print, or web project?

▶ **Review answers**

1   Whatever modifications you make to an image in your library—cropping, rotation, corrections, retouching, or effects—Lightroom records the editing information only in the catalog. The original image file remains unchanged.

2   The fundamental workflow for Adobe Photoshop Lightroom is to:

•   Import digital images into your image library from your hard disk, your camera, a memory card reader, or other storage media.

•   Review, sort, and organize your photos using keyword tags, flags, ratings, and collections.

•   Enhance images by correcting color and tone settings, by retouching, cropping, and applying effects.

•   Optionally, use an external image editor for additional pixel-based editing.

•   Present your images as slide show, print layout, or web gallery.

•   Export photos as e-mail attachments, or create backup copies to CD/DVD ROM.

3   You can hide any of the panels and panel groups surrounding the work area. The working view automatically expands into the space available. The work area is the only part of the Lightroom workspace that you cannot hide from view.

4   The difference between grouping images in a collection and applying keyword tags is that, in a collection, you can change the order of the photos displayed in the Grid view and the Filmstrip, and you can remove an image from the group.

5   Layouts and settings applied to your presentation are saved with the collection. You can return to the collection to refine your work, to add to it, or to tweak output settings.

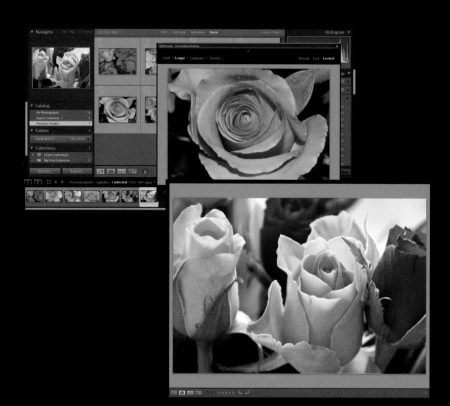

Make working with Lightroom even more pleasurable—and ultimately more productive—by personalizing the workspace so that you always have your favorite tools at hand. Lightroom streamlines your workflow, allowing you to move effortlessly between the different modules and viewing modes and freeing you up to spend less time in front of the computer and more time behind the lens!

2 | Introducing the Workspace

Whether you prefer to use menu commands, keyboard shortcuts, or buttons and sliders—whether you use a small screen or a large one, one monitor or two, you can customize the flexible Lightroom workspace to suit the way *you* work. With a keystroke or a single click you can switch between a variety of screen and view modes or move between the task-specific modules. You can hide or collapse control panels to rearrange the workspace layout and dim or completely darken the interface around an image to better preview your work. Customize each of the modules individually so that you always have your favorite tools and controls at hand, arranged just the way you like them.

To help familiarize you with the Lightroom workspace, this lesson will focus on the interface elements and skills that are common to all the workspace modules:

- Toggling between screen modes.
- Adjusting the workspace layout.
- Showing and hiding panels and panel groups.
- Collapsing or expanding panels.
- Changing and customizing view modes.
- Working with a second display.
- Personalizing the workspace.
- Choosing interface options.
- Using keyboard shortcuts.

You'll probably need between one and two hours to complete all the exercises in this lesson.

Getting started

Before you begin, make sure that you have correctly copied the Lessons folder from the CD in the back of this book onto your computer's hard disk and created the LR2CIB Library Catalog file. See "Copying the Classroom in a Book files" and "Creating a catalog file for working with this book" on page 3.

1 Start Lightroom.

2 In the Adobe Photoshop Lightroom - Select Catalog dialog box, make sure the file LR2CIB Library Catalog.lrcat is selected under Catalog Location, and then click Continue.

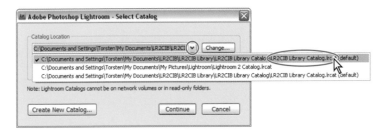

3 If the Back Up Catalog dialog box appears, click Skip Now.

4 Lightroom will open in the screen mode and workspace module that were active when you last quit. If necessary, click Library in the Module Picker to switch to the Library module.

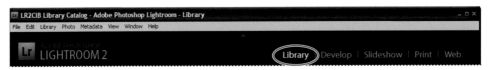

5 Choose File > Import Photos From Disk.

6 In the Import Photos Or Lightroom Catalog dialog box, navigate to the Lessons folder you copied into the LR2CIB folder on your hard disk. Select the Lesson 2 folder, and then click Import All Photos In Selected Folder (Windows) / Choose (Mac OS).

7 In the Import Photos dialog box, choose Add Photos To Catalog Without Moving from the File Handling menu. Choose None from both the Develop Settings menu and the Metadata menu. Type **Lesson 2** in the Keywords text box, and choose Minimal from the Initial Previews menu. Make sure your settings are exactly as shown in the illustration below, and then click Import.

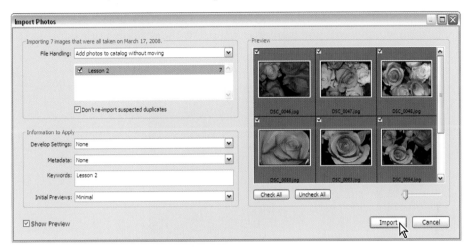

You have imported the photos into your library.

8   If necessary, press the F6 key to show the Filmstrip.

You can see thumbnails of your images in the Grid view of the Library module and in the Filmstrip. You are now ready to start the exercises in this lesson.

Toggling screen modes

Lightroom can operate in any of three *screen modes*. In the default mode the Lightroom workspace appears inside a regular document window that you can resize and position wherever you like on your computer screen. In the two other screen modes, the workspace expands to fill the entire screen—either with or without a visible menu bar—maximizing the space available for working with your images. You can switch between screen modes at any time.

Whether you're working in Windows or Mac OS, the Lightroom workspace looks almost identical. Any variation you may notice is due only to the different user interface standards adopted on each platform.

1   Ensure that you are in default screen mode: choose Window > Screen Mode > Normal.

In Normal screen mode on Windows, the Lightroom workspace appears inside an application window with the menu bar just below the window's title bar.

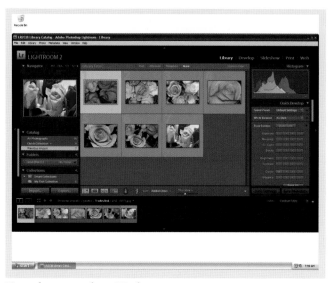

Normal screen mode on Windows.

In Normal screen mode on Mac OS, the Lightroom workspace appears inside a document window with the menu bar across the top of the screen.

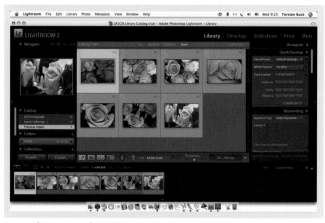

Normal screen mode on Mac OS.

2   Choose Window > Screen Mode > Full Screen With Menubar.

In Full Screen With Menubar screen mode on Windows, the Lightroom workspace expands to fill the screen with the menu bar across the top of the screen and the Windows task bar across the bottom.

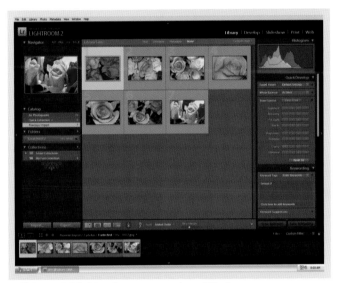

Full Screen With Menubar screen mode on Windows.

In Full Screen With Menubar screen mode on Mac OS, the Lightroom workspace expands to fill the screen with the menu bar across the top of the screen and the Dock—if not currently hidden—across the bottom.

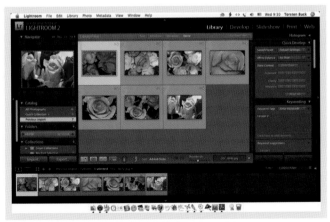

Full Screen With Menubar screen mode on Mac OS.

3   Choose Window > Screen Mode > Full Screen.

In Full Screen mode on Windows, the Lightroom workspace fills the entire screen with both the menu bar and the Windows task bar hidden.

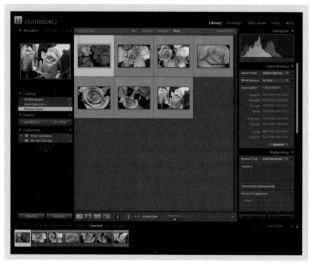

Full Screen mode on Windows.

In Full Screen mode on Mac OS, the Lightroom workspace fills the entire screen with both the menu bar and the Dock hidden.

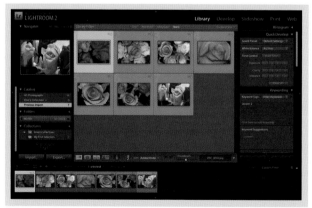

Full Screen mode on Mac OS.

💡 *To access menu commands while in Full Screen mode move the pointer to the top edge of the screen; the menu bar appears.*

4   Press Alt+Ctrl+F / Option+Command+F to return to Normal screen mode.

5   Choose Window > Screen Mode > Full Screen And Hide Panels, or use the keyboard shortcut Shift+Ctrl+F / Shift+Command+F.

6   In Grid view, double-click any of the thumbnails to enter Loupe view.

A variant of the Full Screen mode, Full Screen And Hide Panels is ideal for viewing an image as large as possible in Loupe view, as shown in the illustration below. By pressing T on your keyboard you can even hide the Toolbar below the work area, so that you see nothing but your photo. You will learn more about showing and hiding panels later in this lesson.

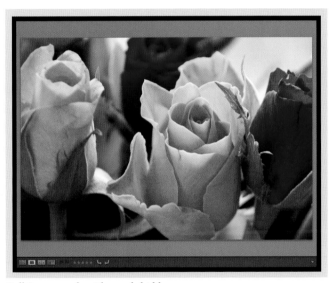

Full Screen mode with panels hidden.

7   Press F on your keyboard. This is the keyboard shortcut for Window > Screen Mode > Next Screen Mode. Press F repeatedly to cycle through the three screen modes. As you switch between the screen modes, you'll notice that the panels around the work area remain hidden.

8   To reveal all hidden panels, press Shift+Tab once or twice. If the Toolbar is hidden, press T to show it.

9   Press Alt+Ctrl+F / Option+Command+F to return to Normal screen mode.

Adjusting the workspace layout

Resizing and repositioning the Library window

1   In Normal screen mode in Windows, you can resize and reposition the application window as you are used to doing with other applications. To resize the window, do any of the following:

•   Move the pointer to any edge of the window. When the pointer changes to a horizontal or vertical double-arrow icon, you can drag the window's edge.

•   Move the pointer to any corner of the window. When the pointer changes to a diagonal double-arrow icon, you can drag the corner.

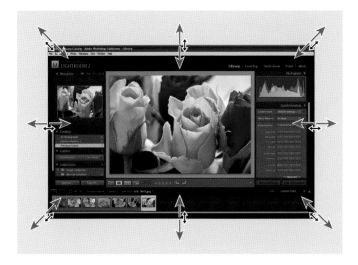

•   Click the Maximize button (■), located next to the Close button at the right of the title bar; the window expands to fill the entire screen, though you are still in Normal screen mode with both the title bar and the menu visible. While the window is maximized, you can no longer resize it as described above, or reposition it by dragging the title bar.

•   Click the Restore Down button (■) to return to the previous window size.

♀ *As a quick alternative to clicking the Maximize / Restore Down button, double-click the title bar.*

2 In Normal screen mode in Mac OS, resize the window by dragging its lower right corner.

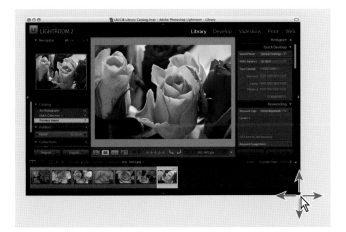

3 Click the green Zoom button (⊙), located next to the Close and Minimize buttons at the left of the title bar. The window expands to fill the screen. Click the Zoom button again to return to the previous window size.

4 Reposition the window by dragging the title bar.

Using a secondary display

If you have a second monitor connected to your computer, you can use it to display an additional view that is independent of the module and view mode currently active on your main monitor. Choose between Grid, Loupe, Compare, and Survey views for your secondary display. You also have the option to display a secondary view in a palette that can be resized and repositioned rather than filling the second screen.

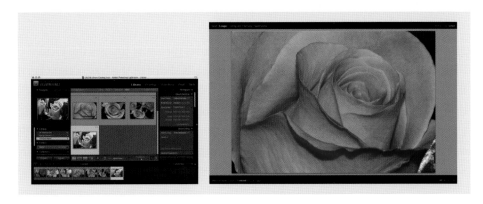

If you have only one monitor connected to your computer, you can open the additional display in a separate window that you can resize and reposition as you work.

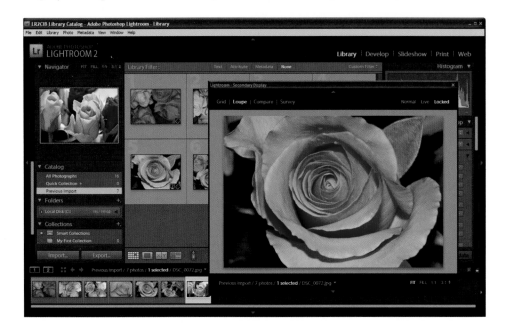

1   To open a separate window—whether you're using one or two monitors—click the Use Second Monitor / Show Second Window button (■), located at the top left of the Filmstrip.

2   In the top panel of the secondary display, click Grid or press Shift+G.

> 💡 *You can use keyboard shortcuts to change the view in the second window—Shift+G for Grid, Shift+E for Loupe, Shift+C for Compare, and Shift+N for Survey. If the second window is not already open, you can use these keyboard shortcuts to quickly open it in the view mode of your choice.*

3   The Grid view in the secondary display shows the same images the Grid view or the Filmstrip in the main window. Use the Thumbnails slider in the lower right corner of the secondary display to change the size of the thumbnail images. Use the scrollbar on the right side, if necessary, to scroll to the end of the Grid view. The source indicator and menu on the left side of the lower panel work the same way as they do in the Filmstrip, and the top and bottom panels can be hidden and shown as they can in the main window. You'll learn more about working with panels later in this lesson.

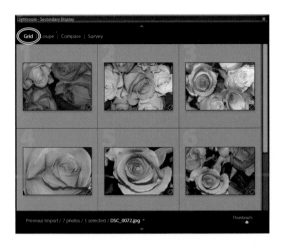

4 Select an image, and then click Loupe in the top panel of the secondary display to display the photo in Loupe view. Make sure that Normal is selected in the view mode picker on the right side of the top panel.

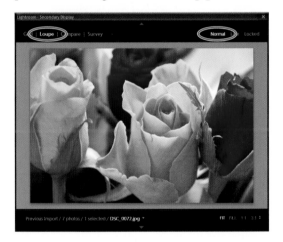

In Normal mode, the Loupe view in the second window always displays the active image from the main Grid view—when in Grid view on the main screen—or Filmstrip.

5 Use the arrow keys to select either the previous or next photo in the Filmstrip. The new selection becomes the active image and the secondary display is updated accordingly.

Note: If your secondary display is open in a window and not on a second screen, you may need to click inside the main window or on its title bar to change the focus of any keyboard input.

6   Click Live in the view mode picker on the right side of the second window's top panel. In Live mode, the secondary display shows the image that is currently under your pointer in either the Filmstrip, Grid, Loupe, Compare, or Survey view in the main window. You can choose a different zoom level from the menu at the lower right of the secondary window.

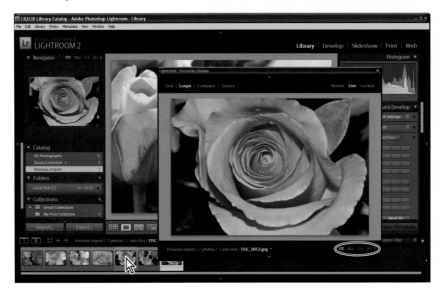

7   Select an image in the Filmstrip, and then click Locked in the view mode picker on the right side of the second window's top panel. The current image will now remain in the display until you switch back to Normal or Live mode. Change the zoom level by choosing from the options at the right of the lower panel: click Fit, Fill, or 1:1, or choose a zoom ratio from the menu at the far right. Drag the zoomed image to reposition it in the view or click it to return to the previous zoom level.

8   (Optional) Right-click / Control-click the image to choose a different background color or texture from the context menu. These settings will apply to the second window independently of the options chosen for the main window.

9   Choose Compare from the view picker in the top panel of the secondary window. In the main window, select two or more images in the Grid view or the Filmstrip. The image in the left pane of the Compare view is the *Select* image; the one in the right pane is the *Candidate*. You can change the candidate image by clicking the Select Previous Photo button (⬅) or the Select Next Photo button (➡). If you selected more than two images, only images from the selection are considered as candidates. To replace the Select image with the current Candidate, click the Make Select button (▰).

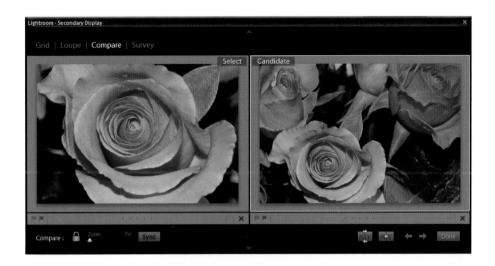

10   Use the Survey view to compare more than two images at once. In the main window, select three or more images in the Grid view or the Filmstrip and click Survey in the top panel of the second window. To remove an image from the Survey view, move the pointer over the unwanted image and click the Close button (✕) that appears in the lower left corner of the image. You'll learn more about using the Compare and Survey views later in this book.

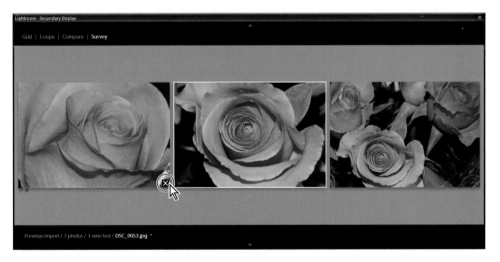

11   Close the secondary display by disabling the menu option Window > Secondary Display > Show.

Resizing panels

You've learned how to switch between screen modes and about using a secondary display; now you'll customize the layout of the workspace. You can adjust the width of the side panel groups and the height of the Filmstrip panel, or hide any of them completely, to suit the way you work and make more space available for the task at hand.

1   Move the pointer over the right edge of the left panel group. The pointer changes to a horizontal double-arrow (↔) / horizontal double-arrow with bar (↔). Drag to the right and release the mouse button when the panel group has reached its maximum width. The work area contracts to accommodate the expanded panel. You might use this arrangement to maximize the Navigator preview.

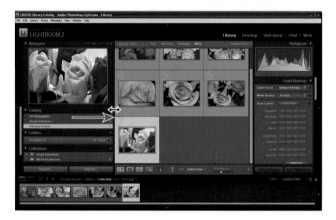

2   Click Develop in the Module Picker to switch to the Develop module. You will notice that the left panel group returns to the width it was when you last used the Develop module. Lightroom remembers your customized panel layout for each module independently. As you move between modules, the workspace is automatically rearranged to suit the way you like to work in each module.

3   Press Alt+Ctrl+Up Arrow / Option+Command+Up Arrow to return quickly to the previous module.

4   In the Library module, drag the right edge of the left panel group to resize it to its minimum width.

Note: Lightroom remembers your custom layout for the right panel group in the same way. You can set up a different layout for each module.

5   Move the pointer over the top edge of the Filmstrip panel. When the pointer changes to a vertical double-arrow ($\updownarrow$) / vertical double-arrow with bar ($\updownarrow$), drag the top edge down until the Filmstrip reaches its minimum height. The work area expands to fill the available space.

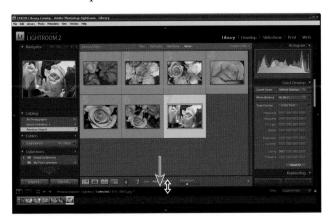

6   Switch back to the Develop module. The Filmstrip remains unchanged as you move between modules. Whichever module you switch to, the Filmstrip will remain at its current height until you resize it.

7   Move the pointer over the top edge of the Filmstrip panel. When the pointer changes to a vertical double-arrow ($\updownarrow$) / vertical double-arrow with bar ($\updownarrow$), double-click the top edge of the Filmstrip to reset the panel to its previous height. Switch back to the Library module.

Note: For the side panel groups, double-clicking the border will produce a different result. This is discussed in the next section, "Showing and hiding panels or panel groups."

8   Drag the top border of the Filmstrip to its maximum height. The thumbnails are enlarged and, if necessary, a scrollbar appears along the bottom of the Filmstrip. Scroll to view all the thumbnails.

9   Move the pointer over the top edge of the Filmstrip panel. When the pointer changes to a vertical double-arrow ($\updownarrow$) / vertical double-arrow with bar ($\updownarrow$), double-click the top edge of the Filmstrip to reset it to its previous height.

Note: You can't change the height of the top panel, but you can hide or reveal it as you wish.

Showing and hiding panels or panel groups

As you have seen, one way of making more space for your work area is to resize the side panel groups and the Filmstrip. Another way is to completely hide panels from view. You can hide any of the panels surrounding the work area in the workspace. In some screen modes Lightroom even hides the title bar, the menu bar, and the Windows task bar or the Dock.

1   To hide the left panel group, click the Show/Hide Panel Group icon (◀) in the left margin of the workspace window. The panel group disappears and the arrow icon is reversed.

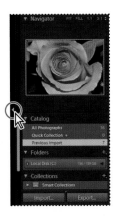

2   Click the Show/Hide Panel Group icon again to reveal the left panel group.

Click the Show/Hide Panel Group icon in the right margin of the workspace window to show and hide the right panel group. Likewise, the arrows in the top and bottom margins of the workspace show or hide the top panel and the Filmstrip.

You don't need to be accurate when you click the Show/Hide Panel Group icons. In fact, you can click anywhere in the workspace margins to hide and show panels.

3   Press the F7 key, or disable the menu option Window > Panels > Show Left Module Panels, to hide the left panel group. To show the group again, press F7, or choose Window > Panels > Show Left Module Panels.

Note: In Mac OS, some function keys are assigned to specific operating system functions by default. If pressing a function key in Lightroom does not work as expected, either press the fn key (not available on all keyboard layouts) together with the respective function key, or change the keyboard behavior in the system preferences.

4   Press the F8 key, or disable the menu option Window > Panels > Show Right Module Panels, to hide the right panel group. To show the group again, press F8, or choose Window > Panels > Show Right Module Panels.

5   Press the F5 key, or disable the menu option Window > Panels > Show Module Picker, to hide the top panel. To show it again, press F5, or choose Window > Panels > Show Module Picker. Press the F6 key, or disable the menu option Window > Panels > Show Fimstrip, to hide the Filmstrip. To show it again, press F6, or choose Window > Panels > Show Filmstrip.

6   Press the Tab key, or choose Window > Panels > Toggle Side Panels, to hide or show both side panel groups together. Press Shift+Tab, or choose Window > Panels > Toggle All Panels, to hide or show the side panel groups, the top panel, and the Filmstrip all at once.

Lightroom offers even more options for showing and hiding panels or panel groups— you can have them show and hide automatically in response to the movements of the pointer.

7   Right-click / Control-click the Show/Hide Panel Group icon (◀) in the left margin of the workspace window. Choose Auto Hide & Show from the context menu.

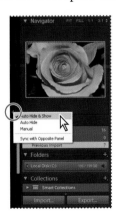

8   Hide the left panel group by clicking the Show/Hide Panel Group icon (◀). Move the pointer over the icon, or anywhere in the left margin of the workspace. The left panel group automatically slides into view, partly covering the work area. You can click to select catalogs, folders, and collections; the left panel group will remain visible as long as the pointer remains over it. Move the pointer outside the left panel group and it will disappear again. To show or hide the left panel group regardless of the current panel settings, press the F7 key.

9 Right-click / Control-click the Show/Hide Panel Group icon (◄) in the left margin of the workspace window and this time choose Auto Hide from the context menu. Now the panel group disappears when you are done with it and does not reappear when you move the pointer into the workspace margin. To show the left panel group again, click in the workspace margin, or press the F7 key.

10 To turn off automatic show and hide, right-click / Control-click the Show/Hide Panel Group icon (◄) in the left margin of the workspace and choose Manual from the context menu.

11 To reset the left panel group to its default settings, activate Auto Hide & Show in the context menu. If necessary, press the F7 key or the F8 key to show the left and right panel groups.

Keep it in mind that Lightroom remembers your customized panel layout for each module independently, including your preferred show and hide options, so you can set these options differently to suit the way you like to work in each module. Options you choose for the Filmstrip and the top panel remain unchanged as you move between modules.

Working with the left and right panel groups

Up to this point in our lesson, we've dealt with the left and right panels only as groups. Now you'll learn to work with the individual panels within the groups.

Expanding and collapsing panels

1 If you are not already in the Library module, switch to it now. Create more space to work with the side panel groups by hiding both the top panel and the Filmstrip.

In the Library module, the left panel group contains the Navigator, Catalog, Folders and Collections panels. Each panel within a group can either be *expanded* to show its content or *collapsed* so that only the panel header is visible. A triangle next to the panel name indicates whether a panel is expanded or collapsed.

2 To expand a collapsed panel, click the triangle next to its name; the triangle turns downward and the panel expands to show its content. Click the triangle again to collapse the panel.

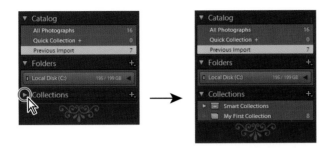

💡 *You don't need to be accurate when you click the triangle. Clicking anywhere in the panel header will do, as long as you don't click any other control that might be located in the panel header, such as the Plus icon (+) in the header of the Collections panel.*

Folders within a panel—such as the Smart Collections folder in the Collections panel— can be expanded and collapsed by clicking the triangle next to the folder name, or by double-clicking the folder header.

3   Panels that are currently expanded and fully visible in the panel group show a check mark in front of their names in the Window > Panels menu. Choose a panel from that menu to toggle its display status.

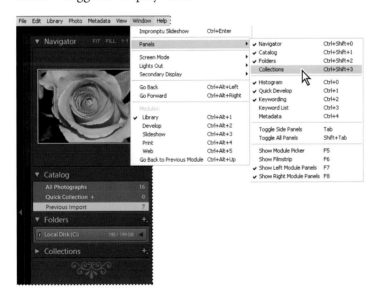

4   In the Window > Panels menu, look at the keyboard shortcuts for expanding and collapsing the individual panels. For the panels in the left group, the keyboard shortcuts begin with Shift+Ctrl / Command+Control followed by a number. The panels are numbered from the top down, so you press Shift+Ctrl+0 / Command+Control+0 for the Navigator panel, Shift+Ctrl+1 / Command+Control+1 for the Catalog panel, and so on. For the panels in the right group, the keyboard shortcuts begin with Ctrl / Command followed by a number. Press Ctrl+0 / Command+0 to collapse the Histogram panel. Press the same keyboard shortcut again to expand it. These keyboard shortcuts may be assigned to different panels in another workspace module, but this should not be too confusing if you remember that the panels are always numbered from the top of the group, starting at 0.

You can expand and collapse all panels (except the topmost in each group) with one command, or have all the panels other than the one you're working with (and the top panel in the group) close automatically. The top panel in each group has a special role and is not affected by these commands.

5   To collapse all panels in either side group, right-click / Control-click the header of any panel—other than the top panel in the group—and choose Collapse All from the context menu. The top panel remains unchanged.

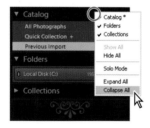

💡 *You can also right-click / Control-click in the empty area below the last panel to bring up this context menu.*

6   To expand all panels in either side group, right-click / Control-click the header of any panel—other than the top panel in the group—and choose Expand All from the context menu. Once again, the top panel remains unchanged.

7   To close all the panels in a group other than the one you're working with, right-click / Control-click the header of any panel—other than the top panel in the group—and choose Solo Mode from the context menu. Only one panel will remain open. The triangles next to the panel names change in appearance, from solid to dotted, when Solo mode is activated. Click the header of a collapsed panel to expand it. The previously expanded panel collapses automatically.

8   Disable Solo mode.

Alt-click / Option-click the header of any panel to quickly activate or disable Solo mode.

Hiding and showing panels

If you use some panels in a group less often than others, you can hide them from view to create more space to expand the remaining panels in the group.

1   To hide all the panels in a group other than the topmost, right-click / Control-click the header of any panel and choose Hide All from the context menu.

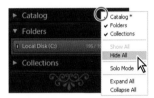

All the panels in the group, except the Navigator panel at the top, are now hidden.

2   To show all panels, right-click / Control-click inside the empty space below the visible panels and choose Show All from the context menu.

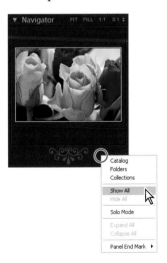

3   To show or hide an individual panel, choose it from the same context menu. Panels that are currently visible have a checkmark in front of their names.

Customizing the appearance of the panel groups

By default, Lightroom displays an ornament—the panel end mark—below the bottom panel in each group. You can select any of the designs that come preinstalled in Lightroom, change the panel end mark to one of your own design, or choose not to display a panel end mark at all.

1   To change the panel end mark, right-click / Control-click inside the empty space below the panels. Choose an ornament from the Panel End Mark submenu in the context menu, or select None.

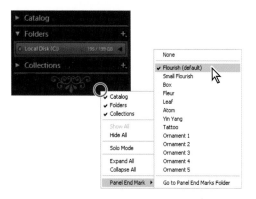

The same panel end mark is used for both side panel groups in all the modules. To use your own PDF, JPEG, GIF, PNG, TIFF, or PSD image, place it in the Panel End Marks Folder. To find the Panel End Marks Folder, choose Go To Panel End Marks Folder from the Panel End Mark submenu. The names of any images you place in the Panel End Marks folder will appear grouped below the pre-installed end marks in the menu. The panel end marks that come pre-installed in Lightroom are no more than 56 pixels high, but you can use a taller image if you wish. If you image is too wide Lightroom will automatically scale it to fit the width of the panel. Your end mark design may contain transparent pixels.

You can also change the Panel End Mark—and the size of the font used in the panels—in the Preferences dialog box.

2   Choose Edit > Preferences / Lightroom > Preferences. In the Preferences dialog box, click the Interface tab. You'll find the Panel End Mark menu in the Panels options.

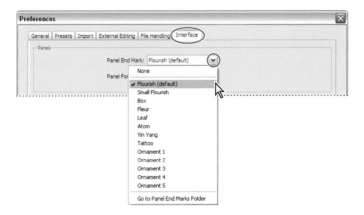

From the Panel Font Size menu you can choose either Small (the default) or Large, although the difference is subtle.

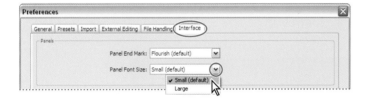

Changes to the font size will take effect next time you launch Lightroom.

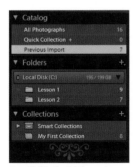
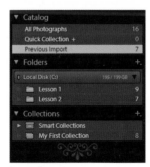

Small (default) font size.　　*Large font size.*

3　Without making any changes, click Cancel / the Close button (⊝) to close the Preferences dialog box.

Working with the main display area

The main display area—the work area—in the center of the application window is where you select, sort, and compare the images in your library, and preview the work in process as you make adjustments and create presentations. The work area serves different purposes in each of the Lightroom workspace modules. The Library and Develop modules offer a choice of view modes to suit a range of tasks, from organizing your collections to editing the individual photos. In the Slideshow, Print, and Web modules, the work area presents a working preview of your project.

View modes

In the Library module, you may see the Filter bar at the top of the work area. You can use filters to limit the photos that will be displayed in the Grid view and the Filmstrip to those with a specified star rating, flag status, or particular metadata content. You'll learn more about the Filter bar controls in Lesson 5, "Organizing and Selecting."

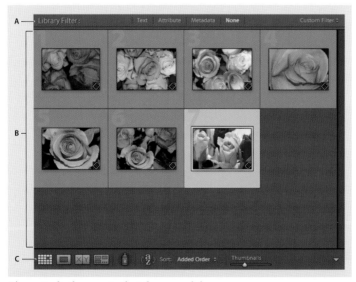

The main display area in the Library module:
A. Filter bar. B. Work area (Grid view active). C. Toolbar.

1   If you are not already in the Library module, switch to it now. If the Filter bar is visible at the top of the work area, hide it by pressing the backslash character (\) or by disabling the menu option View > Show Filter Bar.

Across the bottom of the work area is the Toolbar. The Toolbar is common to all the workspace modules but contains different tools and controls for each.

2   If the Toolbar is not already visible, press T to show it. Press T again to hide it.

3   Switch to the Develop module. If the Toolbar is not already visible, press T to show it. Switch back to the Library Module. You'll notice that in the Library module the Toolbar is still hidden; Lightroom remembers the Toolbar setting for each module independently. Press T to show the Toolbar in the Library module.

4   Double-click an image in Grid view to switch to Loupe view. The Loupe view is available in both the Library and Develop modules, but the controls available in the Toolbar differ for each.

5   You can hide or show individual tools by choosing their names from the menu at the right end of the Toolbar. Tools that are currently visible in the Toolbar have a checkmark in front of their names.

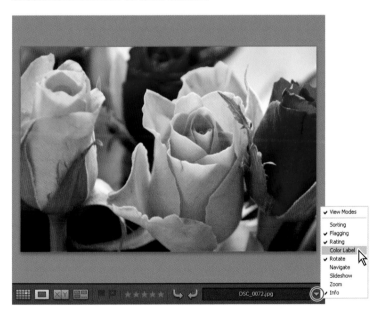

Note: If you have selected more tools than can be displayed in the width of the Toolbar, you can hide either of the side panel groups to increase the Toolbar's width, or disable tools that you don't need at the moment.

In Loupe view, you can view your images at different levels of magnification. The zoom controls in the top right corner of the Navigator panel in the left panel group enable you to switch quickly between preset magnification levels. Choose from Fit, Fill, 1:1, or choose another zoom ratio from a list of 8 options.

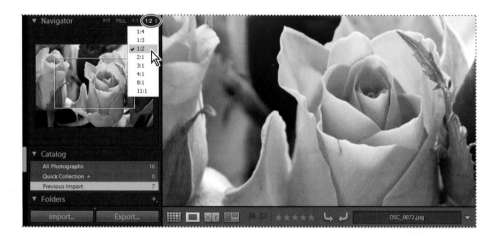

You can toggle between zoom levels using the Toggle Zoom Command, or pressing Z on your keyboard. To better understand the Toggle Zoom View command, you should be aware that the magnification controls in the Navigator panel are organized into two groups: Fit and Fill are in one group, and the zoom ratio settings are in the other. The Toggle Zoom View command toggles between the magnification levels last used in each group.

6   Click Fit in the zoom controls in the top right corner of the Navigator panel. Now click the 1:1 control. Choose View > Toggle Zoom View, or press Z. The zoom setting reverts to Fit. Press the Z key; the zoom setting reverts to 1:1.

7   Click Fill in the zoom controls in the top right corner of the Navigator panel. Now choose a zoom ratio from the menu at the far right of the Navigator panel header; we used 2:1. Click the image in the Loupe view. The zoom setting reverts to Fill. In Loupe view, clicking the image is equivalent to pressing the Z key, or choosing View > Toggle Zoom View, except that the zoomed view of the image will be centered on the area you clicked.

8   When working with a magnified view, drag the zoom rectangle in the Navigator preview, or drag in the Loupe view to change the image area currently visible in the work area. At higher zoom levels you may find using the Navigator panel more convenient, while dragging the image in the Loupe view is better suited to working at lower zoom levels.

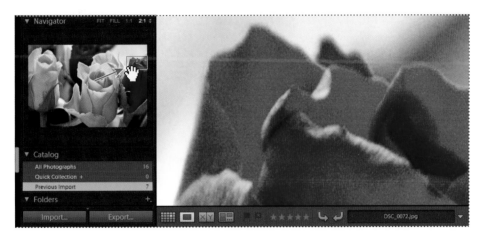

9   When zoomed in, press the Home key to position the zoom rectangle in the top left corner of the image. Now press the Page Down key repeatedly to scroll through the magnified image one section at the time. When you reach the bottom of the image the zoom rectangle will jump to the top of the next column. To start in the lower right corner of the image, press the End key and use the Page Up key to step through the image. This feature can be very helpful if you want to make sure you inspect the entire image area.

The zoom controls and the Navigator panel work the same way for the Loupe view in both the Library and Develop modules.

The other two view modes, Compare view and Survey view, will be covered in Lesson 4, "Reviewing," and Lesson 6, "Developing and Editing."

Grid and Loupe view options

You can customize the information displayed for each image in the Grid and Loupe views. Choose your preferences from the many options in the Library View Options dialog box. For Loupe view and the thumbnail tooltips you can activate two sets of options and use a keyboard shortcut to switch between them.

1   Press G to switch to Grid view in the Library module.

2   Choose View > View Options. The Library View Options dialog box will appear with the Grid View tab already selected. Position the Library View Options dialog box so you can see some of the images in the Grid view.

3   Disable the Show Grid Extras option in the top left corner of the Grid View tab. This will disable most of the other options.

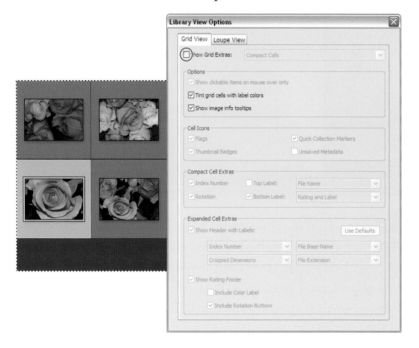

4   The only options still available are Tint Grid Cells With Label Colors and Show Image Info Tooltips. If they are not already activated, click the checkboxes beside both of these options. As the images have not yet been assigned color labels, activating the first option has no visible effect in the Grid view. Right-click / Control-click any thumbnail in the Grid view—you can do this while the Library View Options dialog box is open—and choose a color from the Set Color Label menu. A color-labeled image that is currently selected will show a thin colored frame around the thumbnail; a color-labeled image that is not selected has a tinted cell background.

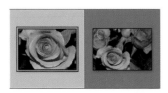

5   Position the pointer over a thumbnail in the Grid view or the Filmstrip; a tooltip appears. In Mac OS you'll need to click anywhere in the Lightroom workspace window to bring it to the front before you can see the tooltips. By default, the tooltip will display the file name, capture date and time, and the cropped dimensions. You can specify the information to be displayed in the tooltip by choosing from the Loupe View options.

6   In Mac OS, if the Library View Options dialog box is now hidden behind the main application window, press Command+J to bring it back to the front.

7   Activate the Show Grid Extras option and choose Compact Cells from the menu beside it. Experiment with each setting to see its effect in the Grid view display. Activate and disable the settings for Options, Cell Icons, and Compact Cell Extras. Position the pointer over the various icons in the image cells to see tooltips with additional information.

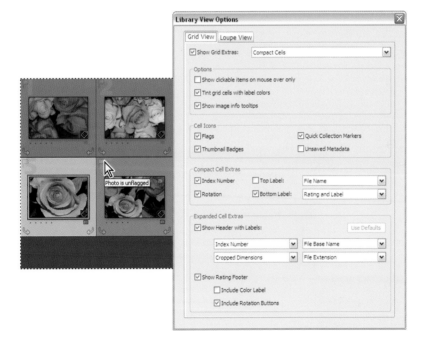

8   Under Compact Cell Extras, click the Top Label menu to see the long list of choices available. For some choices, such as Title or Caption, nothing will be displayed until you add the relevant information to the image's metadata.

9   Now choose Expanded Cells from the Show Grid Extras menu. Experiment with the Expanded Cell Extras to see the effects in the Grid view. Click any of the

Show Header With Labels menus to see the many choices available to customize the information that is displayed in the cell headers.

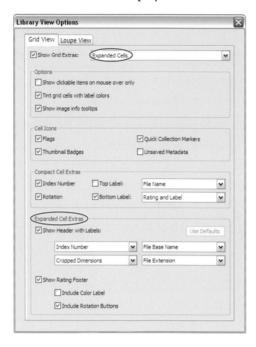

10 Click the Loupe View tab. The work area switches from Grid to Loupe view so you can preview the effects of the changes you'll make in the Library View Options dialog box.

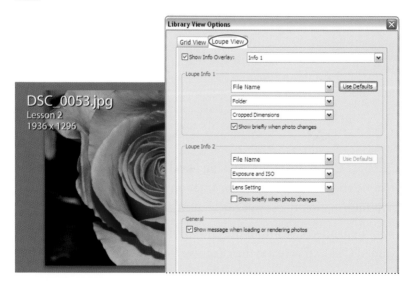

For the Loupe view, you can activate the Show Info Overlay option to display image information in the top left corner of the view. Choose items from the menus in Loupe Info 1 and Loupe Info 2 to create two different sets of information, and then choose either set from the Show Info Overlay menu. When you choose an information item such as Capture Date and Time, Lightroom extracts those details from the image metadata. If the image's metadata does not contain the specified information, nothing will be displayed for that item.

You can reset either group to its default state by clicking the Use Defaults button. Activate the Show Briefly When Photo Changes option to show the info overlay for only a few seconds when a new image is displayed in the Loupe view.

Activate the Show Message When Loading Or Rendering Photos option to display a notification in the lower part of the view while the image preview is updated. It is recommended that you keep this option activated so that you don't inadvertently make judgments about the quality of an image before the update is complete.

11 Click the Close button to close the Library View Options dialog box.

12 You can choose which of the two information sets will be displayed by choosing an option from the View > Loupe Info menu, or by pressing the I key to cycle the info overlay through Loupe Info 1, Loupe Info 2, and its disabled state.

13 Switch to the Grid view. From the View > Grid View Style menu you can choose whether or not to display additional information, using either the Compact Cells layout or the Expanded Cells layout. Press the J key to cycle through the Compact Cells layout, with and without additional information, and the Expanded Cells layout.

Dimming lights

Lightroom gives you the option to darken the workspace so that you can concentrate on the image or images with which you're working. In the Library and Develop modules, everything is dimmed or darkened except your selected photos. In the other three modules, everything except the presentation preview in the work area is dimmed or darkened. All of the tools and controls will still work in the Lights Dim or Lights Off modes—if you can find them! You could pick up the crop tool for example, and then switch to either the Lights Dim or Lights Off mode to help you concentrate on achieving the best result.

1   To dim the lights, press the L key or choose Window > Lights Out > Lights Dim.

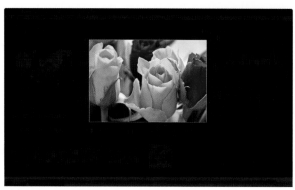

The Lights Dim mode helps you focus on your image.

2   If you're in the Grid view, double-click an image to switch to Loupe view. Click the image to switch between zoom levels. If you can see the Filmstrip, click to select a different image. Switch to a different module. If you remember the keyboard shortcuts they can really come in handy now.

3   To darken the workspace around the image completely, press the L key again or choose Window > Lights Out > Lights Off—if you can still see the menu bar.

4   To return to the normal display mode, press the L key a third time, or choose Window > Lights Out > Lights On.

Lightroom achieves the dimming and darkening effects by means of a black overlay applied to the interface—at a default opacity of 80% for Lights Dim and 100% for Lights Off. You can choose instead to have the workspace fade to white or a shade of grey. This might be useful, for example, if your images contain a lot of black or dark colors. You can also adjust the level of opacity for the Lights Dim mode so that you can still see the controls if necessary.

5   To change the Lights Out screen color or to adjust the opacity for the Lights Dim mode, choose Edit > Preferences / Lightroom > Preferences. In the Preferences dialog box, click the Interface tab and in the Lights Out options, choose a new opacity value from the Dim Level menu. From the Screen Color menu, choose white or a shade of grey.

6   Click OK / the Close button (⊖) to close the Preferences dialog box, and press the L key repeatedly to see your new settings in effect. Return to step 5 to modify your settings or reinstate the defaults.

Personalizing the identity plate

If you're using Lightroom to make presentations to clients on your computer, or if you'd simply like to personalize the workspace, you can change the graphic that is displayed as an Identity Plate in the top panel.

1   If the top panel is not currently visible, press the F5 key, or choose Window > Panels > Show Module Picker.

2   Choose Edit > Identity Plate Setup / Lightroom > Identity Plate Setup. Position the Identity Plate Editor dialog box so you can see both the dialog box and the identity plate in the top panel.

3   If not already selected, activate the Use A Styled Text Identity Plate option. Then activate the Enable Identity Plate option. You'll notice an immediate change in the appearance of the identity plate.

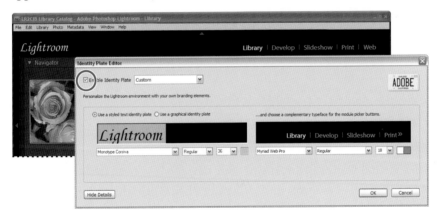

Note: If your Identity Plate Editor dialog box differs from the one shown in the illustration above—apart from the name used in the text box on the left—, click the Show Details button in the lower left corner.

To personalize the identity plate, you can either use styled text or place a graphic of your choice. If you wish, you can also change the typeface and text color used for the Module Picker at the other end of the top panel to better suit your design.

4   Select the text in the text box and replace it with your own.

💡 *If your text is too long to be fully visible in the text box, resize the dialog box or reduce the font size until you've finished editing.*

5   Press Ctrl+A / Command+A to select your new text, and choose a typeface, font style, and font size from the menus beneath the text box. Use your company's corporate typeface or your own favorite —not necessarily mutually exclusive choices. Click the color box beside the font size menu and choose a new color from the Colors palette. Keep an eye on how your choices look in the top panel. Click OK to apply your changes or Cancel to reject them.

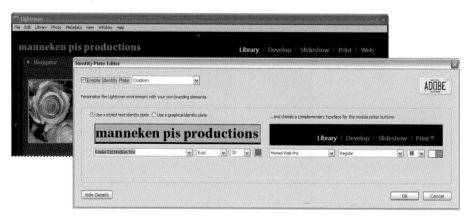

You can use more than one typeface, font style, size, or color in your identity plate text. Simply select a portion of your text and make the desired changes.

6   (Optional) You can also change the typeface, font style, and font size used for the text in the Module Picker to better suit your new identity plate design. You'll notice that there is a second set of controls in the Identity Plate Editor dialog box for this purpose. Click the first color box to change the color used to highlight the name of the active module and the second color box to change the color used for the names of the others.

7   To use an image as your identity plate, activate the Use A Graphical Identity Plate option, and then click the Locate File button. In the Locate File dialog box, navigate to your Lesson 2 folder, select the file Identityplate.png, and click Choose.

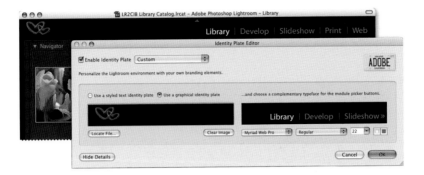

Note: On Windows, you can choose a JPEG, PNG, GIF, BMP, or TIFF image for your graphical identity plate. The image can contain transparent pixels and should not be more than 48 pixels in height. On Mac OS, images in PSD or PDF format are also supported and the image height can be up to 57 pixels.

8 (Optional) You can save several identity plate setups as presets that can be easily accessed for different situations. Choose Save As from the Enable Identity Plate menu, enter a name for your identity plate preset and click Save. Your identity plate presets will appear in the Enable Identity Plate menu.

9 Disable the Enable Identity Plate option, and then click OK to close the Identity Plate Editor dialog box.

Keyboard shortcuts

This concludes your introduction to the Lightroom workspace. You've learned how to switch between the different screen and view modes and how to arrange the workspace layout to suit the way you work in each module. You know how to hide, show, collapse, or expand panels and panel groups, how to customize the Toolbar, and how to use a secondary display. Finally, you have personalized the Lightroom workspace with your own identity plate.

Just one more tip and you are ready for the review questions starting on the next page.

Press Ctrl+/ (Windows) / Command+/ (Mac OS) to see a list of keyboard shortcuts for the active module. When you're done reviewing the keyboard shortcuts, click to dismiss the list.

Review

▶ ## Review questions

1   How would you view an image at the largest size possible on your screen?

2   How do you adjust the size of the thumbnail images in the Grid view, the Navigator panel, and the Filmstrip?

3   What are the keyboard shorcuts to show or hide the four panels that surround the Lightroom workspace?

4   What do you do if you can't see the tool you're looking for in the Toolbar?

5   How can you personalize the Lightroom interface?

▶ ## Review answers

1   In the Grid view, double-click a thumbnail to enter the Loupe view. Choose Window > Screen Mode > Full Screen And Hide Panels, or use the keyboard shortcut Shift+Ctrl+F / Shift+Command+F. A variant of Full Screen mode, Full Screen And Hide Panels is ideal for viewing an image at the largest size possible on your display. Press the T key to hide the Toolbar, leaving nothing on screen but your photo.

2   To change the size of the Grid view thumbnails on your main screen, use the Thumbnails slider in the Toolbar. In Grid view on a secondary display use the slider in the lower right corner of the window. The thumbnail images in the Navigator panel and the Filmstrip are resized automatically as you resize the left panel group or the Filmstrip.

3   The keyboard shortcuts to show or hide the top panel, the Filmstrip, the left panel group, and the right panel group are F5, F6, F7, and F8, respectively.

4   Check what module and view mode you are in. The Toolbar contains different tools for different views and modules. Click the triangle at the right of the Toolbar and activate the missing tool in the tools menu. If the tool is activated and you still can't see it, there may be too many active tools to fit across the Toolbar. Disable tools you are not using in the tools menu and they will be removed from the Toolbar.

5 Lightroom offers several options to personalize the interface:

- You can change the identity plate, the graphic that is displayed at the left corner of the top panel. You can either use styled text or place your own graphic.

- It's also possible to change the typeface and text color used for the Module Picker at the other end of the top panel to better suit your new identity plate.

- You can customize the panel end mark displayed in the left and right panel groups. Choose from the preinstalled designs or use one of your own.

- You can set the color and texture of the background that shows behind the images in many of the working views.

- Set the level of opacity for the Lights Dim modes in the Preferences dialog box.

- Show or hide different workspace panels to suit different tasks. Set panels to show and hide automatically. You can arrange the workspace differently in each of the Lightroom modules so that when you switch between modules, your tools are always set out the way you like them.

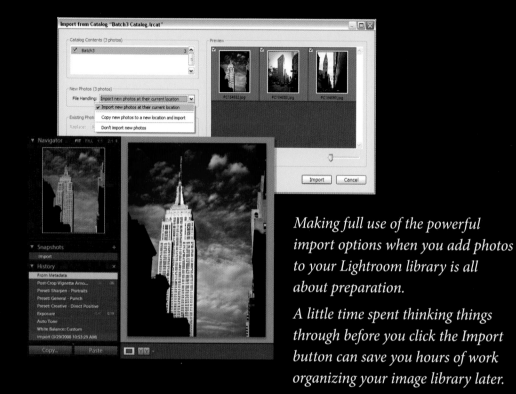

Making full use of the powerful import options when you add photos to your Lightroom library is all about preparation.

A little time spent thinking things through before you click the Import button can save you hours of work organizing your image library later.

3 Importing

When you import photos Lightroom is in fact simply adding entries for those images to its library catalog file. These catalog entries include references to the locations of your image files. You can think of them as records of the images' addresses, whether they reside on your hard disk or on external storage media. During the import process, you can choose whether Lightroom leaves your image files at their current locations—preserving the folder structure to which you are accustomed—or helps you to reorganize them by copying or moving them to new locations before recording their addresses.

An important part of the import process involves using Lightroom to add keywords and other information to those catalog entries to make it easier for you to find and organize your images when you need to work with them. For this reason it might be a good idea to revisit this lesson after completing Lesson 5, "Organizing and Selecting."

This lesson will familiarize you with the many options available to you as you add more photos to your Lightroom library:

- Importing images from a camera or card reader.
- Importing images from a hard disk or removable media.
- Choosing file handling options.
- Organizing, renaming, and processing images automatically.
- Applying metadata and keyword tags as part of the import process.
- Initiating backup strategies.
- Setting Lightroom to import automatically.
- Transferring images between computers and from other applications.

Getting started

Before you begin, make sure that you have correctly copied the Lessons folder from the CD in the back of this book onto your computer's hard disk and created the LR2CIB Library Catalog file. See "Copying the Classroom in a Book files" and "Creating a catalog file for working with this book" on page 3.

1 Start Lightroom.

2 In the Adobe Photoshop Lightroom - Select Catalog dialog box, make sure the file LR2CIB Library Catalog.lrcat is selected under Catalog Location, and then click Continue.

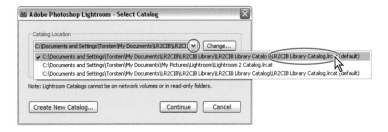

3 If the Back Up Catalog dialog box appears, click Skip Now.

4 Lightroom will open in the screen mode and workspace module that were active when you last quit. If necessary, click Library in the Module Picker to switch to the Library module.

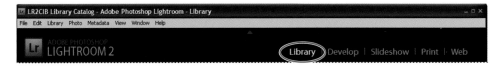

The import process

Lightroom allows a great deal of flexibility in the importing process. You can download images directly from a digital camera or card reader, import them from your hard disk or external storage media, and transfer them from another Lightroom catalog or from other applications. Import at the click of a button, use a menu command, or simply drag and drop. You can even have Lightroom import automatically when you connect your camera or move files into a watched folder.

Whether you're downloading photos from your camera or importing them from a hard disk or DVD you'll be working with the Import Photos dialog box, so we'll begin there. Even the Auto Import setup shares most of the same options.

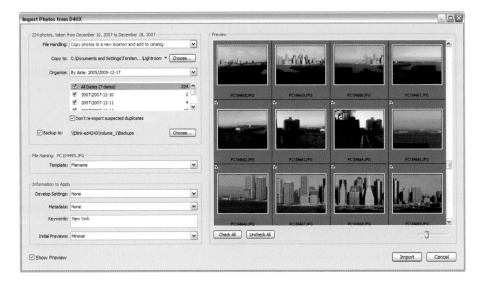

Importing photos from a digital camera

If you have a digital camera or a memory card at hand, you can step through this exercise using your own photos. If not, you can simply read through the steps and study the illustrations—much of the information in this exercise is equally applicable to importing from other sources.

To begin with, you'll configure the Lightroom preferences so that the import process is triggered automatically when you connect your camera or a memory card to your computer.

1   Choose Edit > Preferences (Windows) / Lightroom > Preferences (Mac OS). In the Preferences dialog box, click the Import tab. If not already selected, activate the option Show Import Dialog When A Memory Card Is Detected by clicking the checkbox.

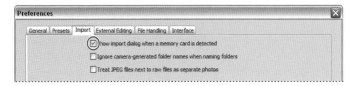

Some cameras generate folder names on the memory card. If you don't find these folder names helpful for organizing your images, activate the option Ignore Camera-Generated Folder Names When Naming Folders. You'll learn more about folder naming options later in this lesson.

If your camera records Raw images, it may also generate a JPEG version of each photo. If you wish to import both files, activate the option Treat JPEG Files Next To Raw Files As Separate Photos; otherwise, Lightroom will display only the Raw images in the Import Photos dialog box.

For the purposes of this exercise, you can disregard the Import DNG Creation options. For information about DNG files, see "About file formats" on page 100.

2   Click OK / the Close button (●) to close the Preferences dialog box.

3   Connect your digital camera or card reader to your computer, following the manufacturer's instructions.

4   This step may vary depending on your operating system and the image management software on your computer:

•   In Windows, if the dialog box shown in the illustration below appears, click Cancel.

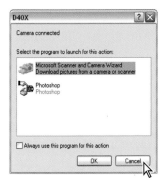

• If you have more than one Adobe image management application installed on your computer and the Adobe Downloader dialog box appears, choose Adobe Photoshop Lightroom 2 from the list and click OK.

• If the Import Photos dialog box appears, continue to step 5.

• If the Import Photos dialog box does not appear, choose File > Import Photos From Device.

5 If you don't see a Preview pane displaying thumbnails of your photos, activate the Show Preview option by clicking the checkbox in the lower left corner of the Import Photos dialog box.

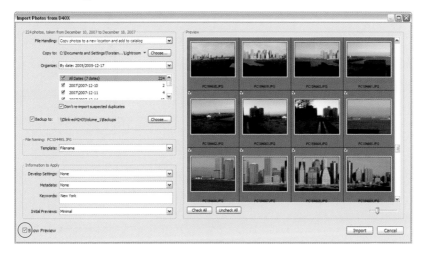

It is preferable that you keep this option activated so that you can always confirm visually that the images you are about to import are those you expect. A check mark in the top left corner of a thumbnail indicates that the photo will be imported. By default, all the photos on your memory card will be check-marked for import. You can exclude an image by clicking its checkbox to remove the check-mark. You can change the size of the thumbnails with the slider below the preview area.

You can select multiple images and then change all their checkmarks simultaneously. To select a range of images, select the first image in the range by clicking the thumbnail or the surrounding image cell, then hold down the Shift key and select the last image in the range. Select individual additional photos by Ctrl-clicking / Command-clicking their thumbnails. Then, click the checkmark of any selected image to change the settings for all selected images.

Remember that in the process of importing, Lightroom is actually only adding entries to the library catalog, including addresses for your images. When you import a photo from your hard disk or from external storage media, Lightroom offers you the option to add it to your catalog without moving it from its current location. You do not have this option when you import an image from a camera. An image on a camera's memory card does not have a very permanent address because memory cards are expected to be erased and reused—so when you import from a camera, Lightroom offers to copy your photos to a more permanent location before adding their addresses to the library catalog.

Therefore, the next step in the process is to specify a destination folder to which your images should be copied. This is the time to give some thought to how you are going to organize your photos on your computer hard disk. For now, leave the Import Photos dialog box open; you will choose a destination folder and go on to deal with the rest of the import options in the following exercises.

About file formats

Lightroom supports the following file formats:

Camera raw formats

Camera raw file formats contain unprocessed data from a digital camera's sensor. Most camera manufacturers save image data in a proprietary camera format. Lightroom reads this data and processes it into a full color photo. You use the controls in the Develop module to process and interpret the raw image data for your photo. For a list of supported cameras and camera raw formats, see www.adobe.com/go/learn_ps_cameraraw.

Digital Negative format (DNG)

The Digital Negative (DNG) file format is a publicly available archival format for raw files generated by digital cameras. By addressing the lack of an open standard for the raw files created by individual camera models, DNG helps ensure that photographers will be able to access their files in the future. You can convert proprietary raw files to DNG within Lightroom. For more information about the Digital Negative (DNG) file format, visit www.adobe.com/dng. You'll find comprehensive information and a link to a user forum.

(Continued on next page.)

About file formats (cont.)

TIFF format

Tagged-Image File Format (TIFF, TIF) is used to exchange files between applications and computer platforms. TIFF is a flexible bitmap image format supported by virtually all paint, image-editing, and page-layout applications. Also, virtually all desktop scanners can produce TIFF images. Lightroom supports large documents saved in TIFF format (up to 100 million pixels with pixel dimensions of no more than 10,000 on a side). However, most other applications, including older versions of Photoshop (pre-Photoshop CS), do not support documents with file sizes greater than 2 GB. The TIFF format provides greater compression and industry compatibility than Photoshop format (PSD), and is the recommended format for exchanging files between Lightroom and Photoshop. In Lightroom, you can export TIFF image files with a bit depth of either 8 bits or 16 bits per channel.

JPEG format

Joint Photographic Experts Group (JPEG) format is commonly used to display photographs and other continuous tone images in web photo galleries, slideshows, presentations, and other online services. JPEG retains all color information in an RGB image but compresses file size by selectively discarding data. A JPEG image is automatically decompressed when opened. In most cases, the Best Quality setting produces a result indistinguishable from the original.

Photoshop format (PSD)

Photoshop format (PSD) is the standard Photoshop file format. To import and work with a multi-layered PSD file in Lightroom, the file must have been saved in Photoshop with the Maximize PSD and PSB File Compatibility preference turned on. You'll find the option in the Photoshop file handling preferences. Lightroom saves PSD files with a bit depth or 8 bits or 16 bits per channel.

Note: Lightroom does not support CMYK files, Adobe Illustrator files, files with dimensions greater than 65,000 pixels per side or larger than 500 million pixels, or video files, including video files acquired by digital still cameras.

—From Lightroom Help

Organizing your copied photos in folders

Although there is no technical reason why you can't choose a different destination folder for each import, it's much easier to keep your hard disk organized if you create a single folder to contain all the images that are associated with a particular catalog. Within this folder you can create a new subfolder for each batch of images downloaded from your camera or copied from other external media.

Before beginning the lessons in this book, you created a folder named LR2CIB inside your *[username]*/My Documents (Windows) or *[username]*/Documents (Mac OS) folder on your computer. This folder already contains subfolders for your LR2CIB Library Catalog file and for the image files used for the lessons in this book. For the purposes of this exercise, you'll specify the LR2CIB folder as the destination for the images that you import from your camera's memory card:

1   From the File Handling menu in the Import Photos dialog box, choose Copy Photos To A New Location And Add To Catalog; then click the Choose button immediately below the File Handling options menu.

2   In the Browse For Folder / Choose Folder dialog box, navigate to your LR2CIB folder. Click the Make New Folder / New Folder button and type **Imported From Camera** as the name for your new folder, and then press Enter (Windows) / click the Create button (Mac OS).

3   Make sure the new Imported From Camera folder is selected in the Browse For Folder / Choose Folder dialog box, and then click OK / Choose. Note that the new destination folder is indicated below the File Handling options menu in the Import Photos dialog box. Click the small arrow to the left of the choose button; you'll see that the new destination folder has been added to this menu to allow easy access for future imports.

The next step is to choose from the Organize menu, which offers various options to help you organize the photos in folders as you copy them onto your hard disk:

•   **Into One Folder** With the current settings, the images would be copied directly into the new Imported From Camera folder. You have the option to create an additional subfolder for each import.

- **By Date:** *[Date Format]* The remaining options are all variations on organizing your photos by date. The images would be copied into the Imported From Camera folder and placed into one or more subfolders based on capture dates. The option "By Date: 2005/12/17" for example, creates one folder per year containing one folder per month containing one folder per day for each capture date.

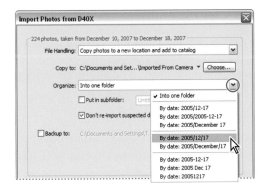

You should think about which system of folder organization best suits your needs before you begin to import photos from your camera for your own purposes and maintain that system for all your subsequent imports. For the purposes of this exercise, choose the first option.

4   Choose Into One Folder from the Organize menu.

5   (Optional) Click the Put In Subfolder checkbox and type **Lesson 3 Import**.

Backup strategies

Your next choice is whether or not to make backup copies of the images from your camera at the same time as Lightroom adds them to the library catalog and creates primary copies in the location you have just specified. It's a good idea to create backup copies on a separate hard disk or on external storage media so you don't lose your images should your hard disk fail or in case you accidently delete them.

1   In the Import Photos dialog box, activate the backup option by clicking the Backup To checkbox.

2   Click the Choose button to specify a location for your backup copies.

3   In the Browse For Folder / Backup Folder dialog box, navigate to the folder where you wish to create the backup copies of your images. Then, click OK / Choose.

This backup is mainly a precaution against loss of data due to disk failure or human error during the import process. It is not meant to replace the standard backup procedure you have in place—or should have in place—for the files on your hard disk. It's worthwhile to archive each photo shoot by burning your images to DVD's, which you can store separately. This will also help you organize your image library in Lightroom because you'll feel more secure trimming your collection down to the best images knowing that you have a backup before you press the delete key.

Renaming files as they are imported

The cryptic file names created by digital cameras are not particularly helpful. Lightroom can rename your images for you as they are imported. You can choose from a list of predefined naming options, or create your own customized naming templates.

1   In the Import Photos dialog box, choose Custom Name - Sequence from the Template menu under File Naming. Type a descriptive name in the Custom Text box that appears below the Template menu—we used **New York**— and then press the Tab key on your keyboard. The name that will be applied to first image imported is indicated above the Template menu. You can enter a number other than 1 in the Start Number text box; this is useful if you import images that belong in the same series in more than one batch.

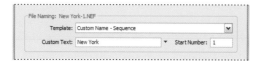

2 Click the small triangle to the right of the Custom Text box; your new custom text has been added to a list of recently entered names. You can choose a custom text from this list if you import another batch of files that belong in the same series. This not only saves time and effort but helps you ensure that subsequent batches are named identically. Should you ever wish to clear the list, choose Clear List from the menu.

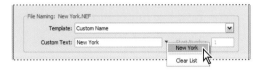

3 Next, choose Custom Name (x of y) from the Template menu. You'll notice that the sample file name indicated above the Template menu has been updated to reflect the change.

4 Finally, choose Edit from the Template menu to open the Filename Template Editor. In the Filename Template Editor dialog box you can set up a filename template that makes use of metadata information stored in your image files—such as file names, capture dates, or ISO settings—adding automatically generated sequence numbers and any custom text you specify. A filename template includes placeholders—or *tokens*—that will be replaced by actual values during the importing and renaming process.

For example, you could rename your photos: New York-01, New York-02, and so on by setting up a filename template with a custom text token followed by a hyphen (-) and a 2-digit sequence number token.

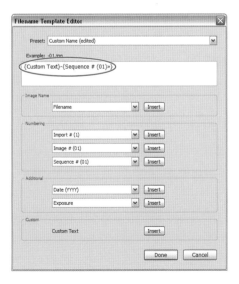

After closing the Filename Template Editor you would type **New York** in the Custom Text box just as you did previously in this exercise; "New York" would replace the custom text token in the filename template and the sequence number would be added automatically.

5   Click Cancel to close the Filename Template Editor without making any changes.

For more information on using the Filename Template Editor please refer to Lightroom Help.

Despite all of the options available for renaming your images during the import process, there's only so much information you can squeeze into a single file name. It might be better to take a minimal approach to renaming your photos during import and instead take advantage of the other file management capabilities of Lightroom. Metadata and keyword tags are far more powerful and versatile tools for organizing and searching your image library. You'll learn about using metadata and keyword tags in the following exercises and in Lesson 5, "Organizing and Selecting."

An option you should consider—if your camera supports it—is to set your camera to generate file names with unique sequence numbers. When you clear your memory card, or change memory cards, your camera will continue to generate unique sequence numbers rather than start counting from one again. This way, the images you import into your library will always have unique file names.

You have now completed this exercise in importing photos from a digital camera or a memory card. You will learn about the remaining options in the Import Photos dialog box in the exercises to follow.

6   For now, click Cancel to close the Import Photos dialog box without actually importing any images.

Importing images from a hard disk

When you import photos from your hard disk or from external storage media, Lightroom offers you more options for organizing your original files than those that were available when importing from your camera.

If you wish, you can still choose to copy your images to a new location during the import process but you also have the option to add them to your catalog without moving them from their current locations. You might choose the latter option if the images you wish to import are already organized in a satisfactory folder hierarchy.

For images that are already located on your hard disk you have an extra option: to *move* them to a new location, removing them from the original location at the same time. This option might appeal if the images on your hard disk are not already organized in a satisfactory manner.

1   To import images from your computer hard disk or from a CD, DVD, or other external storage media, either choose File > Import Photos From Disk, press Ctrl+Shift+I / Command+Shift+I, or simply click the Import button below the left panel group in the Library module.

2   In the Import Photos Or Lightroom Catalog dialog box, navigate to the Lessons folder you've already copied into the LR2CIB folder on your hard disk. Select the Lesson 3 folder and click Import All Photos In Selected Folder / Choose.

3   From the File Handling menu in the Import Photos dialog box, choose Add Photos To Catalog Without Moving, an option that wasn't available when you imported images from your camera. Do not click Import yet!

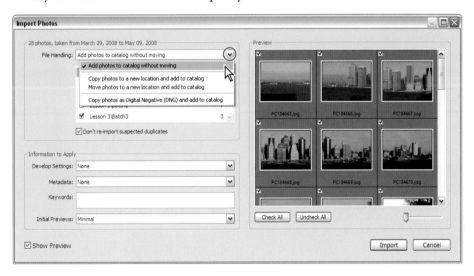

4   Notice the list of folder names beneath the File Handling menu. The number to the right of each folder name indicates the number of images within that folder. The Lesson 3 folder contains nine images and three subfolders. The subfolders Batch1, Batch2, and Batch3 contain nine, seven, and three images respectively, bringing the total number of images in the Lesson 3 folder to 28.

5 Click the All Folders (4 Folders) checkbox to disable it, and then click the checkbox beside the Lesson 3/Batch1 subfolder.

6 Click the All Folders name in the list box, rather than the associated checkbox, and use the scrollbar in the Preview pane to scroll down through the preview display—or use the slider to reduce the size of the thumbnails—so that you can see more of the images. All but the selected Batch1 photos are now grayed out.

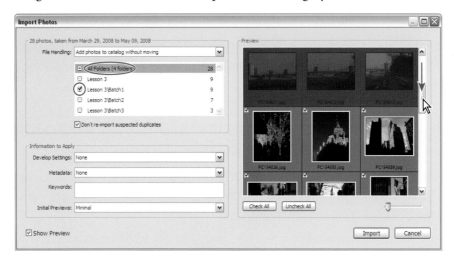

7 Before moving on, take a moment to review the options in the File Handling menu:

• Choose the option Add Photos To Catalog Without Moving to preserve the current folder structure and location of the images you're importing.

• Choose the option Copy Photos To A New Location And Add To Catalog to create copies of your images as you import them, leaving the originals in their current locations and preserving their original folder hierarchy. If you activate this option, you can choose from further options in the Organize menu: copy the photos into a single folder, into subfolders based on their creation dates, or into a folder structure that replicates their original arrangement.

• Choose the option Move Photos To A New Location And Add To Catalog to move the images to a new location on your hard disk and delete them from their original locations. For this option, you can also select one of the three folder arrangements from the Organize menu.

• Choose the option Copy Photos As Digital Negative (DNG) And Add To Catalog to create copies of your images in DNG file format and then import those copies to a new location.

Applying metadata

Lightroom uses the metadata information attached to image files to enable you to quickly find and organize your photos. You can search your image library and filter the results by keyword, creation date, flag status, color label, shooting settings, or any combination of a wide range of other criteria. You can also choose specific information about your images from this metadata and have Lightroom display it as a text overlay applied to each image in a slideshow, web gallery, or print layout.

Some metadata is automatically generated by your camera when you take a photo. You can also add your own information as part of the import process, making it even easier to locate and organize your images on your own terms.

1   In the Information To Apply options pane, choose New from the Metadata menu.

2   In the New Metadata Preset dialog box, type a descriptive name for these nine photos in the Preset Name box (we used "New York trip Dec 2007"). Then enter metadata information that is applicable to the images as a group, such as copyright information. You can customize the metadata for each individual image later, adding information such as titles and captions. Click Create to close the New Metadata Preset dialog box.

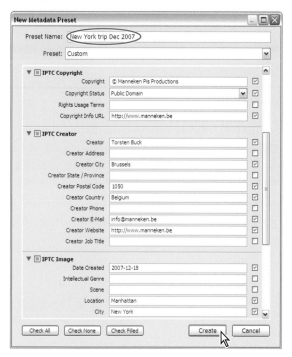

Note: You may need to use the scrollbar to see all the metadata categories in the New Metadata Preset and Edit Metadata Presets dialog boxes.

💡 *You can edit your metadata presets later by choosing Edit Presets from the Metadata menu in the Import Photos dialog box. In the Edit Metadata Presets dialog box you can edit, rename, or delete presets, or save modified settings as a new preset.*

3 Confirm that your new metadata preset is selected in the Metadata menu. Type **Lesson 3, New York** in the Keywords text box, choose None from the Develop Settings menu, and choose Minimal from the Initial Previews menu. Check that your settings are the same as those shown in the illustration below, and then click Import.

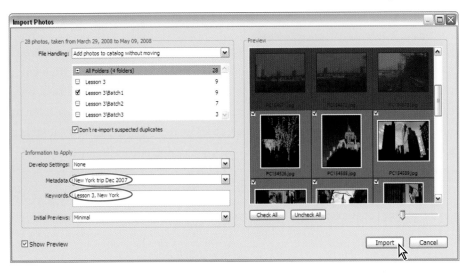

Lightroom will import the photos into your library catalog and display thumbnail images in the Grid view and the Filmstrip.

4 Right-click / Control-click any of the images in the Grid view and choose Show In Folder In Library from the context menu. In the Folders panel in the left panel group, the Batch1 subfolder inside the Lesson 3 folder is highlighted and the image count indicates that it contains your 9 newly imported photos.

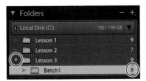

5 Right-click / Control-click the Batch1 subfolder in the Folders panel and choose Show In Explorer / Show In Finder from the context menu.

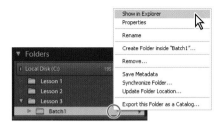

The Lesson 3 folder will open in a Windows Explorer / Finder window with the Batch1 folder highlighted.

Importing via drag and drop

Perhaps the easiest way to add photos to your image library is to drag-and-drop a selection of files—or even an entire folder—directly into Lightroom.

1 The Windows Explorer / Finder window showing your Lesson 3 folder should still be open from the previous exercise. Position the window so that you can see the Grid view in the Lightroom workspace beside it.

2 Drag the Batch2 folder from the Windows Explorer / Finder window onto the Grid view. The Import Photos dialog box opens when you release the mouse button.

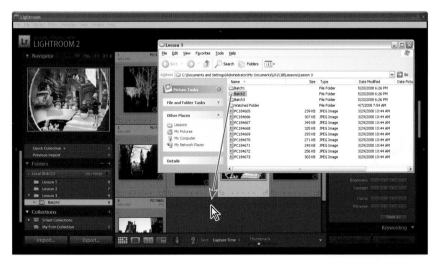

3   In the Import Photos dialog box, the Batch2 subfolder is now selected in the folder list below the File Handling menu and the 7 photos stored in that folder are displayed in the Preview pane. You'll notice that the rest of the settings from your last import remain unchanged:

•   Add Photos To Catalog Without Moving is still selected in the File Handling menu.

•   The Information To Apply settings are the same; your customized metadata preset is selected and the keywords box still contains the text "Lesson 3, New York".

•   The Show Preview option is still activated.

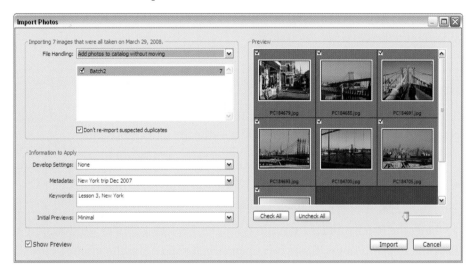

4   Before importing the new images into Lightroom, you could modify any of these settings. For this exercise, leave all the settings as they are.

5   Click Import.

6   The Batch2 subfolder is now listed in the Folders panel and the 7 newly imported photos are displayed in the Grid view and the Filmstrip.

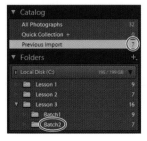

7   Switch back to Windows Explorer / the Finder and drag the Batch2 folder onto the Grid view in Lightroom again. A dialog will appear listing the photos that won't be imported because they are already present in the catalog. Click Show In Library to see the photos that are already in the catalog in the Grid view. Note the Already In Catalog entry selected in the Catalog panel. Right-click / Control-click an image in the Grid view and choose Show In Folder In Library from the context menu to find the Batch2 folder in the Folders panel.

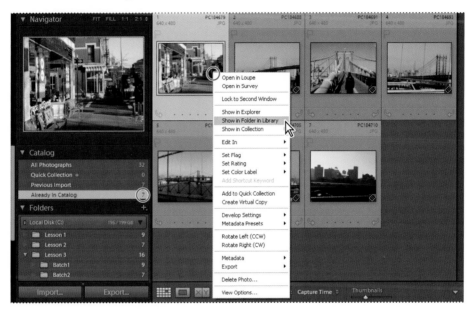

Importing from other catalogs

If you work on a laptop while you're on location and need to merge your new photos with the Lightroom library on your desktop computer, or if you work in a situation where more than one person will be using the same images in Lightroom on different computers, you can move photos from one computer to another using the Export As Catalog and Import From Catalog commands. Your images will be transferred with all of your edits, adjustments, and settings in place—including any keywords or other metadata you may have added.

Lesson 10, "Backup and Exporting" will discuss exporting photos as a catalog; for this lesson you'll import photos from a catalog you'll find in the Batch3 folder inside the Lesson 3 folder on your hard disk.

1   Choose File > Import From Catalog.

2   In the Import From Lightroom Catalog dialog box, navigate to the Batch3 folder inside the Lesson 3 folder on your hard disk. Select the file Batch3 Catalog.lrcat inside the Batch3 folder and click Choose.

3   In the Import From Catalog dialog box, choose Add New Photos To Catalog Without Moving from the File Handling menu, and then click Import.

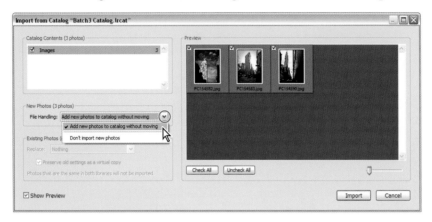

The Don't Import New Photos option in the File Handling menu is useful when you have exported images from one computer, modified them on a different computer, and then wish to re-import them without importing any new images.

4   If you see the Photo Is Missing icon (⊞) in the top right corner of the images in the Grid view, click the icon, click Locate in the Confirm dialog box, navigate to the Images folder inside the Batch3 folder, select the missing photo, activate the Find Nearby Missing Photos option, and then click Select.

5   The Batch3 subfolder is now listed in the Folders panel and three newly imported photos are displayed in the Grid view and the Filmstrip.

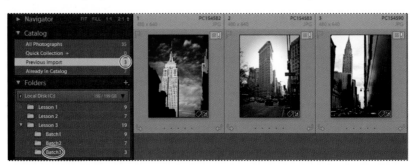

Re-importing existing photos

If you wish to re-import photos that already exist in your library, select from the following options in the Existing Photos area of the Import From Catalog dialog box:

• From the Replace menu, choose Metadata, Develop Settings, And Negative Files to override all the settings in the current catalog. If you choose this option, you might want to activate the option Preserve Old Settings As A Virtual Copy to keep a backup. You can also activate the option Replace Non-Raw Files Only to avoid replacing raw negatives. If changes to raw negative files affect only metadata, selecting this option helps save time.

• From the Replace menu, choose Metadata And Develop Settings Only to leave the negative files (the source photos) unchanged. If you choose this option, you might want to activate the option Preserve Old Settings As A Virtual Copy to keep a backup.

• From the Replace menu, choose Nothing to import only new photos.

• If photos in the current catalog are missing and can be found in the imported catalog, indicate whether you want to update the metadata and Develop settings for these files. Activate the option Preserve Old Settings As A Virtual Copy to keep a backup. If the photos missing in the current catalog appear in the imported catalog, specify whether the missing files should be copied and where they should be copied to.

—From Lightroom Help

When you import images from a Lightroom catalog, you do not have the option to apply develop settings or to add keywords and other metadata during the import process as you do when you import from your camera or hard disk. When you export a catalog, keywords and other metadata are transferred with the images. When importing from a catalog these keywords and other metadata are preserved. You'll notice that metadata has already been added to the photos you have just imported; you can add to it if you wish.

6   Select one of the images in the Grid view. In the Keywording panel in the right panel group, you can see that the keywords "Lesson 3" and "New York" have already been applied. If you wished, you could add more keywords to each of the images individually, such as **Empire State Building**, **Flatiron Building**, and **Chrysler Building**.

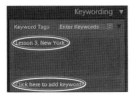

7   Expand the Metadata panel in the right panel group. If necessary, collapse the other panels in the group or scroll down so that you can see the contents of the Metadata panel. Note that additional metadata has been added to the images. You can edit the metadata to your liking.

The imported images have also been edited and the edit history has been imported with them.

8   Select one of the images in the Grid view, and then switch to the Develop module. If necessary, scroll down in the left panel group so that you can see the contents of the History panel. Click the Import entry at the bottom of the History panel to see how the image looked originally. Then, choose Edit > Undo to return to the edited version.

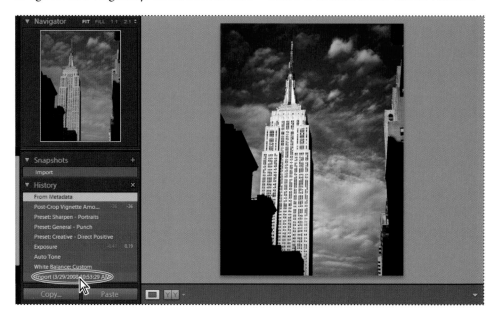

💡 *You can also import from a Lightroom version 1.x catalog. On Windows, you can import from a Photoshop Elements catalog if Lightroom detects that Photoshop Elements is installed on your computer. Importing from Photoshop Elements is not supported on Mac OS.*

Importing from a watched folder

You can set Lightroom to watch a specified folder on your hard disk and automatically import any photos that are placed in that folder. When you add or save photos to the watched folder Lightroom will move them to a new location and add them to the library catalog. You can even have Lightroom automatically rename the files and add metadata information in the process.

1   To set up the Auto Import options, choose File > Auto Import > Auto Import Settings.

2   In the Auto Import Settings dialog box, click the top Choose button to designate a watched folder.

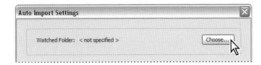

3   In the Browse For Folder / Auto-Import From Folder dialog box, navigate to the Lesson 3 folder. Select the folder named Watched Folder inside the Lesson 3 folder, and then click OK / Choose.

4   Click the Choose button under Destination to specify a folder to which Lightroom will move your photos in the process of adding them to the library catalog. In the Browse For Folder / Choose Folder dialog box, navigate to the Lessons folder. Select the Lesson 3 folder (you will specify to create a subfolder inside the Lesson 3 folder in the next step), and then click OK / Choose.

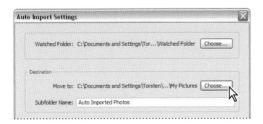

5   Under Destination in the Auto Import Settings dialog box, type **Batch4** in the Subfolder Name text box. Lightroom will create this subfolder inside the Lesson 3 folder.

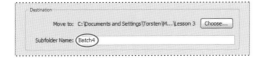

6   Choose Filename from the File Naming menu.

7   Under Information, choose the metadata preset you created earlier in this lesson from the Metadata menu and type **Lesson 3, New York** in the Keywords text box. Choose None from the Develop Settings menu and Minimal from the Initial Previews menu. Click OK to close the Auto Import Settings dialog box.

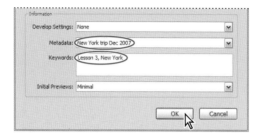

💡 *You can choose a preset to be applied to your photos during the import process from the Develop Settings menu. You could, for example, create a develop settings preset customized for a particular camera and apply that preset when importing photos taken with that camera. Refer to Lesson 6, "Developing and Editing," for more information on develop settings presets.*

8   Choose File > Auto Import > Enable Auto Import.

9   Switch to Windows Explorer / the Finder and navigate to the Lesson 3 folder. Note that the Watched Folder is empty and that as yet there is no Batch4 folder inside the Lesson 3 folder.

10   Select the 9 image files in the Lesson 3 folder and drag them to the Watched Folder.

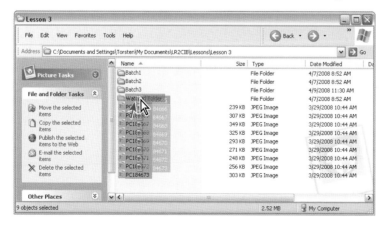

11 If you can see the Lightroom workspace in the background you will notice the 9 photos being imported. When Lightroom has finished importing, you'll see the newly created folder named Batch4 inside the Lesson 3 folder. The Watched Folder is empty once more and the 9 lesson images have been moved into the Batch4 folder.

12 Return to Lightroom and switch to the Library module. The Batch4 subfolder is now listed in the Folders panel and the 9 newly imported photos are displayed in the Grid view and the Filmstrip.

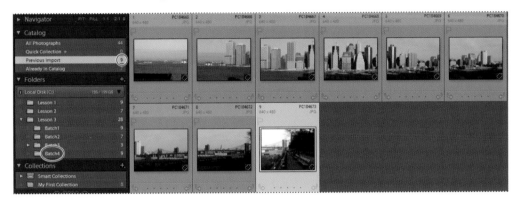

Specifying initial previews when importing

As photos are imported, Lightroom can immediately display a photo's embedded preview, or display higher-quality previews as the program renders them. You can choose the rendered size and quality for previews using the Standard Preview Size and Preview Quality menus in File Handling tab of the Catalog Settings (Lightroom > Catalog Settings). Please keep in mind that embedded previews are created on-the-fly by cameras and are not color managed therefore they don't match the interpretation of the camera raw files made by Lightroom. Previews rendered by Lightroom are color managed.

In the Import Photos dialog box, do one of the following:

• To immediately display images using the smallest previews embedded in the photos, choose Initial Previews > Minimal. Lightroom renders standard-size previews when needed.

• To display the largest possible preview available from the camera, choose Initial Previews > Embedded & Sidecar. This may take longer to display than a Minimal preview but is still faster than rendering a standard-size preview.

• To display previews as Lightroom renders them, choose Initial Previews > Standard. Standard-size previews use the ProPhoto RGB color space.

• To display previews that are a 1 to 1 view of the actual pixels, as in the Develop module, choose Initial Previews > 1:1.

—From Lightroom Help

Now that you've configured the Auto Import settings you can import images into your Lightroom library by simply dragging them onto the watched folder. This makes importing photos directly from a camera or memory card reader even easier; there's no need to attend to a dialog box and yet your images can be renamed and have custom metadata added automatically.

Tethered shooting

Another use for the watched folder is a process known as tethered shooting. You connect—or tether—your digital camera to your computer and the camera saves the images directly to the computer's hard disk rather than its memory card. To do this you'll need a camera that supports tethered shooting and the associated image capture software, which will allow you to designate your watched folder as the destination to which the camera will save your photos.

Tethered shooting is supported by Canon EOS cameras in conjunction with the Canon EOS Viewer Utility software. For Nikon cameras you can use the Camera Control component of the Capture NX software. Camera Control's Download Options dialog box lets you specify the location for the photos downloaded from the camera and apply additional metadata to the images. Make sure to choose Do Nothing from the When A New Image Is Received From The Camera menu. Lightroom will remove the images from the Watched Folder as soon as it detects them.

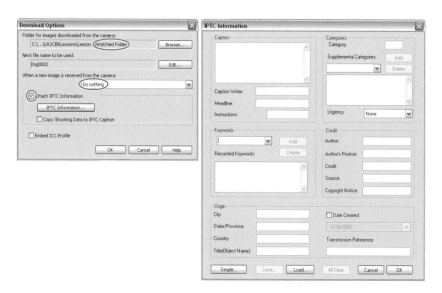

There are also third party software solutions available to enable tethered shooting for a range of other digital cameras. To find out what's available, search *tethered shooting* on the Internet.

With tethered shooting you can view a photo on your computer screen immediately after you shoot it—a vastly different experience from seeing it on your camera's LCD screen—and have Lightroom rename the file, add metadata, and organize it in your library then and there. If necessary, you can adjust your camera settings (white balance, exposure, focus, depth of field, and others), before taking the next shot. The better the quality of the captured image the less time you'll need to spend adjusting it later.

Review

▶ **Review questions**

1   In what circumstances would you choose to copy imported images to a new location on your hard disk and when would you want to add them to your library catalog without moving them?

2   Which file formats are supported by Lightroom?

3   What is DNG?

4   How can you transfer photos—together with their metadata and develop settings—between Lightroom libraries on separate computers?

5   What is tethered shooting and what are its advantages?

▶ **Review answers**

1   When importing photos from a camera or memory card Lightroom does not offer the option to import them at their current location. In the import process Lightroom needs to record a location for each file in the library catalog and as memory cards are expected to be erased and reused the images need first to be copied to a more permanent location.

Copying or moving images might also be useful when they are not already arranged on the hard disk or removable media in an orderly manner. Lightroom can be used to organize the files into an ordered folder hierarchy during the import process. Images that are already arranged in a useful way on the hard disk or removable media can be added to the library catalog in their current locations

2   Lightroom supports the following file formats: most camera raw formats, Digital Negative (DNG), TIFF, JPEG, and Photoshop PSD. Some file format exceptions apply: Lightroom does not support CMYK files, Adobe Illustrator files, files with dimensions greater than 65,000 pixels per side or larger than 500 million pixels, or video files, including video files acquired by digital still cameras.

3   The Digital Negative (DNG) file format is a publicly available archival format for raw files generated by digital cameras. By addressing the lack of an open standard for the raw files created by individual camera models, DNG helps ensure that photographers will be able to access their files in the future. You can convert proprietary raw files to DNG within Lightroom.

4   On one computer, export the images from Lightroom as a catalog file. On the other computer, choose File > Import From Catalog to import the photos into the Lightroom library together with their develop settings and metadata.

5   Tethered shooting is the process of connecting a camera directly to a computer and using image capture software to download photos to the computer's hard disk as they are shot. Images can be viewed immediately on a large screen so that decisions can be made about camera settings as the shoot progresses. By downloading the images to a watched folder they can be imported into Lightroom at once. Lightroom will automatically rename the files and apply keywording and metadata presets as specified.

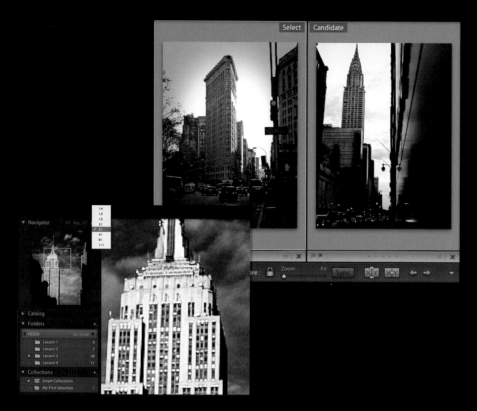

The Lightroom Library module offers you a variety of ways to review and evaluate your images: you can sort and group thumbnails in the Grid view, examine a single photo up close in Loupe view, assess images side by side in Compare view, or hone a selection of shots in Survey view.

4 Reviewing

It's a good policy to spend some time reviewing newly imported images. A little time spent sorting and organizing photos at this stage will make it much easier to manage and work with your growing image library. In the Library module you can inspect and compare the images that you've just imported; then sort, mark, and group them so that they are easy to find when you need them.

In this lesson you'll become familiar with using different tools and techniques for reviewing your images and navigating through your photo catalog:

- Working in the different Library module views.
- Navigating through your catalog.
- Using the Navigator panel.
- Comparing photos.
- Flagging rejects and deleting images.
- Using the Quick Collection.
- Converting and clearing the Quick Collection.
- Creating Stacks.
- Hiding the Filmstrip and adjusting its size.
- Applying the Filmstrip Source Filters.
- Rearranging photos in the Grid view.

You'll probably need between one and two hours to complete all the projects in this lesson.

Getting started

This lesson assumes that you are already familiar with the Lightroom workspace and with moving between the different modules. If you find that you need more background information as you go, refer to Lightroom Help or the previous lessons in this book.

Before you begin, make sure that you have correctly copied the Lessons folder from the CD in the back of this book onto your computer's hard disk and created the LR2CIB Library Catalog file. See "Copying the Classroom in a Book files" and "Creating a catalog file for working with this book" on page 3.

1   Start Lightroom.

2   In the Adobe Photoshop Lightroom - Select Catalog dialog box, make sure the file LR2CIB Library Catalog.lrcat is selected under Catalog Location, and then click Continue.

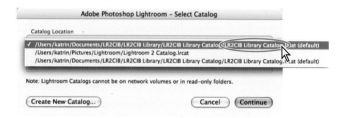

3   If the Back Up Catalog dialog box appears, click Skip Now.

4   Lightroom will open in screen mode and workspace module that were active when you last quit. If necessary, click Library in the Module Picker to switch to the Library module.

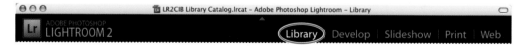

First you'll import the Lesson 4 images into the Lightroom library.

Importing images into the library

1 In the Library module, choose File > Import Photos From Disk.

2 In the Import Photos Or Lightroom Catalog dialog box, navigate to the Lessons folder you copied into the LR2CIB folder on your hard disk. Select the Lesson 4 folder, and then click Import All Photos In Selected Folder (Windows) / Choose (Mac OS).

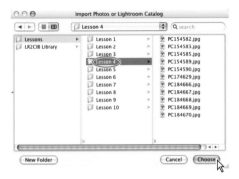

3 In the Import Photos dialog box, make sure the Show Preview option in the lower left corner of the dialog box is activated so you can see thumbnail images of the photos you're about to import. For this exercise, leave all eleven photos selected.

4 Choose the option Add Photos To Catalog Without Moving from the File Handling menu. Choose None from both the Develop Settings menu and the Metadata menu. Type **Lesson 4** in the Keywords text box, choose Minimal from the Initial Previews menu, and then click Import.

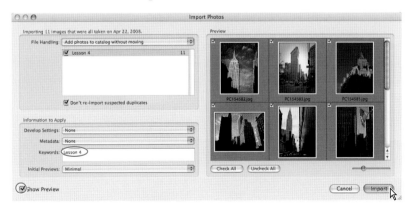

The eleven photos—images of New York architecture—appear in the Grid view of the Library module as well as in the Filmstrip.

Viewing and managing your images

In the Library module, Lightroom offers a variety of viewing modes, tools, and options to help you examine, compare, sort, mark, and group your images. During the import process you applied common metadata in the form of keyword tags to the selection of images as a whole. As you review your photos in the Library module you can add another layer of organization to your catalog, flagging some of the images as picks and others as rejects, assigning ratings, and applying tags and labels to individual files or to subsets of the imported selection.

The Library module also provides the sophisticated search functions and customizable filters that will enable you to leverage the metadata you attach to your images. You can sort your images by category, subject, or any other association and create Collections and Smart Collections to group them—making it easy to find exactly the photos you want no matter how extensive your catalog.

In this Lesson, you'll explore the different ways to preview and arrange your images.

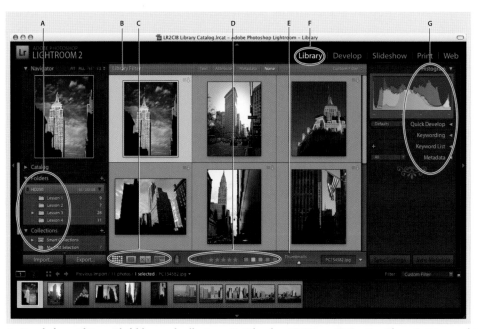

*A. Panels for working with folders and collections. **B.** Filter bar. **C.** Views. **D.** Sorting Flags, Ratings, and Color Labels. **E.** Thumbnail size slider. **F.** Library Module active in the Module Picker. **G.** Panels for adjusting images and working with keywords and metadata.*

Switching views

In the Library module you can move between four viewing modes to suit different phases of your workflow. Press the G key for Grid view (▦) to see thumbnails of your images while you search, apply flags, ratings and labels, or create collections. Use the keyboard shortcut E to inspect a single photo at a range of magnifications in Loupe view (▣). Press C to see two images side by side in Compare view (XY) or use the keyboard shortcut N to evaluate several images at once in Survey view (▦).

The Toolbar displays a different set of controls for each view mode.

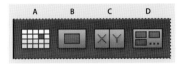

A. Grid view (G). *B. Loupe view (E).*
C. Compare view (C). *D. Survey view (N).*

The Grid view

By default your images will be displayed in Grid view after they've been imported.

> *To navigate from one image to the next in the Grid view and the Filmstrip, use the arrow keys on your keyboard.*

1   Click the triangle at the right end of the Toolbar and ensure that View Modes is activated in the tools menu. If you are working on a small screen, you can disable all the other options except Thumbnail size and Info for this lesson.

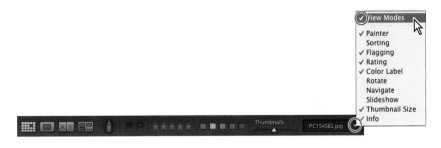

2   If Grid view is not already selected, click the Grid view button (⊞). Adjust the size of the thumbnails by dragging the Thumbnails slider so that you can see about two rows of thumbnails in the Grid view without having to scroll down.

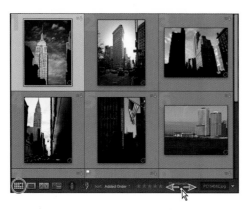

3   To specify how your photos will be displayed in the Grid view image cells, choose View > View Options. The Library View Options dialog box appears.

4   For the purposes of this exercise, activate the Show Grid Extras option and choose Compact Cells from the menu beside it. Customize the settings for Options, Cell Icons, Compact Cell Extras, and Expanded Cell Extras to your liking. As a guide for your choices, please refer to "View Options for the Grid view" on the next page. When you're done, close the Library View Options dialog box.

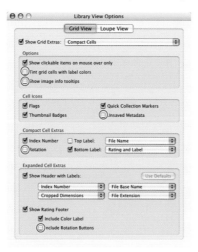

View Options for the Grid view

You can choose from a range of options that affect the way your photos are displayed in the Grid view—from simplified image cells containing nothing but the image thumbnails to expanded cells displaying your choice of image information, status indicators, labels, and clickable controls.

Show Grid Extras: Displays your choice of labels, markers, and controls in each image cell. If this option is disabled most of the other Grid view options are unavailable.

Compact Cells: Shows simple cells with less information so more thumbnails are visible in the Grid.

Expanded Cells: Expands the image cells to include more information in cell headers and footers.

Show Clickable Items On Mouse Over Only: Displays rotation controls, flags, and labels only when you move the pointer over an image cell. Disable this option to show these controls at all times.

Tint Grid Cells With Color Labels: Tints the image cell around a photo to indicate its color label.

Show Image Info Tooltips: Displays a brief description of an item when you hold the pointer over it. Shows image info and the names of the controls, status badges, and indicators in the image cell.

Flags: Activates clickable flag status indicators in the upper left corner of the image cells.

Quick Collection Markers: Shows a clickable Quick Collection marker in the upper right corner of each thumbnail. Images with a solid grey dot are part of the Quick Collection.

Thumbnail Badges: Displays indicator badges on the thumbnail images indicating which photos have keywords attached and which have been adjusted or cropped.

Unsaved Metadata: An icon with a down arrow in the upper right of a cell indicates that an image has changes in its metadata that have not yet been saved to file. An up arrow icon shows that the image file's metadata has been changed in an external application and an exclamation mark icon indicates that a photo's metadata has unsaved changes made in both Lightroom and an external application.

Index Number: Shows image cell numbers indicating the order of the photos in the Grid view.

Rotation: Displays Rotation buttons in the lower corners of the image cells.

Top Label and **Bottom Label:** Displays your choice of image information and attributes above and below the thumbnail in a compact image cell.

Show Header With Labels: Displays up to four labels in the headers of expanded image cells showing the information you specify. Choose from a menu of image information and attributes.

Use Defaults: Restores the Header Label options to their default settings.

Show Rating Footer: Shows the rating stars—and optionally the color label and rotation buttons—in the footers of expanded image cells.

You can quickly activate and disable groups of the options you just set in the Library View Options dialog box by choosing from the Grid View Style menu.

5   To switch to Expanded Cell viewing mode, select Expanded Cells from the View > Grid View Style menu. Ensure that the option Show Extras is activated in the same menu.

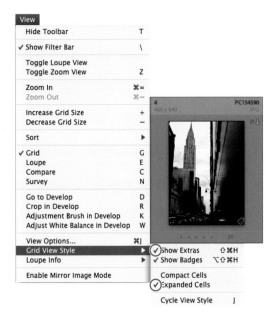

Note: To quickly cycle through the different Grid view styles, press the J key repeatedly or choose View > Grid View Style > Cycle View Style.

Zooming with the Navigator in Loupe view

In Loupe view you can look closely at one photo at a time at a wide range of zoom levels. Use the Loupe view to help you to evaluate your images as you sort them in the Library module and to inspect and adjust them in the Develop module.

> *In the Grid View tab of the Library View Options dialog box, the Show Grid Extras option enables you to display a range of information with your images. In the Loupe View tab, activate Show Info Overlay to display the same kind of information overlaid on your images in the Loupe view. By default, the Loupe view info overlay in disabled.*

In the Navigator panel you can set the level of magnification for the Loupe view and find your way around a zoomed image with ease. Like the Loupe view, the Navigator is common to both the Library and Develop modules.

1 Select the first thumbnail image (showing the Empire State building) in the Grid view or the Filmstrip, and then click the Loupe view button (▣) in the Toolbar. You can also switch to Loupe view by double-clicking a thumbnail in the Grid view or the Filmstrip or by pressing the E key on your keyboard.

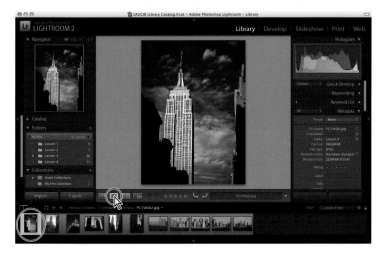

2 If necessary, expand the Navigator panel at the top of the left panel group. The zoom controls for the Loupe view are in upper right corner of the Navigator panel. Click 1:1; as you can see, the resolution of this particular image is quite low.

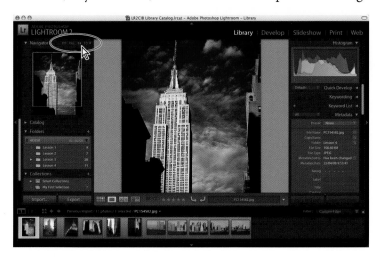

3 Click the small triangle at the right of the Navigator panel header and choose the zoom ratio 3:1 from the menu.

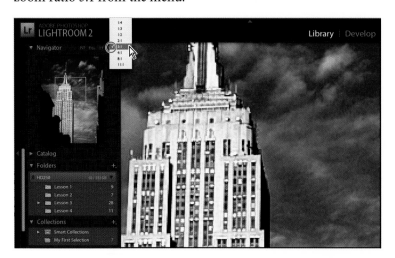

4 When working at such a high level of magnification, the Navigator helps you move around in the image quickly and easily. Click anywhere in the Navigator preview and the zoomed view will be centered on that point. Drag in the Navigator preview to reposition the view. The white rectangle indicates the area currently displayed in the Loupe view. Click in the Loupe view to move back and forth between the last two zoom levels used; when zooming in, the view will be centered on the point you click.

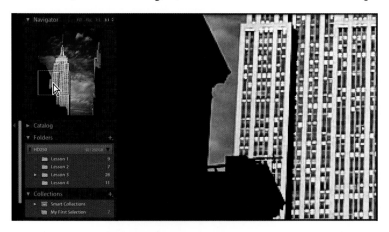

5 In the header of the Navigator panel, click each of the four zoom levels in turn (Fit, Fill, 1:1, and 3:1—the option you chose from the menu). Press the Ctrl / Command key together with the Minus key (-) repeatedly to zoom out through the last four zoom levels used and to finally switch to Grid view; press the Ctrl / Command key together with the Equal key (=) repeatedly to switch back to Loupe view and to progressively zoom in. Finally, set the zoom level to Fit.

💡 *Click the image in Loupe view to switch between zoom levels; double-click the image to switch quickly between the Grid and Loupe views.*

Comparing photos

As the name suggests, the Compare view (⊠⊠) is ideal for examining and evaluating images side by side.

1 Press Control+D / Command+D or choose Edit > Select None.

2 In the Filmstrip, Ctrl-click / Command-click two images or your choice (in the illustration below we first changed the sort order using the controls in the Toolbar and then selected the images of the Flatiron building and the Chrysler building), and then click the Compare View button (⊠⊠) in the Toolbar.

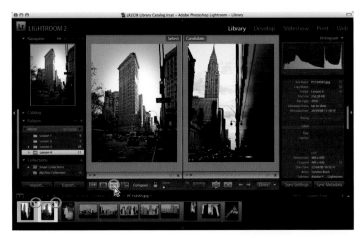

The first image you selected becomes the *Select* image and is displayed in the left pane of the Compare view; the image displayed in the right pane is the *Candidate*. In the Filmstrip the Select image is marked with a while diamond in the upper right corner, and the Candidate image with a black diamond.

To use the Compare view to make a choice from a group of more than two similar photos, select the photos you wish to compare—being sure to select your favored choice first to place it as the Select image, and then add the other images to your selection. Then click the Select Previous Photo and Select Next Photo buttons (⬅➡) in the

Toolbar or press the left and right arrow keys on your keyboard to move between the selected candidates.

Should you decide that the current Candidate is better than the Select image, you can reverse their positions by clicking the Swap button (▣) in the Toolbar.

3   To compare fine detail in the images, zoom in by dragging the Zoom slider in the Toolbar. You'll notice that the images are zoomed together. Drag either of the images in the Compare view and the images move in unison. The closed lock icon to the left of the Zoom tool indicates that the view focus of the two images is locked.

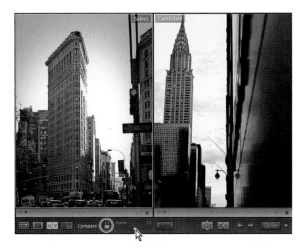

4   If you wish to zoom and move the Select and Candidate images independently, click the lock icon to unlink them.

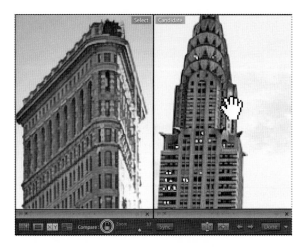

Note: *The Develop module also has a split screen view; for comparing before and after versions of an image as you work on it.*

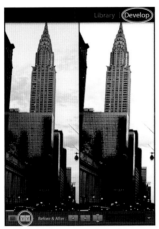

The Before & After view is available only in the Develop module.

Using Survey view to narrow down a selection

The last of the four views in the Library module, the Survey View lets you to see a multiple selection of images together on one screen, and then narrow your choices by dropping one photo after another from the view.

1   In the Filmstrip, sort the images by filename, select the last five images. In the Library module, click the Survey view icon (⊞) or press the N key.

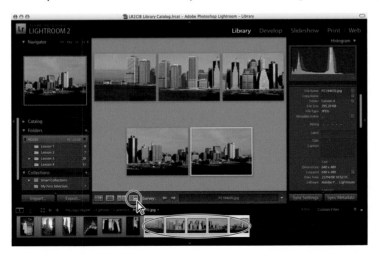

2   Navigate between the images by pressing the arrow keys on your keyboard or click the Select Previous Photo and Select Next Photo buttons (⬅➡) in the Toolbar. *(See illustration below step 3.)*

3   Position the pointer over the last photo. A Deselect Photo icon (⊠) appears in the lower right corner of the image. Click this icon to drop the image from the selection in the Survey view.

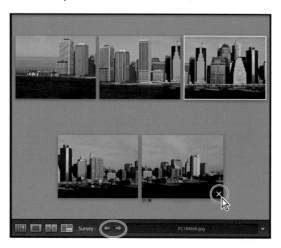

4   Continue to eliminate photos from the Survey view until you've narrowed your selection to the image (or images) you want. For the purposes of this exercise, deselect all but one favorite (we chose the active photo—marked with a white border—in the illustration below).

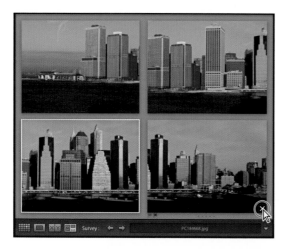

Note: Dropping a photo from the Survey view does not delete it from its folder or remove it from the catalog. The dropped image is still visible in the Filmstrip—it has simply been deselected. You can see that the images that are still displayed in the Survey view are also the only ones still selected in the Filmstrip.

Flagging picks and rejects and deleting images

Now that you have narrowed down a selection of images to one favorite in the Survey view, you can mark your choice with a flag.

Flagging images as picks or rejects as you review them is an effective way to quickly sort your work. A white flag indicates a pick (⚑), a black one with an x marks a reject (⚑), and a neutral grey flag shows that an image has not been flagged (⚑).

1 Still in the Survey view, move the pointer over the remaining photo to see the flag icons below the lower left corner. The grayed icons indicate that the image is not yet flagged. Click the flag to the left. The flag turns white, which marks this image as a pick. In the Filmstrip, you can see that the thumbnail now displays a white flag in the upper left of the image cell.

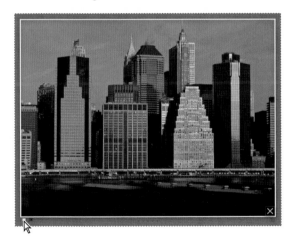

💡 *Press the P key on your keyboard to flag the currently selected image as a pick (⚑), the X key to flag it as a reject (⚑), or press the U key to remove any flags.*

2 Select a different image in the Filmstrip, and then press the X key. The black reject flag icon appears at the lower left corner of the image in the Survey view and at the upper left of the thumbnail in the Filmstrip. The thumbnail of the rejected image is dimmed in the Filmstrip.

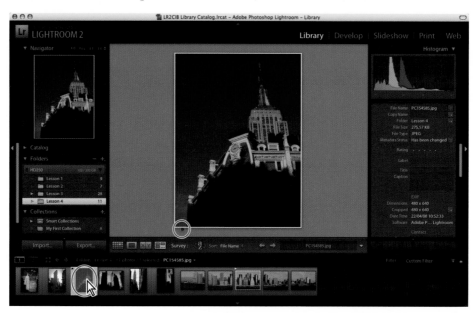

3 Press the Delete key on your keyboard. In the dialog box that appears, click Remove to remove the photo from your catalog without deleting the master image file from your hard disk.

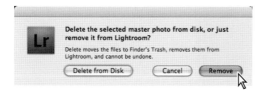

As you have removed the image from the library catalog it is no longer visible in the Filmstrip.

4 Press the G key or click the Grid view icon in the Toolbar to see all the remaining images as thumbnails in the Grid view.

Grouping images in the Quick Collection

Collections are a convenient way to group photos in your catalog, even when the image files are actually located in different folders on your hard disk. You can create a new collection for a particular presentation or use collections to group your images by category or any other association. Your collections are always available from the Collections panel where you can access them quickly.

Note: The Quick Collection is a temporary holding collection: a convenient place to group images while you review and sort your new imports or while you assemble a selection of photos from different folders in your catalog. You can add images to the Quick Collection from the Grid view or the Filmstrip with a single click and remove them just as easily. Your images will stay in the Quick Collection until you are ready to convert it to a permanent grouping that will be listed in the Collections panel. You can access the Quick Collection from the Catalog panel so that you can return to work with the same selection of images at any time.

Moving images into or out of the Quick Collection

1   You'll find a listing for the Quick Collection in the Catalog panel in the left panel group. If necessary, expand the Catalog panel in order to see it.

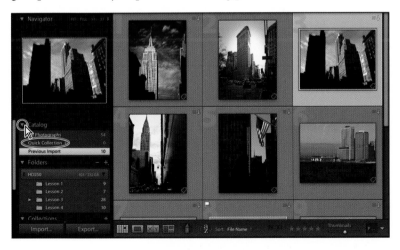

2   In the Grid view, select the portrait format images in cells 1, 2, 4, and 5 by Ctrl-clicking / Command-clicking them.

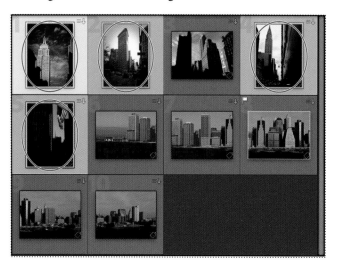

Note: You need to activate the Index Number option in the Library View Options dialog box (in Compact or Expanded Cells layout) to see cell numbers displayed in the Grid view.

3   To add the selected images to the Quick Collection, press the B key or choose Photo > Add To Quick Collection.

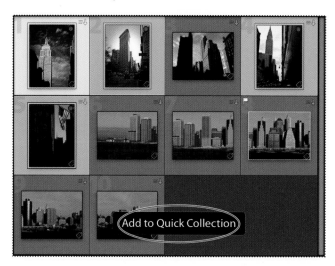

4   The number 4 appears beside the listing for the Quick Collection in the Catalog panel, indicating that the Quick Collection now contains four images. If you have activated the option Show Quick Collection Markers in the Library View Options dialog box, each image in the Quick Collection is marked with a gray dot in the upper right corner of its thumbnail in the Grid view. The same markers are also shown in the Filmstrip unless the Filmstrip height—and with it the thumbnail size—is set to be very small.

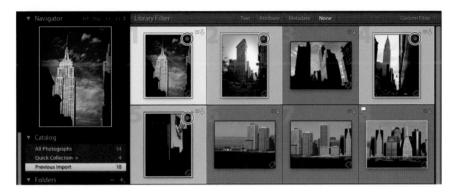

You can remove all selected photos from the Quick Collection by simply clicking the marker on one of the thumbnails or by pressing the B key.

5   For this exercise, remove only the image in cell 5 from the group by first deselecting the other three images and then—with only the image in cell 5 selected—pressing the B key. Your Quick Collection is reduced to three images.

Converting and clearing the Quick Collection

1   Click the Quick Collection entry in the Catalog panel. The Grid view now displays only three images. Until you clear the Quick Collection, you can easily return to this group of images to review your selection.

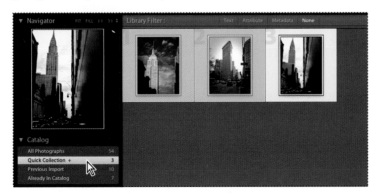

Now that you've honed your selection you can save your images to a more permanent Collection.

2   Choose File > Save Quick Collection.

3   In the Save Quick Collection dialog box, type **New York Skyscrapers** in the Collection Name box. Activate the option Clear Quick Collection After Saving and click save.

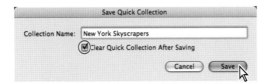

4   In the Catalog panel, you can see that the Quick Collection now has an image count of 0; the Quick Collection has been cleared. Expand the Collections panel if necessary so that you can see the listing for your new collection, which displays an image count of 3.

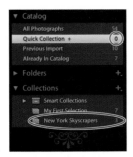

5   In the Folders panel, click the Lesson 4 folder. The grid view once more shows all the photos of New York including those in the skyscrapers collection.

Working with the Filmstrip

No matter which module or view you're working in, the Filmstrip across the bottom of the Lightroom workspace provides constant access to the images in your selected folder or collection.

As with the Grid view, you can quickly navigate through your images in the Filmstrip using the arrow keys on your keyboard. If there are more images than will fit in the

Filmstrip you can use the scroll bar below the thumbnails, drag the Filmstrip by the top edge of the thumbnail frame, or click the shaded thumbnails at either end.

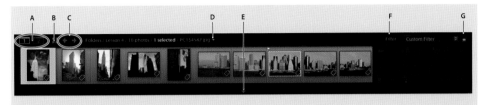

*The Lightroom Filmstrip: **A.** Show/Hide secondary window button **B.** Go to Grid view. **C.** Go Back and Go Forward buttons (to navigate between previously displayed groups of images). **D.** Filmstrip Source Indicator and menu. **E.** Show/Hide Filmstrip control. **F.** Filters. **G.** Turn Filters on/off.*

Hiding the Filmstrip and adjusting its size

1   Click the triangle in the lower border of the workspace window to hide and show the Filmstrip. Right-click / Control-click the triangle to set the automatic show and hide options.

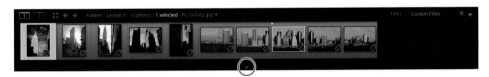

2   Position the pointer over the top edge of the Filmstrip; the cursor becomes a double arrow. Drag the top edge of the Filmstrip up or down to enlarge or reduce the thumbnails. The narrower you make the Filmstrip the more thumbnails it can display.

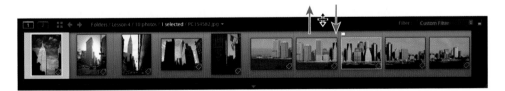

Using filters in the Filmstrip

With so few photos in the Lesson 4 folder it's not difficult to see all the images at once in the Filmstrip. However, when you are working with a folder containing many images it can be inconvenient to scroll the Filmstrip looking for the images you want. Use the

Filmstrip filters to narrow down the images displayed in the Filmstrip to only those that share a specified flag status, rating, color label, or any combination of these attributes.

In the Filmstrip you can see that one of the images in the Lesson 4 folder displays the white Pick flag that you assigned in a previous exercise. If you don't see the flag, activate the option Show Ratings And Picks In Filmstrip in the Interface tab in Lightroom Preferences.

1 From the filters menu at the top right of the Filmstrip, choose Flagged. Only the image with the white flag is displayed in the Filmstrip.

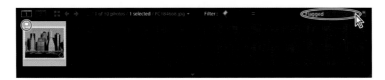

2 The white flag icon is now highlighted among the Filter controls in the top bar of the Filmstrip. You can activate or disable any of the filters you saw in the filters menu by clicking the Filter controls buttons. You can set up a combination of filters and save it as a custom preset. Click to deactivate the white flag filter in the top bar of the Filmstrip or choose Filters Off from the menu to disable all filters. The Filmstrip once more displays all the images in the folder.

Change the sorting order of the thumbnails

Use the Sort Direction control and the Sort Criteria menu in the Toolbar to change the display order of the thumbnails images in the Grid view and the Filmstrip.

1 If the Sort Direction control is not currently visible in the Toolbar, choose Sorting from the tools menu at the right of the Toolbar. Click the Sort Direction control (⭸) to reverse the sorting direction of the thumbnails.

2 Choose Pick from the Sort Criteria menu beside the Sort Direction control.

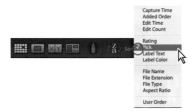

Stacking images

Another effective way of reducing the numbers of images displayed is by grouping similar photos in stacks. This is particularly helpful when you are working with a folder containing hundreds of photos from the same shoot. You can stack a group of images of the same subject or a series shot to test different camera settings. To reduce the clutter in the Filmstrip and the Grid view, only the top image in each stack is displayed.

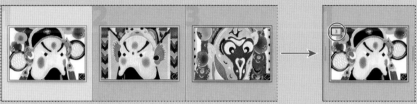

An icon representing a stack of photos is shown in the upper left corner of the thumbnail together with an image count.

To create a stack, do the following:

1 *In Grid view or the Filmstrip, select two or more images.*

2 *Choose Photo > Stacking > Group Into Stack.*

3 *Click the stack icon to expand and collapse the stack.*

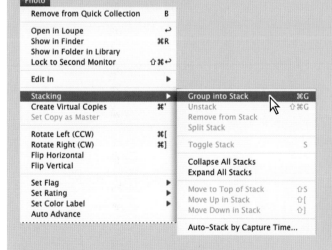

To learn more about Stacks, please refer to Lightroom Help.

The thumbnails are rearranged to display the images with a white Pick flag first in the Grid and the Filmstrip.

You can arbitrarily change the sorting order for images you've group as a Collection.

3 If you are not already in the Grid view, press G on your keyboard or click the Library Grid button at the left of the top bar of the Filmstrip.

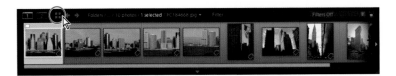

4 Expand the Collections panel in the left panel group and click the New York Skyscrapers collection that you created earlier.

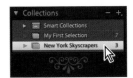

5 In the Grid view, drag the third thumbnail to the left and release the pointer when you see a black insertion bar appear to the left of the first image.

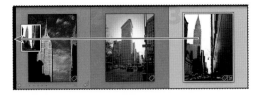

The image snaps to its new location.

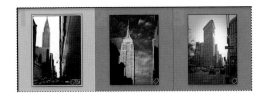

💡 *You can also change the order of the images in a collection by dragging their thumbnails in the Filmstrip.*

6   Your manual sorting order is saved and listed as User Order in the Sort Criteria menu. Choose File Name from the Sort Criteria menu; then return to your manual sorting by choosing User Order.

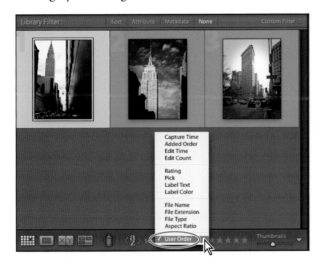

Congratulations; you've finished another lesson. You've gained confidence navigating through your library and learned techniques for reviewing, sorting, filtering, and grouping your images as collections. You'll learn more about structuring and organizing your photo library in the next lesson.

Review

▶ Review questions

1   How would you use each of the views in the Library module?

2   What is the Navigator?

3   Why would you create a Stack?

4   How do you use the Quick Collection?

▶ Review answers

1   Switch to the Grid view (▦) with the keyboard shortcut G, to review, mark, and select images as thumbnails. Switch to the Loupe view (▣) by pressing the E key, to examine a single image at a range of magnification levels and to the Compare view (▥) by pressing C, to evaluate images side by side. Press N to refine a multiple selection in the Survey view (▦).

2   The Navigator is an interactive full image preview that helps you move around easily within a zoomed image in Loupe view. Click or drag in the Navigator preview to reposition the view while a white rectangle indicates the portion of the magnified image that is currently visible in the workspace. The Navigator panel also contains controls for setting the zoom levels for the Loupe view. Click the image in Loupe view to switch between the last two zoom levels set in the Navigator panel.

3   Stacks can be used to group similar photos and reduce the number of thumbnails displayed at one time in the Grid view and the Filmstrip. Only the top image in a stack appears in the thumbnail display but the stack can be expanded and contracted by clicking the thumbnail.

4   To create a Quick Collection, select one or more images and then press the B key or choose Photo > Add To Quick Collection. The Quick Collection is a temporary holding area; you can continue to add—or remove—images until you are ready to save the grouping as a more permanent Collection. You'll find the Quick Collection listed in the Catalog panel.

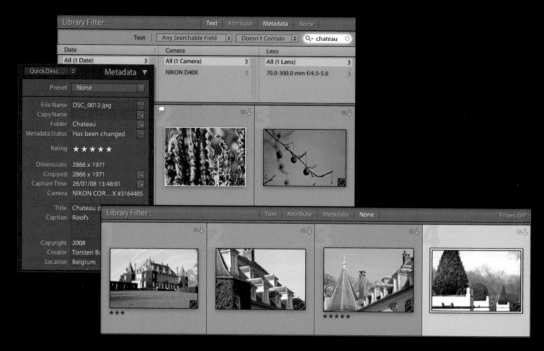

Lightroom delivers powerful, versatile tools to help you organize your image library and sophisticated search features that put the photos you want at your fingertips when you need them.

5 | Organizing and Selecting

As your photo library grows larger it will become increasingly important that you're able to locate your images quickly. Lightroom offers a range of options for organizing your image files and folders before you even click the import button. By the time they appear in the library, your photos can be automatically backed up, renamed, tagged with keywords and custom metadata information, and sorted into the folder system you prefer.

Once you've imported your photos you have even more options. You can add custom information to each file individually or apply the same metadata to a whole batch of images, making it easier and more intuitive to find just the images you want to compile collections sorted by subject, date, or shared keywords and metadata. You can manage and synchronize your folders or move files between them without leaving the Library module.

This lesson will familiarize you with the techniques you'll use to manage your library:

- Creating a folder structure.
- Moving files and synchronizing folders.
- Understanding Collections.
- Working with keywords and keyword sets.
- Using Flags, Ratings, and Color Labels.
- Adding and editing Metadata.
- Using the Painter tool.
- Finding and filtering files.
- Reconnecting renamed and missing files.

Getting started

This lesson assumes that you are already familiar with the Lightroom workspace and with moving between the different modules. If you find that you need more background information as you go, refer to Lightroom Help or the previous lessons in this book.

Before you begin, make sure that you have correctly copied the Lessons folder from the CD in the back of this book onto your computer's hard disk and created the LR2CIB Library Catalog file. See "Copying the Classroom in a Book files" and "Creating a catalog file for working with this book" on page 3.

1   Start Lightroom.

2   In the Adobe Photoshop Lightroom - Select Catalog dialog box, make sure the file LR2CIB Library Catalog.lrcat is selected under Catalog Location, and then click Continue.

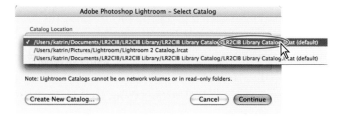

3   If the Back Up Catalog dialog box appears, click Skip Now.

4   Lightroom will open in the screen mode and workspace module that were active when you last quit. If necessary, click Library in the Module Picker to switch to the Library module.

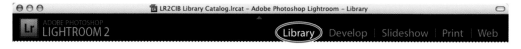

Importing images into the library

The first step is to import the images for this lesson into the Lightroom library.

1   If you're not already in the Library module, switch to it now.

2   Choose File > Import Photos From Disk.

3   In the Import Photos Or Lightroom Catalog dialog box, navigate to the Lessons folder you've already copied into the LR2CIB folder on your hard disk. Select the Lesson 5 folder, and then click Import All Photos In Selected Folder / Choose.

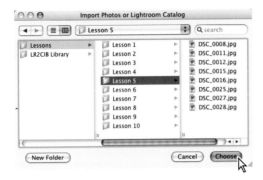

4   In the Import Photos dialog box, make sure the Show Preview option in the lower left corner of the dialog box is activated so that you can see thumbnail images of the photos you're about to import. For this exercise, leave all eight photos selected.

5   Choose Add Photos To Catalog Without Moving from the File Handling menu. Choose None from both the Develop Settings menu and the Metadata menu. Type **Lesson 5** in the Keywords text box, and choose Minimal from the Initial Previews menu. Then, click Import.

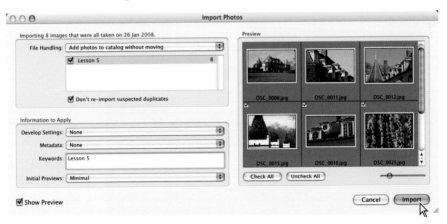

The lesson photos—architectural images of a chateau and details from the gardens—appear in the Grid view of the Library module and in the Filmstrip.

Organizing folders

In the Folders panel in the left panel group, you can organize your photo library at the most basic level by rearranging files and folders on your hard disk without ever leaving the Lightroom workspace. Each time you import images Lightroom lists the folder that contains those images (and the volume that contains that folder) in the Folders panel, where you can create or delete folders on the hard disk at the click of a button and move files and folders by simply dragging them.

Note: Lightroom maintains a single catalog entry for each photo you import, recording the location of the original image file on your hard disk. When you use the Folders panel to move a file between folders on the hard disk the catalog entry for that file is automatically updated with its new address. A master image cannot be added to the catalog twice, so you can't create copies of an image in separate folders—when you use the Folders panel to move an image file between volumes Lightroom will update its catalog entry and delete the master file from its original location.

Creating subfolders

In this exercise you'll use the Folders panel to organize the photos in the Lesson 5 folder into basic categories. You'll move the images of the chateau into a subfolder to sort them from those showing details of the gardens.

1 In the Grid view, each image cell displays an index number in the top left corner. Ctrl-click / Command-click to select the photos that feature the chateau in cells 1, 2, 3, and 5.

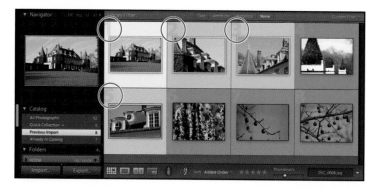

Note: If you can't see the image cell index numbers, activate the Index Number option in the Grid view tab of the Library View Options dialog box (View > View Options).

2 In the Folders panel, select the Lesson 5 folder. Click the Create New Folder button (+) in the Folders panel header and choose Add Subfolder from the menu.

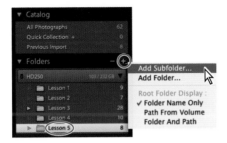

3 In the Create Folder dialog box, type **Chateau** as the folder name, activate the Include Selected Photos option, and then click Create.

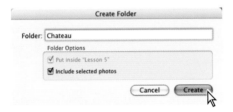

4 In the Folders panel, expand the Lesson 5 folder to see the folder "Chateau" nested inside it. Click the new subfolder to check that it contains the four images you selected in step 1.

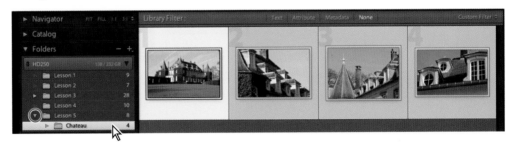

💡 *To change the name of a folder in the Folders panel, right-click / Ctrl-click its name, and then choose Rename from the context menu. Be aware that when you rename files and folders in the Folders panel, the changes affect the files and folders on the hard disk.*

Making changes to a folder's content

When you arrange and modify files and folders in the Folders panel the changes are made on your hard disk. Inversely, the Folders panel needs to be updated to reflect any changes you make to the location, name, or contents of a folder from outside the Lightroom workspace. In this exercise you'll experience this first hand by deleting an image in Windows Explorer / the Finder.

1   Click the Lesson 5 folder in the Folders panel.

2   Right-click / Ctrl-click one of the images in the Grid view and choose Show In Explorer / Show In Finder from the context menu.

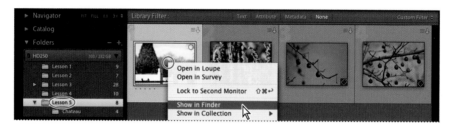

3   The Explorer / Finder window opens. In the Lesson 5 folder, select the file DSC_0028.jpg. Also note the subfolder "Chateau" inside the Lesson 5 folder.

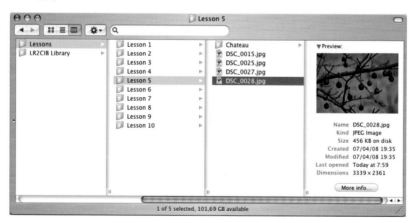

4   In the Explorer / Finder window, right-click / Ctrl-click the image and choose Delete / Move To Trash. Then, switch back to Lightroom.

5   Back in the Lightroom workspace, note that the image you just deleted in the Explorer / Finder window now has a question mark icon in the upper right corner of its grid cell. This indicates that Lightroom still has an entry for the image in its library catalog but the link to the original file has been broken.

6 Click the question mark icon. A dialog box opens offering you the option to locate the missing file and reestablish its link to the catalog. Click Cancel.

As you deleted the file intentionally you should now remove it from the library catalog. You can remove a missing photo from your catalog by selecting its thumbnail in the Grid view or the Filmstrip and pressing Alt+Backspace / Option+Delete or by choosing Photo > Remove Photos From Catalog. Don't remove the photo from the catalog yet—if you've done so already, choose Edit > Undo Remove Images. In the following exercise you'll learn a different technique for updating the catalog by synchronizing folders.

Synchronizing folders

When you synchronize the folders in the Lightroom catalog with the folders on your hard disk you have the option to remove catalog entries for files that have been deleted, import photos that have been added to your folders, or scan for files with updated metadata. You can specify which folders and subfolders will be synchronized and which new images you want added to your library.

1 Make sure that the Lesson 5 folder is still selected in the Folders panel.

2 Choose Library > Synchronize Folder.

3 In the Synchronize Folder 'Lesson 5' dialog box, activate the option Remove Missing Photos From Catalog (1), disable Scan For Metadata Updates, and then click Synchronize.

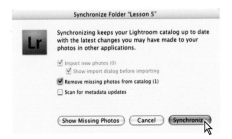

The missing image has now been removed from your catalog and all your links have been restored.

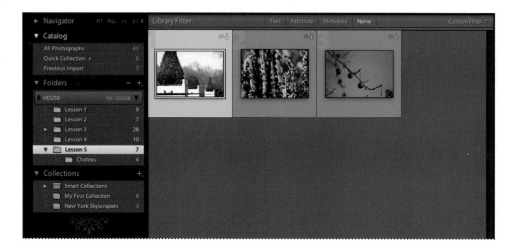

💡 *Activate the Import New Photos option in the Synchronize Folders dialog box to automatically import any files that have been added to a folder without yet having been added to your image library. Optionally, activate Show Import Dialog Before Importing. Activate the Scan For Metadata Updates to check for files with metadata that has been modified in another application.*

Using collections to organize images

Although a well organized system of folders provides a good foundation for your image library, grouping photos into collections in Lightroom is a far more efficient and flexible way to classify your images and offers many more options when you need to access them.

Collections are virtual groupings of the photos in your library based on your own associations rather than on the actual location of the files. A collection may contain images selected from any number of different folders on your hard disk and although a single master image is located in only one folder it can be included in any number of collections. The same photo might appear in a collection of images with architectural content and also in a compilation of shots suggesting an Autumn theme. It may be listed in a collection you assembled for a client presentation and in another you created for a holiday slideshow.

Grouping your images as collections in your library doesn't rearrange the files and folders on your hard disk and removing a photo from a collection won't remove it from the library catalog or delete it from the hard disk.

Note: Once you have grouped a selection of photos as a collection you can rearrange the order in which they will appear in a presentation or on a printed page. The new sorting order is saved with the collection.

There are three types of collection: Collections, Smart Collections and the Quick Collection.

The Quick Collection

The Quick Collection is a temporary holding collection; a convenient place to group images while you gather photos from different folders. You can access the Quick Collection from the Catalog panel so that you can return to work with the same selection of images at any time. Your images will stay in the Quick Collection until you are ready to convert your selection to a permanent collection that will then be listed in the Collections panel.

Note: There is only one Quick Collection. You can create as many collections and smart collections as you wish, but if the Quick Collection already contains a selection of images you'll need to convert it to a permanent collection and clear its contents before you can use it for a new project.

To add a selected image or group of images to the Quick Collection, press the B key or choose Photo > Add To Quick Collection. To remove a selection from the Quick Collection, press the B key again or choose Photo > Remove From Quick Collection. In the Grid view, a photo that is listed in the Quick Collection is indicated by a solid grey circle in the upper right corner of the thumbnail.

For more information on the Quick Collection, please refer to "Grouping images in the Quick Collection" in Lesson 4.

Collections

You can create as many permanent collections as you wish. Use a collection to assemble the images you need for a particular project or to group photos by subject or any other another association.

> *Remember that although the master image file is located in only one folder in your library, the photo can be part of many collections. This makes grouping your images in collections far more versatile than sorting them into categorized folders.*

When you create a collection of images for a slideshow or a web page, all the work you do on your presentation will be saved with the collection in the catalog file. In fact, a single collection can incorporate your settings from the Develop module, a slide layout and playback options applied in the Slideshow module, a gallery design you set up in the Web module, and a page layout modified in the Print module. You can also create an output collection for a print job that will include your color management and printer settings.

To create a collection, click the New Collection button (+) in the Collections panel header, and then choose Create Collection from the menu, or choose Library > New Collection. Enter a name in the Create Collection dialog box and click Create. Your new collection will be added to the list in the Collections panel. Drag photos onto the folder in the Collections panel to add them to the collection.

> *To create a permanent collection containing the images currently in the Quick Collection, right-click / Control-click the Quick Collection folder in the Catalog panel, and then choose Save Quick Collection from the context menu.*

Smart collections

A smart collection searches the metadata attached to your photos and gathers together those images that meet a specified set of criteria. Any newly imported photo matching the criteria you've set up for a smart collection will be added to that collection automatically.

You can specify the search criteria for your smart collection by choosing options from the menus in the Create Smart Collection dialog box (Library > New Smart Collection).

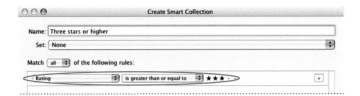

You can add more search criteria by clicking the + button to the right of any of the rules. In the illustration below a second rule has been added to search for images containing "New York" in any searchable text. Hold down the Alt / Option key and click the Plus button (+) to refine a rule. In the illustration, a refined rule has been added to search for images which were either captured or edited this year.

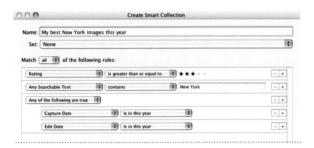

Applying keyword tags

Perhaps the most direct way to tag and later identify your photos is by adding keywords—text metadata applied to describe the subject of an image or to categorize it in other terms. For example, the image in the illustration below could be tagged with the keywords Architecture and Belgium and could therefore be located by searching for either or both of those tags. If the Thumbnail Badges option is activated in the Library View Options dialog box, photos with keyword tags are identified by a thumbnail badge icon in the lower right corner of the thumbnail.

You can apply keywords to your photos individually or tag an entire series of images with shared metadata in one operation, thereby linking them by association and making them easier to access amongst all the photos that make up your library. Keywords added to images in Lightroom can be read by Adobe applications such as Bridge, Photoshop, and Photoshop Elements and by other applications that support XMP metadata.

Viewing keyword tags

As the imported images are all marked with the thumbnail badge icon, we know that they already contain edited metadata. Let's review the keywords already attached to these photos.

1 Make sure that you are still in the Grid view, and then select the Lesson 5 folder in the Folders panel.

2 In the right panel group, expand the Keywording panel.

Clicking the thumbnail badge icon of an image in Grid view will automatically expand the Keywording panel. If you can't see the thumbnail badge icons, make sure the Thumbnail Badges option is activated in the Library View Options dialog box.

3 If necessary, expand the Keyword Tags pane at the top of the Keywording panel. By selecting each thumbnail in the Grid view in turn you can see that all images in the Lesson 5 folder share the keyword "Lesson 5."

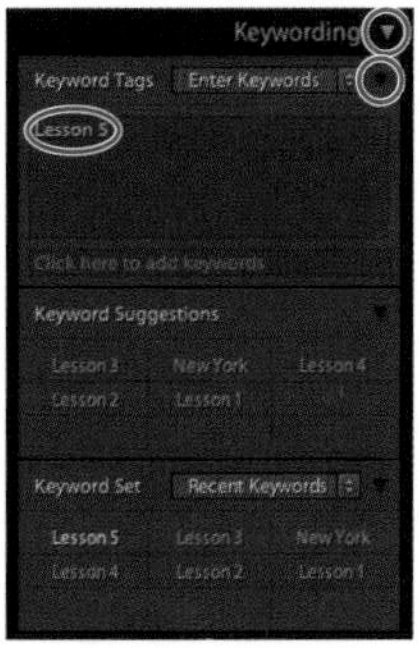

To view the keyword tags for more than one photo at a time, select the photos in the Grid view and check the Keywording panel. An asterisk appears beside any keyword tags not shared by all the selected photos. In the Keyword List panel just below the Keywording panel, a checkmark in front of a keyword indicates that the keyword is shared by all the images in the selection and a dash indicates that a keyword is not common to all the images.

Adding keyword tags

You have already had an opportunity to add keywords to your images during the process of importing them into your Lightroom library. The Import Photos dialog offers the option to apply keywords or a more extensive metadata preset to each image imported.

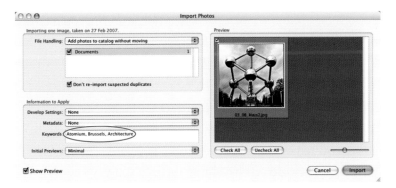

Once the images have been added to your Lightroom library, you can add keywords in the Keywording panel in the Library module.

1   In the Folders panel select the Chateau subfolder inside the Lesson 5 folder. Then, choose Edit > Select All.

2   In the Keywording panel, click the grey text Click Here To Add Keywords in the text box below the Keyword Tags pane. Then, type **Architecture, Chateau, Belgium, Europe**, being sure to add the commas as shown.

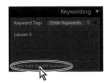 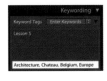

Note: Always use commas to separate keywords. Using periods will not work—Lightroom would treat "Belgium. Europe" as a single keyword.

3   Press Enter / Return. The new keywords are now listed in alphabetical order in the Keyword Tags panel and in the Keyword List panel.

💡 *To remove a keyword from a selected photo or photos, delete the word from the Keyword Tags pane in the Keywording panel, or click the checkbox to disable that keyword in the Keyword List panel.*

💡 *You can also apply keyword tags to selected images by clicking a keyword tag in the Keyword Suggestions pane in the Keywording panel.*

Working with keyword sets and nesting keywords

You can use the Keyword Set pane of the Keywording panel to work with *keyword sets*; groups of keyword tags compiled for a particular purpose. You could create a set of keywords for a specific project, another set for a special occasion, and one for your friends and family. Lightroom provides three basic keyword sets. You can use these sets as they are or as starting points for creating sets of your own.

1 Choose Wedding Photography from the Keyword Set menu. You can see that the keywords in the set would indeed be helpful in organizing the shots from a big event. Look at the categories covered by the other Lightroom keyword sets. You can use these as templates for your own keyword sets by editing them to suit your needs and saving your changes in a new preset.

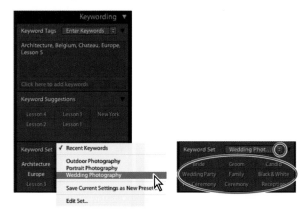

💡 *Keyword sets are a convenient way to have the keywords you need at hand as you work on the different collections in your library. A single keyword tag may appear in any number of keyword sets.*

Note: *If you don't see the Lightroom presets in the Keyword Set menu, open Lightroom Preferences and click the Presets tab. In the Lightroom Defaults options, click Restore Keyword Set Presets.*

2 Choose Recent Keywords from the Keyword Set menu.

3 Choose Edit > Select None.

4 If necessary, expand the Keyword List panel, located below the Keywording panel. In the Keyword List panel, right-click / Control-click the keyword "Europe" and choose Create Keyword Tag Inside 'Europe' from the context menu.

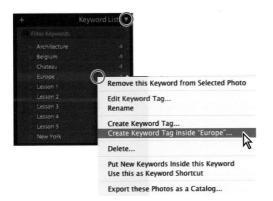

💡 *To add a new Keyword tag to the list, click the Plus icon on the upper left corner of the Keyword List panel.*

5 In the Keyword Tag text box, type **Germany**. In the Synonyms text box just below, type **Deutschland, Allemagne**. Make sure all the Keyword Tag Options are activated as shown in the illustration, and then click Create.

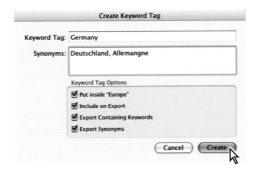

Include On Export: Includes the keyword tag when exporting photos.

Export Containing Keywords: Includes the parent tag when exporting photos.

Export Synonyms: Includes the synonyms associated with the keyword tag when exporting photos.

6 Expand the keyword "Europe" in the Keyword List panel. Note that the keyword "Europe" now contains the nested keyword "Germany."

Searching by keywords

If you have taken the time to organize your images by adding keywords and other metadata it will be very easy to find exactly the photo you're looking for. The Filter bar across the top of the Grid view provides everything you need to set up sophisticated and detailed searches of your library.

1   If the Filter Bar ist not already visible in the Grid view, choose View > Show Filter Bar, or press the Backslash key (\). Choose Text from the Library Filter options in the center of the Filter bar. Choose Keywords from the first menu and note the options available in the second menu. You can enter your search text in the text box to the right of the menus, and then press Enter to filter your images.

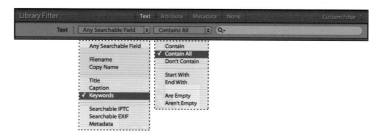

2   Disable the Text filter by clicking Text in the Library Filter options in the Filter bar. As you can see, the Text Filter menus offer a variety of options for searching your images by keyword. Next, we'll look at the Attribute filters.

> 💡 To transfer lists of keywords between computers or share them with colleagues who are also working in Lightroom, use the Export Keywords and Import Keywords commands in the Metadata menu.

Using Flags and Ratings

The Attribute filters in the Filter bar allow you to search and sort your images according to attributes such as flags and ratings.

1   In the Filter bar, choose Attribute from the Library Filters. The Filter bar expands to display controls for sorting your images by flag status, star rating, color label, copy status, or any combination of these attributes.

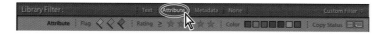

Flagging images

Assigning flags to sort the good images from the rejects can be a good way to begin organizing a group of photos. An image can be flagged as a pick (▱), a reject (▰), or left unflagged (▱).

1 If the Toolbar is not already visible, press the T key.

Note: In the Grid and Loupe views, you'll find tools for adding ratings, flags, and color labels in the Toolbar. In the Compare and Survey views you can change these attributes using the controls beneath the images. You can also flag a selected images by choosing from the Photo > Set Flag menu.

2 Click the triangle at the right side of the Toolbar and activate the Flagging tool from the menu. The Flag As Pick and Flag As Reject buttons appear in the Toolbar.

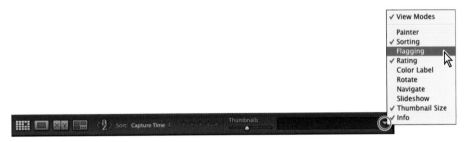

3 In the Folders panel select the Lesson 5 folder. In the Grid view, click to select the photo of the dry ferns (DSC_0025.jpg). If you have the Flags option activated in the Library View Options dialog box, a grey flag icon in the upper left corner of the thumbnail indicates that this image is unflagged. If necessary, hover over the image cell to see the flag icon, or deselect Show Clickable Items On Mouse Over Only in the Library View Options dialog box.

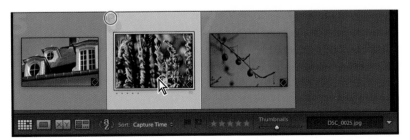

4 To change the flag status to Flagged, click the Flag As Pick button (▱) in the Toolbar.

> 💡 *Lightroom offers many ways to flag a photo. Choose Photo > Set Flag > Flagged or press the P key on your keyboard. Click the flag icon at the top left corner of the image cell to toggle between Unflagged and Pick status. To flag an image as a reject, choose Photo > Set Flag > Rejected, press the X key, or Alt-click / Option-click the flag icon in the corner of the image cell. Yet another way to change an image's flag status is to right-click / Control-click the flag icon in the corner of the image cell and choose Flagged, Unflagged, or Rejected from the context menu.*

5 Note that the photo is now marked with a white flag icon in the upper left corner of the image cell.

6 Click the white flag button in the Attribute Filter bar. The Grid view displays only the image that you just flagged. The view is now filtered to display only flagged images from the Lesson 5 folder.

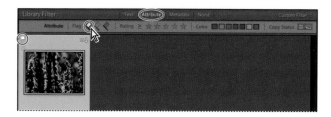

7 Click the grey flag button—the flag in the center—in the Attribute Filter bar. The Grid view now displays any photos flagged as Picks and all unflagged photos, so once again we see all of the images in the Lesson 5 folder.

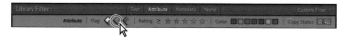

> 💡 *The Refine Photos command enables you to use flags to sort through your photos quickly. Choose Library > Refine Photos, and then click Refine. Unmarked photos are flagged as rejects and picks are reset to unflagged status.*

8 In the Filter bar, click Attribute to disable the Attribute filters.

Assigning ratings

A quick and easy way to sort your images as you review and evaluate them is to assign each photo a rating on a scale from one to five stars.

1   In the Grid view, select the first image of the chateau, named DSC_0008.jpg.

2   Press the 3 key on your keyboard. The message "Set Rating to 3" appears briefly and the photo is now marked with three stars in the lower left of its image cell.

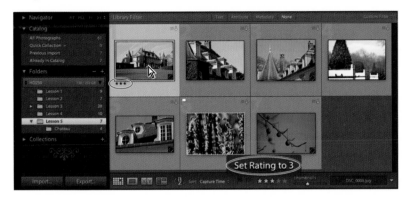

Note: If you don't see the star rating in the image cell, choose View > View Options and make sure Rating And Label is activated in the image cell display options.

It's easy to change the rating for a selected image; simply press another key between 1 and 5 to apply a new rating or press the 0 key to remove the rating altogether.

3   Click the triangle at the right of the Toolbar and make sure Rating is activated in the menu.

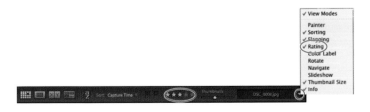

4   Click the stars in the Toolbar to change the rating. Click the current star rating to remove it.

💡 *You can also assign ratings by clicking the stars under the thumbnail image or in the Metadata panel. Choose from the Photo > Set Rating menu, or right-click / Control-click the thumbnail and choose from the Set Rating menu in the context menu.*

Specifying Color labels

Color labeling can be a very versatile tool for organizing your workflow. Unlike flags and ratings, color labels have no predefined meanings; you can attach your own meaning to each color and customize different label sets for specific tasks. While setting up a print job you might assign a red label to an image you wish to proof, a blue label to one that requires retouching, or a green label to mark an image that has been approved. For another project, you could use color labels to indicate levels of urgency.

Applying Color Labels

You can use the colored buttons in the Toolbar to assign color labels to a your images. If you don't see the color label buttons, click the triangle at the right of the Toolbar and choose Color Label from the menu. You can also click the color label icon displayed in a photo's image cell and choose a label from the menu. To assign a color label to an image using menu commands, choose Photo > Set Color Label and choose from the menu. In the menu, you'll notice that four of the five color labels have keyboard shortcuts.

Note: To see—and set—color labels in the Grid view image cells, choose View > View Options or right-click / Control-click any of the thumbnails and choose View Options from the context menu. The Library View Options dialog box appears. In the Grid View tab, activate the Show Grid Extras option. In the Compact Cell Extras area, you can choose Label or Rating And Label from either the Bottom Label or Top Label menus. In the Expanded Cell Extras area, activate the Include Color Label checkbox.

Editing Color Labels and using Color Label Sets

You can rename the color labels to suit your own purposes and create separate label sets for different parts of your workflow.

1 *Select an image in the Grid view and choose Photo > Set Color Label. The options in the menu for the default label set are Red, Yellow, Green, Blue, Purple, and None. Change the color label set by choosing Metadata > Color Label Set > Review Status. Choose Photo > Set Color Label again and you'll notice the options in the menu have changed: To Delete, Color Correction Needed, Good To Use, Retouching Needed, To Print, and None.*

2 *The Review Status label set gives you an idea of how you might assign your own label names to help you keep organized. You can use this label set as it is or as a starting point for creating your own sets. Choose Metadata > Color Label Set > Edit. The Edit Color Label Set dialog box appears.*

3 *Select the text "To Delete" beside the red color dot and type **Cropping Needed**. Choose Save Current Settings As New Preset from the Presets menu and type **My Review** in the New Preset dialog box. Click Create, then click Change to close the Edit Color Label Set dialog box.*

4 *Choose Photo > Set Color Label and you can see that the new label "Cropping Needed" now appears in the menu. To rename or delete a color label set, choose Metadata > Color Label Set > Edit and choose Delete Preset or Rename Preset from the Presets menu in the Edit Color Label Set dialog box.*

Specifying Color labels (cont.)

Searching by color label

1 Make sure that the Lesson 5 folder is selected in the Folders panel. Select all the images in the Grid view or the Filmstrip and apply a red label by clicking the red button in the Toolbar.

2 Select any two images and change the label by clicking the green button in the Toolbar. Select another of the red labeled images and click the color label indicator in its image cell. Choose Retouching Needed: the name assigned to a blue label in your customized label set.

3 In the Filter bar, click Attribute to see the Attribute filter controls. Click the red button. The images in the Lesson 5 folder are filtered so that only those with red labels appear in the Grid view. Click the green button. The Grid view now shows images with either red or green labels. Click the red and green buttons again to disable these filters and click the blue button; only one image is displayed in the Grid view.

4 Right-click / Control-click the blue button in the Filter bar and choose None from the menu. There are no color filters active and all the images in the Lesson 5 folder appear in the Grid view. The grey button at the right of the color label buttons filters for images without color labels (there are none in this folder).

*5 Select the image with the blue color label; then expand the Metadata panel in the right panel group. About half-way down the Metadata panel, below the Rating entry is the Label text box. You can see that the label for the selected image is "Retouching Needed". Click to select the text and type **Crop and Retouch**. Then press Enter / Return. The selected thumbnail in the Grid view has lost its blue label.*

6 Click the white button in the Attribute filter bar. This control filters for any image with a custom label so the Grid view now displays only one image. Right-click / Control-click the white button in the Filter bar and choose None from the menu. Select all the photos in the Grid view; then click on the color label in any of the thumbnails—if necessary, activate the option in the Library View Options dialog box to show the color labels in the Grid view—and choose None from the menu to remove the labels from all the images.

***Note:** The Attribute filters, including the Color Label filters, are also available in the bar above the thumbnails in the Filmstrip.*

Adding Metadata

You can leverage an image's metadata—information that is attached to the image file—to help you organize and manage your photo library. Much of the metadata, including capture date, exposure time, focal length and other camera settings, is generated by your camera. You can also add your own metadata to help you search and sort your catalog. In fact, you did just that when you applied keywords, ratings, and color labels to your images.

In addition, Lightroom supports the information standards evolved by the International Press Telecommunications Council (IPTC). This standard includes metadata entries for descriptions, keywords, categories, credits, and origins.

Storage of Metadata

File information is stored using the Extensible Metadata Platform (XMP) standard. XMP is built on XML. In the case of camera raw files that have a proprietary file format, XMP isn't written into the original files. To avoid file corruption, XMP metadata is stored in a separate file called a sidecar file. For all other file formats supported by Lightroom (JPEG, TIFF, PSD, and DNG), XMP metadata is written into the files in the location specified for that data. XMP facilitates the exchange of metadata between Adobe applications and across publishing workflows. For example, you can save metadata from one file as a template, and then import the metadata into other files. Metadata that is stored in other formats, such as EXIF, IPTC (IIM), and TIFF, is synchronized and described with XMP so that it can be more easily viewed and managed. To find out more about Metadata, please refer to Lightroom Help.

—From Lightroom Help

You can use the Metadata panel in the right panel group to inspect or edit the metadata attached to a selected image.

1 Select the photo in image cell 3 (DSC_0012.jpg).

2 Expand the Metadata panel. If necessary, collapse the other panels in the right group or hide the Filmstrip so that you can see as much of the contents of the Metadata panel as possible. Choose Default from the Metadata Set menu in the Metadata panel header.

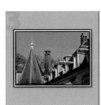
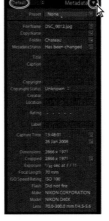

Even in the default metadata set, the Metadata panel exposes a great deal of information about the image. Although most of this metadata has been generated by the camera, some of it can be very useful in sorting your photos; you could filter images by capture date, search for shots taken with a particular lens, or easily separate photos taken on different cameras. However, the default setting displays only a subset of the metadata available in an image file.

3   Click the Metadata Set menu in the Metadata panel header and choose All. Scroll down in the Metadata panel to get an idea of the kinds of information that can be applied to an image.

4   For the purpose of this exercise, choose Quick Describe from the Metadata Set menu.

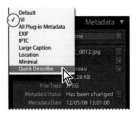

5   In the Quick Describe metadata set, the Metadata panel shows the Filename, Copy Name (if the image is a virtual copy), Folder, Rating, and some EXIF and IPTC metadata. You can use the Metadata panel to add titles and captions to a photo, attach details about the photographer and the location where the photo was shot, or change the rating.

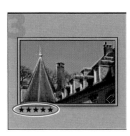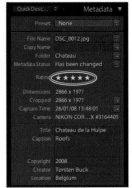

6   Control-click / Command-click the image in grid cell 2 to add it to the selection. In the Metadata panel most of the fields now show the entry <mixed>.

The folder name and the camera model are the only items shared by both files.

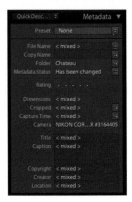

Changes made to any of the items in the metadata panel, even those with mixed values, will affect both of the selected images. This is a convenient way to edit items such as copyright details for a whole batch of images at the same time.

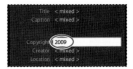

Using the Painter tool

Of all the features Lightroom provides to help you organize your growing image library, the Painter tool (🖌) is the most flexible. By simply dragging the Painter tool across your images you can add metadata, apply flags, labels, ratings, keywords, and developing settings, and even rotate your photos or add them to the Quick Collection.

The appearance of the Painter tool spray can icon changes slightly depending on the task at hand. When you pick the Painter tool up from its well in the Toolbar, the Toolbar is rearranged. From the Paint menu beside the empty tool well you can choose which settings or attributes you wish to apply to your images. The options are: Keywords,

Labels, Flag, Rating, Metadata, Settings, Rotation, and Target Collection. The illustration below shows the corresponding spray can icons.

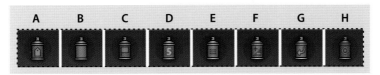

*A. Keywords. **B.** Labels. **C.** Flag. **D.** Rating.*
*E. Metadata **F.** Setting. **G.** Rotation. **H.** Target Collection.*

In this exercise you'll use the Painter tool to mark images with a color label.

1   Make sure you are still in the Grid view and that none of the images are selected. If you don't see the Painter tool in the Toolbar, click the triangle at the right side of the Toolbar and choose Painter from the tools menu.

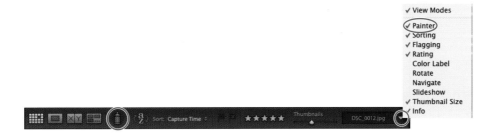

2   Click the Painter tool in its well in the Toolbar, choose Label from the Paint menu, and click the red color label button.

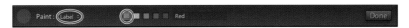

3   The Painter tool is now 'loaded'. Move the pointer over the images in the Grid view and a red spray can icon appears.

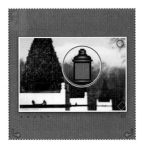

4   Click one of the images in the Grid view and the red label will be applied. While over a red labeled image thumbnail, the cursor icon changes from a spray can to an eraser. Click the image again to remove the color label and the spray can icon returns.

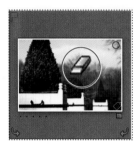

5   Click the image once more—but this time drag the spray can across several images. You have applied the red color tag to all these images with one stroke. Click the last image and drag the eraser tool back over the same images to remove the label.

6   Click Done at the right side of the Toolbar to deselect the Painter tool and return the Toolbar to its normal state.

Finding and filtering files

Now that you're familiar with the different techniques for categorizing and marking your photos, it's time to see some results. Next you'll look at how easy it is to search and sort your images once they have been prepared in this way. You can now filter your images by rating or label or search for a specific set of keywords and other metadata.

There are a numerous ways to find the images you need but one of the most convenient is to use the Filter bar across the top of the Grid view.

Using the Filter bar to find photos

1   If the Filter bar is not visible at the top of the Grid view, press the backslash key (\) or choose View > Show Filter Bar.

The Filter bar contains three filter groups: Text, Attribute, and Metadata filters. Click any of these options and the Filter bar will expand to display the settings and controls for setting up a filtered search. You can use these filters separately or combine them for a more sophisticated search.

Text: Search any metadata text including filenames, captions, keywords, and the EXIF and IPTC metadata.

Attribute: Filter a search by flag status, star rating, color label, or copy status.

Metadata: Set up to eight columns of metadata criteria to refine your search. Choose from the menu at the right end of a column header to add or remove a column.

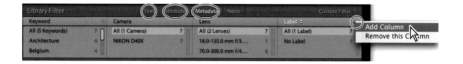

2 If the Text and Metadata filters are active, click to disable them. Click to activate the Attribute filters. If any of the flag filters is still active from the previous exercise, choose Library > Filter By Flag > Reset This Filter.

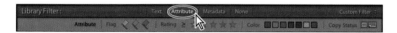

3 In the Rating controls, click the first star to search for any image with a rating of one star or higher. The grid view displays only the images to which you've currently a star rating applied.

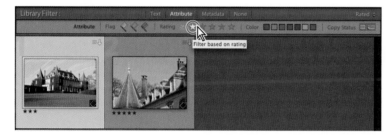

4 There are many options for refining your search. Click Text in the header of the Filter bar to add an additional filter. In the Text filter bar, click to open the menu on the left. Apart from the default search target Any Searchable Field, the menu offers you options to narrow the search to Filename, Copy Name, Title, Caption, Keywords, or searchable IPTC and EXIF metadata.

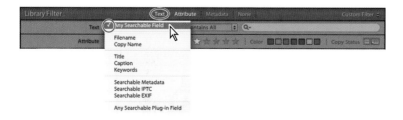

5   Click the other menu in the Text filter and choose "Doesn't Contain."

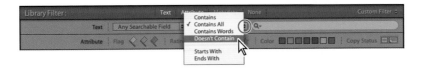

6   In the search text box, type **chateau** (you might remember adding this keyword to the images in the Chateau subfolder), and then press Enter. Disable the Rating filter in the Attribute filter controls by clicking the highlighted star.

7   Click Metadata in the header of the Filter bar to add an additional filter. In the Metadata filter controls, click on any of the column headers and choose Shutter Speed from the menu.

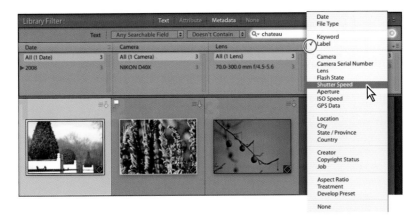

💡 *In the search text box, add an exclamation mark (!) before any word to exclude it from the results. Add a plus sign (+) before any word to apply the "Starting With" rule only to that word. Add a plus sign (+) after any word to apply the "Ending With" rule only to that word.*

8   In the Shutter Speed column, select any of the listed shutter speeds (or more than one by Ctrl-clicking / Command-clicking). Only images that do not contain "Chateau" in any searchable text field and were taken with the selected shutter speed will be displayed in the Grid view and the Filmstrip.

As you can see, there are endless possibilities for combining filters to find just the image you're looking for.

9   Click None in the Filter bar to disable all filters.

Using the filters in the Filmstrip

The Attribute filter controls are also available above the thumbnails in the Filmstrip. As in the Filter bar the Filter Presets menu lists filter presets and offers the option to save your filter settings as a custom preset, which will then be added to the menu.

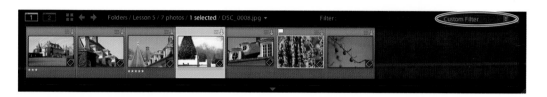

1   Experiment by choosing each of the Filter Presets menu options in turn.

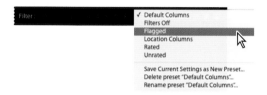

Default Columns: Opens the four default columns of the Metadata search options: Date, Camera, Lens, and Label.

Filters Off: Turns off all filters and collapses the Filter bar.

Flagged: Displays photos with a Pick flag.

Location Columns: Filters photos by Country, State/Province, City, and Location metadata.

Rated: At the current settings, displays photos with a star rating of one or higher.

Unrated: Displays photos that have no star rating.

Note: : If you don't see any filter presets in the presets menu, open Lightroom Preferences and click the Presets tab. In the Lightroom Defaults options, click Restore Library Filter Presets.

2   Choose Flagged from the Filter Presets menu. The only photo displayed is an image you flagged as a pick in a previous exercise.

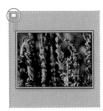

3   Choose Filters Off to display all the images in the Lesson 5 folder.

💡 *To save time and effort setting up searches, save your filter settings as a new preset. Specify criteria for any combination of Text, Attribute, and Metadata filters. Then choose Save Current Settings As New Preset from the Custom Filter menu in the Filter Bar or the Filmstrip.*

Renaming and reconnecting missing files

Remember that when you import a photo into your library, Lightroom adds the image file's name and address to the library catalog file. If you rename or move a photo while you're outside the Lightroom workspace the link to the catalog will be broken and Lightroom may no longer be able to locate the image file. The photo's thumbnail will be marked with a missing file icon to alert you.

1   Right-click / Control-click the photo in grid cell 4 and choose Show In Explorer / Show In Finder from the context menu.

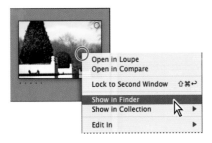

2   In the Explorer / Finder window, change the name of the selected file (an image of three trees) to **tree.jpg**.

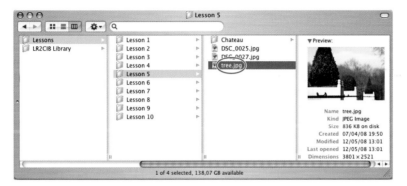

3   Back in the Grid view in Lightroom, you'll notice the broken link icon in the upper right corner of the image cell. Click the icon, and then click Locate in the dialog box.

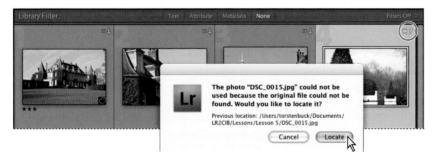

4   In the Locate file dialog box, select the renamed file and then click Select.

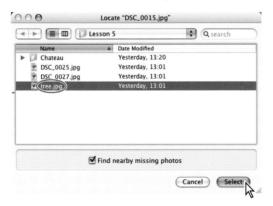

💡 *Activate the option Find Nearby Missing Photos if you moved several or even an entire folder of images to a new location. Lightroom will find the remaining missing photos in the same folder automatically.*

5 Click Confirm to verify that this is the correct file despite the changed name. You have now reestablished the link to your renamed file; the broken link icon is gone.

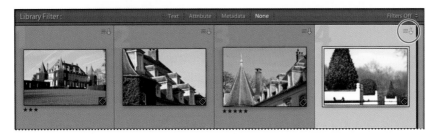

Note: In the Folders panel a question mark on a folder icon indicates that the link between the folder and the Lightroom catalog file is broken. To reestablish the link, right-click / Control-click the missing folder and choose Locate Missing Folder from the menu.

This concludes the lesson on organizing your image library. You've learned about structuring your folders, sorting and grouping images into collections, and a variety of methods for tagging and marking your photos to make them easier to find by applying a range of search filters.

However, it's worth discussing a final step that is invaluable in managing your growing library of photos: perform regular catalog backups. The library catalog contains not only your entire image database but also all the preview images and metadata, together with records of your collections and all your settings from the Develop, Slideshow, Web and Print modules. It is as important to make backups of your catalog as it is to keep copies of your image files.

You'll learn more about backing-up your library in Lesson 10, "Creating Backups and Exporting Photos."

Review

▶ **Review questions**

1   Can you keep multiple copies of the same master image in different folders?

2   What is a Smart Collection?

3   What are keyword tags?

4   What are the three modes in the Filter bar?

▶ **Review answers**

1   You can't keep copies of a master image in separate folders because the same image cannot be added to the Lightroom catalog twice. Although the image must reside in a single folder, it can be included in any number of Collections.

2   A Smart collection can be configured to search the library for images that meet specified criteria. Smart collections stay up-to-date by automatically adding any newly imported photos that meets the same criteria.

3   Keyword tags are text added to the metadata of an image to describe its content or classify it in one way or another. Shared keywords link images by subject, date, or some other association. Keywords help to locate, identify, and sort photos in the catalog. Like other metadata, keyword tags are stored either in the photo file or (in the case of proprietary camera raw files) in XMP sidecar files. Keywords applied in Lightroom can be read by Adobe applications such as Bridge, Photoshop, or Photoshop Elements, and by other applications that support XMP metadata.

4   The Filter bar offers three filter groups: Text, Attribute, and Metadata filters. Using combinations of these filters you can search the image library for metadata text, filter searches by flag, copy status, rating, or label, and specify a broad range of customizable metadata search criteria.

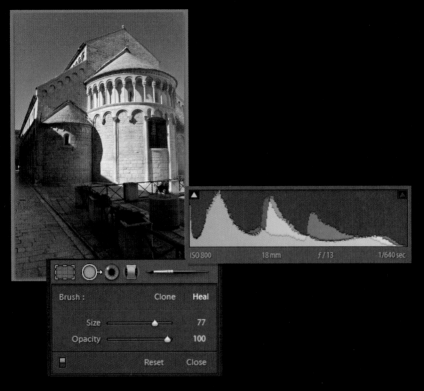

*Fine-tune and polish your
photographs with precise,
easy-to-use tools—secure
in the knowledge that the
modifications you make in
Lightroom won't alter your
master image, whether you're
working on a JPEG, TIFF,
DNG, or camera Raw file.*

6 Developing and Editing

Artificial light sources, unusual shooting conditions, and incorrect camera exposure settings can all cause faults such as tonal imbalances and unwelcome color casts in an image. In the Develop module Lightroom delivers a suite of powerful developing tools to quickly rectify these and other problems in your photos. Take your developing a step beyond just correcting your images; use the Develop module controls creatively to customize your own special effects, and then save them as develop presets.

This lesson introduces you to many of the options available in the developing and editing process—from easy-to-use presets and retouching tools to an array of specialized settings. Along the way you'll pick up a little computer graphics background knowledge as you become familiar with some basic techniques:

- Applying Develop presets.
- Cropping, rotating, and flipping images.
- Using the History and Snapshots panels.
- Removing blemishes.
- Correcting color problems.
- Adjusting the tonal range.
- Sharpening images and removing noise.
- Making discrete color adjustments.
- Working with grayscale and split tone effects.
- Adjusting specific areas of an image.
- Working with an external image editor.

Getting started

This lesson assumes that you are already familiar with the Lightroom workspace and with moving between the different modules. If you find that you need more background information as you go, refer to Lightroom Help or the previous lessons in this book.

Before you begin, make sure that you have correctly copied the Lessons folder from the CD in the back of this book onto your computer's hard disk and created the LR2CIB Library Catalog file. See "Copying the Classroom in a Book files" and "Creating a catalog file for working with this book" on page 3.

1 Start Lightroom.

2 In the Adobe Photoshop Lightroom - Select Catalog dialog box, make sure the file LR2CIB Library Catalog.lrcat is selected under Catalog Location, and then click Continue.

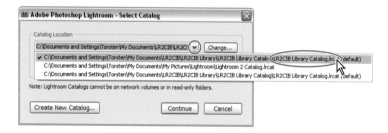

3 If the Back Up Catalog dialog box appears, click Skip Now.

4 Lightroom will open in the screen mode and workspace module that were active when you last quit. If necessary, click Library in the Module Picker to switch to the Library module.

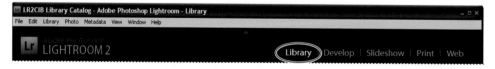

5 Choose File > Import Photos From Disk.

6 In the Import Photos Or Lightroom Catalog dialog box, navigate to the Lessons folder you've already copied into the LR2CIB folder on your hard disk. Select the Lesson 6 folder, and then click Import All Photos In Selected Folder (Windows) / Choose (Mac OS).

7   In the Import Photos dialog box, choose Add Photos To Catalog Without Moving from the File Handling menu. Choose None from both the Develop Settings menu and the Metadata menu. Type **Lesson 6** in the Keywords text box, and choose Minimal from the Initial Previews menu. Make sure your settings are exactly as shown in the illustration below, and then click Import.

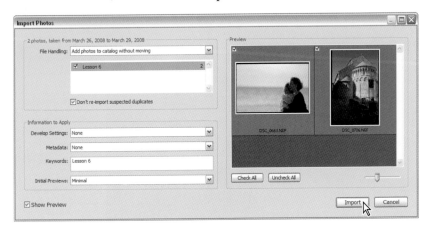

You have imported the photos into your library; you can see thumbnails of the images in the Grid view of the Library module and in the Filmstrip. You are now ready to start the exercises in this lesson.

Quick Develop

In the Library module, the Quick Develop panel in the right panel group provides a range of simple controls that enable you to make color and tonal corrections, apply developing presets, and crop an image without even switching to the Develop module.

1   In the Grid view, double-click the photo DSC_0653.NEF (an image of a mother and child) to see it in Loupe view.

2   In the right panel group, expand the Quick Develop panel.

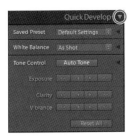

3 From the Saved Preset menu, choose the Creative - Antique Grayscale, Creative - Cyanotype, and Creative - Sepia presets in turn. The Loupe view shows the effect of each develop preset.

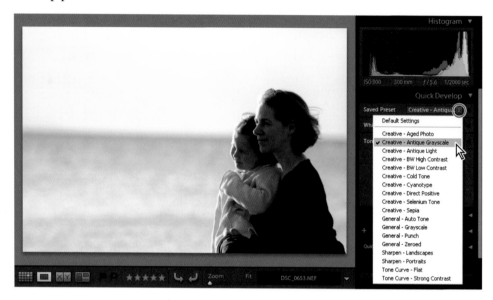

💡 *You can select a series of images in the Grid view or Filmstrip and apply a develop preset—or any other Quick Develop adjustment—to all of them at once.*

Develop presets apply a combination of different developing settings to your images at the same time, enabling you to achieve dramatic results with a single click. As presets are listed in alphabetical order, these Lightroom presets with the prefix "Creative" appear high in the Saved Preset menu but it's actually preferable that you apply them as a last step after you've made any color and tonal corrections that are necessary.

Note: When saving and naming your own presets, you should keep it in mind that they will be listed in alphabetical order. You can group related presets in the list by adding a common prefix or sequential numbering to their names so that they will be listed in the order in which they should be applied.

4 To return the image to its original state, choose Default Settings from the Saved Preset menu.

5 Expand the White Balance pane in the Quick Develop panel. *(See illustration on next page.)* From the White Balance menu, choose the Daylight, Cloudy, and Shade presets in turn. You'll notice that the colors in the image become progressively warmer. Select the white balance you prefer; we chose the Daylight preset.

Adjusting the white balance—and most of the other develop settings—means making some very subjective choices. If you wish to stay fairly close to the look of the original image, start with the As Shot setting in the Saved Presets menu, and then fine-tune the Temperature and Tint settings. If you feel that the white balance was set incorrectly when a shot was taken—perhaps as a result of artificial lighting—or if you wish to create a specific effect, use an appropriate preset from the menu as a starting point.

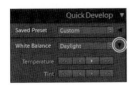

6   Expand the Tone Control pane and click the Auto Tone button. As the original photo was too bright, Auto Tone darkens the whole image considerably—exposing slightly more detail in the sky and water but effectively losing detail from the overly darkened faces. You can use the controls below the Auto Tone button to fine-tune the tonal balance of the image. In this case, you'll increase the detail visible in the shadowed areas of the image—including the faces—by adjusting the Fill Light control. Click the button on the far right three or four times to increase the fill light in relatively large increments.

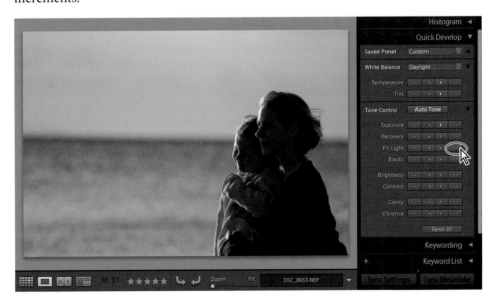

You have already improved the image considerably with just a few clicks but you can do a lot more to enhance this photo in the Develop module. In the next section of the lesson you'll explore the Develop module panels and learn how to use a variety of developing and editing tools. Once you have that background knowledge you can come back and apply what you've learned to get even better results from the Quick Develop panel.

> 💡 *While experimenting with the settings in the Quick Develop panel you can reset any control to its original state by simply clicking the name of the control. Click the Reset All button located at the bottom of the Quick Develop panel to revert the image to its original state.*

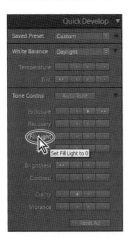

7   Click Develop in the Module Picker or press the D key to switch to the Develop module.

The Develop module

The Develop module contains all the tools and controls you need to correct and enhance your images. To assist and guide your workflow, the tools in the Develop module panels are arranged from top to bottom in the order in which they would ordinarily be used. All of the controls are easy enough for a beginner to use and yet have the depth and power required by the advanced user.

The Develop module offers two working views: the Loupe view and the split-screen Before/After view. The Toolbar across the bottom of the work area contains buttons for switching between the views and a slightly different suite of controls for each viewing mode.

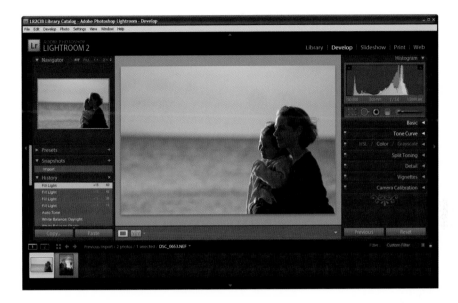

At the top of the left panel group, the Navigator helps you find your way around a zoomed image, previews the effects of the developing presets, and reviews past stages in the developing history. The Navigator panel also contains controls for setting the zoom levels in the working views. The Snapshots panel is used to record important stages in the development of a photo and the History panel keeps track of every modification made to the image—including the changes you made in the Library module.

At the top of the right panel group is the Histogram panel. Immediately below the Histogram is an array of tools for cropping, removing flaws and red eyes, applying graduated adjustments and painting develop settings directly onto an image selectively. Clicking any of these tools opens a drawer with controls and settings for that tool.

Below these editing tools is the Basic panel: your starting point for color correction and tonal adjustments. In many cases this may be the only panel you need to use to achieve the results you want. The remaining panels offer specialized tools for various image enhancement tasks. For example, you can use the Tone Curve controls to increase the contrast in the mid-tones by fine-tuning the distribution of the tonal range or the Detail controls to sharpen an image and reduce noise.

It is not intended that you use every tool on every photo. In many circumstance you may make only a few adjustments to an image. However, when you wish to polish a special photo—or if you need to work with shots captured at less than ideal camera settings—the Develop module contains the all tools you need.

In the next exercise you'll crop and rotate the image, remove some spots, and then move on to the color adjustment tools.

Cropping, rotating, and flipping images

The Crop Overlay tool makes it simple to improve your composition, crop unwanted edge detail, and even straighten your image.

1   If you're not already in Loupe view in the Develop module, press the D key or choose View > Go To Develop to switch to it now. Hide the Filmstrip and the left panel group to make more space in the work area.

2   Click the Crop Overlay tool button just below the Histogram panel, or press R. A crop overlay rectangle is placed over the image in the Loupe view and controls for the tool appear in the right panel group.

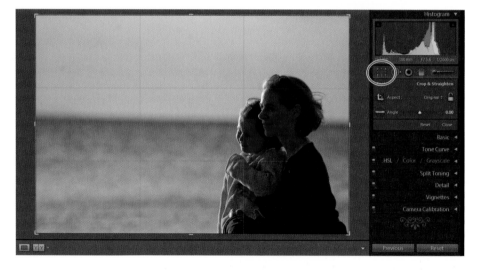

3   From the Aspect menu, choose Original. If the lock button shows and open lock icon, click the lock button to close the lock. The closed lock will constrain the aspect ratio while cropping.

4   Drag the top left handle of the crop overlay rectangle down and to the right. As you drag, you'll notice that the crop rectangle is resized from the center while the image moves so that the cropped portion is always centered in the Loupe view. Release the

mouse button when the horizon is roughly aligned with the guideline two-thirds of the way up the image as shown in the illustration below.

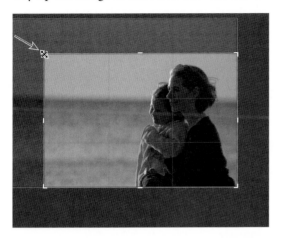

5 Click outside the crop overlay rectangle and drag to rotate the photo. As you drag, additional grid lines appear to help you straighten the image. Release the mouse button when the horizon is aligned with the grid.

6 Click inside the crop overlay rectangle and drag to reposition the image. You'll notice that you can drag the image only until its edge touches the border of the cropping rectangle, which is different from what you might be used to in Photoshop.

7 Reduce the size of the crop overlay rectangle further by dragging the bottom right handle upwards and to the left. Drag the image to reposition it so that the horizon is aligned with the horizontal guide as shown in the illustration below.

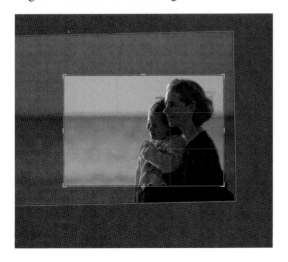

8   To exit cropping mode, press R on your keyboard or click the Crop Overlay tool button again. The cropped image is displayed in the Loupe view. You can return and adjust the crop at any time by clicking the Crop Overlay tool. The entire image will become visible again and you can resize the cropping rectangle or reposition the image as you wish.

9   Choose Photo > Flip Horizontal. This command comes in handy if the composition looks more interesting or fits better with a page layout when the image is reversed.

Undoing, redoing, and remembering changes

Lightroom offers several options for undoing and redoing changes and recalling key stages in the develop process.

Using the Undo and Redo commands

1   Choose Edit > Undo Flip Photos or press Ctrl+Z / Command+Z to undo the last command executed.

The Edit > Undo command lets you step back one command at a time; pressing Ctrl+Y / Command+Shift+Z will redo the last command undone. To jump several steps at once, use the History panel.

The History panel

1   Press F7 or click the triangle in the left border of the workspace to show the left panel group. If necessary, collapse other panels or scroll down to see the History panel.

2   Expand the History panel. You can see a long list of commands that have already been performed.

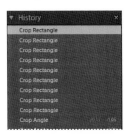

3   Scroll down to the bottom of the list and click the first entry—*Import ([date and time of the import])*—to see the image in its original state in the Loupe view.

Note: If you return an image to a previous state by clicking an entry in the History panel, and then make any adjustment to the image, the more recent entries are replaced by the new command.

4 Watch the Navigator panel as you move the pointer slowly up the list of commands in the History panel. The Navigator preview shows how the image looked at each stage of its developing history.

5 Scroll up to the top of the list and click the last entry—*Crop Rectangle*—to return to the most recent edited state of the image.

Creating snapshots

As the list in the History panel quickly becomes very long and unwieldy, it's a good idea to save key steps in an image's developing history as Snapshots for easy reference.

1 Expand the Snapshots panel and click the snapshot named *Import*, which was created automatically. In the Loupe view, the image reverts to its original state. You can see that even this step has been recorded in the History panel.

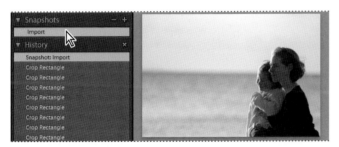

2 Scroll down in the History panel to the point just before you began using the Crop Overlay tool. Right-click / Control-click the most recent *Fill Light* entry (the highest in the list) and choose Create Snapshot from the context menu.

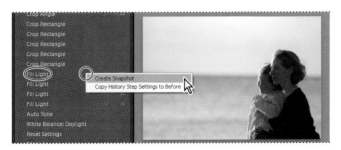

> *By default, the original version of the image as it was imported is shown as the Before version in the Before/After view. To designate a different state in the history of the image as the Before version, right-click / Control-click an entry in the History panel and choose Copy History Step Settings To Before. Repeat this step with the Import snapshot to reset the original state of the image as the Before view. To quickly toggle between the last edited state of an image and the Before view, press the Backslash key (\).*

3 In the Snapshots panel, type **Tonal Adjustments** as the name for your new snapshot and press Enter / Return.

4 In the History panel click the most-recent *Crop Rectangle* entry—just below the *Snapshot: Import* entry—to return to your last editing step. Click the Create Snapshot button (+) in the header of the Snapshots panel to create a new snapshot. Type **Crop and rotate** as the name for this snapshot, and then press Enter / Return.

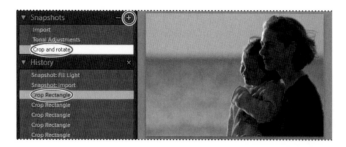

> *To delete a snapshot, select its name in the Snapshots list and click the Delete Selected Snapshot button (-) in the header of the Snapshots panel or right-click / Command-click the snapshot and choose Delete from the context menu.*

You now have a series of snapshots you can use to quickly return to important points in your developing process. In the next exercise, for example, we will return to an uncropped version of the image to demonstrate the spot removal tool.

Creating virtual copies

There may be times when you wish to explore different treatments for an image without losing the work you've already done. You can create *virtual copies* of your photo and make modifications to each one independently just as if you had separate copies of the master file in your image library.

The advantage in working with virtual copies is that you don't use all that extra disk space. You will still have only one copy of the original image file on your hard disk; each time you make a virtual copy Lightroom will simply add another entry for that image to the library catalog. Every change you make to the virtual copy is recorded in the new catalog entry so that not only the master file remains untouched but also your settings for any other virtual copy.

If you include a single photo in more than one collection, any changes you make to that image while you're working in any one of the collections will be visible in the others. If you wish to apply a special effect to a whole collection without affecting the images as they appear elsewhere in your catalog you should use virtual copies. You could include a full-frame, full-color image in a collection assembled for a slideshow and a tightly cropped, sepia-toned virtual copy in another collection you've created for a print layout.

1   In the Snapshots panel, select the Tonal Adjustment snapshot: the last version of the image before it was cropped.

2   Choose Photo > Create Virtual Copy.

3   If necessary, press F6 to show the Filmstrip. You can see that there are now two copies of the same image visible in the Filmstrip.

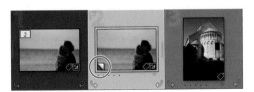

4   Press G on your keyboard to switch to Grid view in the Library module. In Grid view and the Filmstrip, virtual copies are identified by a page peel icon in the lower left corner of the image.

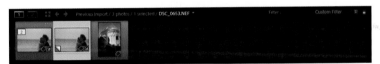

💡 *You can use the Copy Status filter—one of the Attribute filters in the Filter bar—to display master images or virtual copies selectively.*

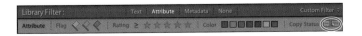

Note: By default, Lightroom will automatically stack the virtual copy with the original in the catalog. If you don't want the original and the virtual copy stacked, choose Photo > Stacking > Auto-Stack By Capture Time. In the Auto-Stack By Capture Time dialog box set the Time Between Stacks to 0.

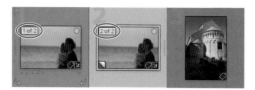

5   Press D on your keyboard to switch back to Loupe view in the Develop module.

6   Press F7 to hide the left panel group.

Removing spots

If you look at the photo carefully you'll notice three unsightly spots in the upper left of the image, caused by dirt on the lens. The Spot Removal tool is ideal for fixing blemishes like these.

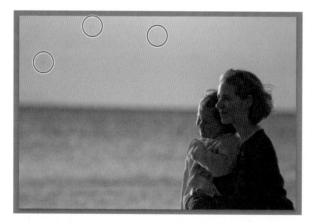

1   In Loupe view in the Develop module, click the Spot Removal tool just below the Histogram panel *(see illustration on next page)*, or press N. You'll notice that an extra pane opens below the tool buttons with controls and settings for the Spot Removal tool.

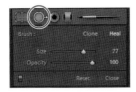

The Spot Removal tool works in either Clone mode or Heal mode. In Clone mode, the tool covers an imperfection in the photo (the target area) with an exact copy of another portion of the image (the sample area). Clone mode is ideal when you need to repair an area in the image which is patterned or where there are distinct repeated details such as bricks, stairs or even foliage. For areas in an image that have smooth color transitions—such as skin in a portrait shot or the sky in our example—use the Heal mode. In Heal mode, the Spot Removal Tool blends the sampled area with the target area rather than replacing it.

2   In the Spot Removal Tool settings, choose Heal from the two brush options.

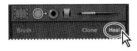

3   Use the sliders to set the brush Size to about 80 pixels and the Opacity to 100%. Click the first blemish near the left margin of the image—but don't drag. Release the mouse button and move the pointer away; you'll notice that Lightroom automatically finds an appropriate area to sample. On your screen you should see something similar to what's shown in the illustration below: the white circle with the cross-hairs is the target area centered on the blemish and the bolder white circle is the sample area.

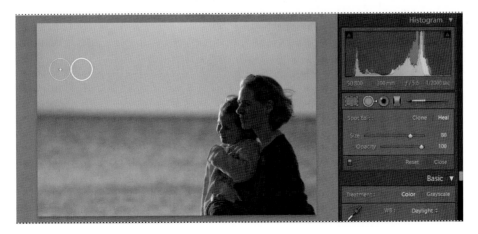

💡 *The best way to evaluate the results of the Heal operation is to set in the Navigator panel the zoom ratio for the Loupe view to 1:1, and then use the Navigator panel to focus on the recent spot correction location.*

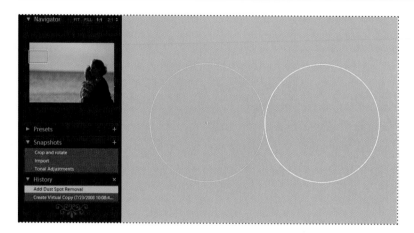

4   If you wish, you can specify the sample area for the Heal brush manually. With the Spot Removal tool, click the next spot and drag to find a sample that blends effectively; you can see the effect on the target area as you drag. Release the pointer when you're satisfied with the result.

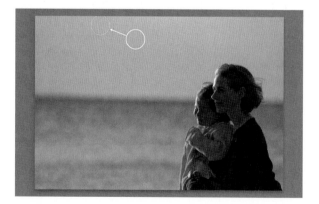

💡 *You can reposition both the sample and target areas for a spot correction by dragging the white circles in the Loupe view. To modify a previous spot correction, first click inside the target circle to activate it. Drag the circles to reposition them or use the sliders to adjust the size and opacity of the correction. Press Backspace / Delete to cancel and remove the spot correction.*

5   Remove the third spot using either of the techniques from the last two steps, and then press N to dismiss the Spot Removal tool. Remember that you can return and adjust the spot corrections at any time by clicking the Spot Removal tool.

Applying basic color corrections

In the Develop module basic color corrections are generally best made in the following order:

• Apply tonal corrections to set the correct white point and maximize the tonal range in the image using the Histogram and the controls in the Basic panel.

• Adjust the overall brightness and contrast using the Brightness control and the Tone Curve panel.

• Apply sharpening and noise reduction in the Detail panel.

• Add special effects such as decorative lens vignetting or specific color adjustments, using the HSL / Color / Grayscale, Split Toning, and Vignettes panels.

The following exercise will take you through a typical image correction process.

Adjusting the white balance and the tonal range

You'll start by adjusting the white balance for the photo of the church using the Histogram and the controls in the Basic panel; then you'll improve the tonal range by lightening the image—especially in the shadow areas.

1   In the Filmstrip, select the photo of the church: DSC_0706.NEF.

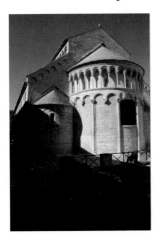

2   As this photo is in portrait format, you can make more space in the Loupe view for the vertical orientation by hiding the top panel (F5) and the Filmstrip (F6). Press T to hide the Toolbar. In the right panel group, expand the Histogram panel and the Basic panel.

3   In the Basic panel you can see that the current White Balance (WB) setting is As Shot. The Temp control shows that the shot was taken at color temperature of 4800 K (kelvin), which appears to be just about correct. However, by my recollection the color of the stonework was actually slightly warmer. Choose Daylight from the White Balance (WB) menu in the Basic panel. The Temp control now shows a color temperature value of 5500 K and the image looks a little too warm. Use the Temp slider to reduce the temperature to about 5250 K.

> 💡 *Enlarge the right panel group to its maximum width to increase the length—and therefore the sensitivity—of the sliders.*

The image is slightly too dark overall. You can see this reflected in the histogram; the tonal range looks a little weighted towards the left. The histogram shows the distribution of brightness—or *luminance*—in the image. The darker a pixel the further left it is recorded in the histogram, a lighter pixel is mapped further to the right. A peak in the histogram represents a large number of pixels of a similar brightness in the image.

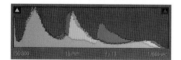

While you're adjusting an image's tonal balance, you can use the histogram as a reference as you work to achieve a more even distribution of tone over the full range from dark to light. If you make an image too dark you'll notice that part of the distribution curve moves out of range to the left of the histogram. This is known as *clipping* and represents a loss of color information from the image. For the pixels in the truncated portion of the curve, differences in brightness have been lost and every pixel is mapped to black; the shadows have been clipped. If you lighten the image too much, the curve is truncated at the right end of the histogram and the highlights are clipped.

Once the histogram is spread over as much of the range as is possible without clipping highlights or shadows, you can redistribute the curve to produce a well balanced image.

4 The small triangles in the upper corners of the histogram are clipping indicators. If the curve is clipped at either end of the histogram the respective indicator turns white. You can see that there is already some truncation of the left end of the curve and a white triangle indicates that the shadows are being clipped. To see which areas of the image are affected, move the pointer over the clipping indicator. Clipped shadows are shown as bright blue in the image and clipped highlights as red. You can see that some color detail is being lost in the railings and planters in the foreground. Click the clipping indicator to highlight the clipped shadows permanently. Press J on you keyboard to turn both clipping indicators on, or right-click / Control-click in the histogram and choose Show Clipping from the context menu. Turn Show Clipping off, if you prefer, before continuing with the next step.

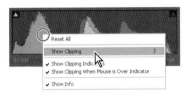

5 The Auto Tone command usually serves as a good starting point for adjusting the tonal range. Watch the histogram as you click the Auto button in the Tone section of the Basic panel. You'll notice that the histogram curve shifts slightly to the right and the image becomes lighter overall. You can see at a glance that the left end of the curve is not as truncated; there is much less clipping of the shadows.

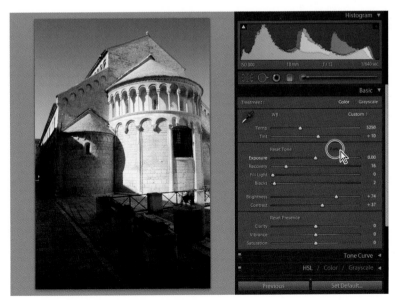

About white balance

To be able to display the full range of color information contained in an image file correctly, it's critical to set the right white balance for the photo. For this reason, it's important to understand what the white balance is. An image's white point reflects the lighting conditions in which the photo was taken. The white point is defined by values on two scales: temperature and tint.

If the red, green, and blue components of a pixel on the screen all have exactly the same values, the pixel appears as a neutral gray—ranging from white to black. The higher the red component, the warmer the image appears. The higher the blue component, the cooler the image. The tint accounts for color shifts in the direction of green or magenta.

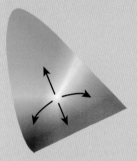

The sensors in a digital camera record the amount of red, green, and blue light that is reflected from an object. A neutral gray reflects all color components of the light source equally. If the light source is not pure white but has a predominant red component for example, a higher amount of red will be reflected to the sensors. Unless the composition of the light source is known—and the *white balance* or *white point* is corrected accordingly—the image will have a red color cast. Different types of artificial lighting have different white points; they provide lighting that is dominated by one color or deficient in another. Weather conditions also have an affect on the white balance.

When shooting in auto white balance mode, your camera tries to estimate the composition of the light source from the color information measured by the sensors. Although modern cameras are doing better at automatically setting the white balance to meet conditions, it is never fail-proof. It is preferable—if your camera supports it—to have the camera measure the white point of the light source; this is usually done by taking a picture of a light gray object under the same lighting conditions as the subject.

As well as the color information recorded by the camera sensors, a Raw image also contains the "As Shot" white balance information. This enables Lightroom to correctly interpret the recorded color information for a given light source. The recorded white point information is used as a calibration point in reference to which the white balance can be corrected and the colors in the image will be shifted accordingly.

(Continued on next page.)

About white balance (cont.)

If there is an area in your photo that you know should appear as a light neutral gray on screen you can use that area to set the point around which the image can be calibrated. Use the White Balance Selector tool, located in the top left corner of the Basic panel, to sample the color information in that area and Lightroom will set the image's white balance accordingly. As you move the White Balance Selector tool across the image you will see a magnified view of the pixels under the eyedropper and RGB values for the central target pixel. To avoid too radical a color shift, try to click a pixel where the red, green, and blue values are as close as possible. Do not use white or a very light color as target neutral; for a very bright pixel a color component might already have been clipped.

Color temperature is defined with reference to a concept known as *black-body radiation* theory. When heated, a black-body will first start glowing red, then orange, yellow, white, and finally blue-white. A color's temperature is the temperature—in kelvin (K)—to which a black-body must be heated to emit that particular color. Zero K corresponds to −273.15 °C or −459.67 °F and an increment of one unit kelvin is equivalent to an increment of one degree Celsius.

What we generally refer to as a warm color (with a higher red component) actually has a lower color temperature (in kelvin) than what we would call a cool color (with a higher blue component). The color temperature of a visually warm scene lit by candlelight is about 1,500 K. In bright daylight you would measure around 5,500 K and light from an overcast sky results in a color temperature in the photo of about 6,000 to 7,000 K.

The Temp slider adjusts the color temperature (in kelvin) of the designated white point, from low at the left side of the range to high on the right side. Moving the Temp slider to the left reduces the color temperature of the white point. In consequence, the colors in the image are interpreted as having a higher color temperature relative to the adjusted white point and are shifted towards blue. The colors displayed inside the Temp slider control indicate the effect a change in that direction will have on the image. Moving the slider to the left will increase the blue in the image, moving the slider to the right will make the image look more yellow and red. The Tint slider works in the same way. For example, to remove a green cast in an image you would move the Tint slider to the right, away from the green displayed inside the slider control. This increases the green component in the white point so the colors in the image are interpreted as less green relative to the adjusted white point.

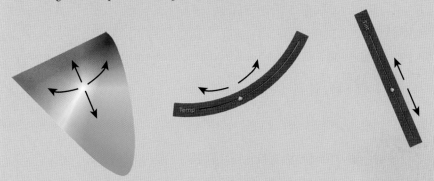

Adjusting the Temp and Tint sliders corresponds to shifting the white point in the color gamut.

6 Move the pointer slowly across the histogram from left to right. You'll see that the range of brightness values in the histogram is divided into four distinct zones, which are highlighted in turn as the pointer moves over them. At the same time, the name of each area is displayed in the lower left corner of the Histogram panel: Blacks, Fill Light, Exposure, and Recovery. You'll notice that these names are shared by four of the controls in the Basic panel.

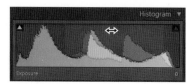

To change the tonal balance within any of these areas you can drag the relevant portion of the curve directly in the histogram. Drag to the right to brighten that portion of the tonal range or to the left to darken it. You could make the same adjustments by using the Exposure, Recovery, Fill Light, and Blacks sliders in the Basic panel.

Note: As you move either the Exposure or Fill Light sliders, the curve in the histogram will shift in the same direction as the slider. By comparison, the Recovery and Blacks sliders appear to work backwards. Increasing the Recovery value reduces the brightness in the Recovery area, shifting the curve to the left and thus recovering highlight information that might otherwise be clipped. Increasing the Blacks value also shifts the curve to the left, darkening the shadows and possibly resulting in more color information being clipped at the left end of the histogram.

Next you'll darken the brightly lit church wall and lighten the shadow area in the lower left of the image using the Exposure and Fill Light sliders.

7 To darken the brightest part of the church wall, drag the Exposure slider to about −0.38. Drag the Fill Light slider to about 25 to lighten the shadowed areas to the left of the building and in the foreground. You'll notice that this has also taken care of the clipped shadows.

Note: In general, clipped shadows in an image are less of a problem than clipped highlights as the resultant image artifacts are usually more noticeable in the lighter areas of an image.

💡 *Hold down the Alt / Option key while dragging the Exposure, Recovery, or Blacks slider to see the clipping mask in the Loupe view.*

8   Press the Backslash key (\) repeatedly to toggle between the edited and unedited versions of the image in the Loupe view. In this way you can quickly evaluate your current improvements against the original image.

The image is now much better lit but appears somewhat flat. Increasing the Clarity can add depth to an image by heightening *local contrast*, the differences in brightness between small adjacent areas of the image. The eye is very sensitive to changes in local contrast. On a larger scale, *contrast* describes the difference between significant bright and dark areas in the image. You'll adjust the contrast globally using the Tone Curve panel later in the lesson.

9   The Clarity setting is best adjusted at a magnification level of 100% or greater. Zoom the photo to 100% by clicking the 1:1 zoom ratio in the Navigator panel. Reposition the image so that you can focus on the colonnades and the lightest part of the curved stone wall. Then set the Clarity to about +50.

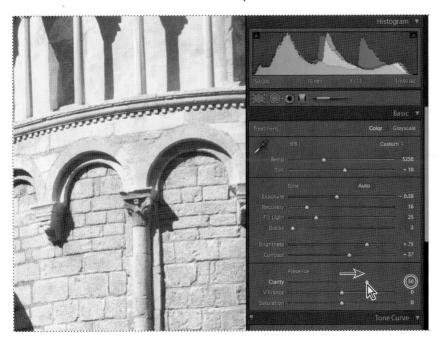

10   Undo and redo the last step a few times to quickly compare the image with and without the increased clarity setting. Drag the image in the Loupe view to review the effect in a different area. Before you continue, make sure the Clarity adjustment is applied.

> You can set every control in the Basic panel using keyboard shortcuts. Press the *Period (.) or Comma (,) keys to cycle forwards or backwards through all the controls in the panel. Use the Plus (+) and Minus (-) keys to change the settings; hold down the Shift key to adjust in higher increments. Press the Semicolon (;) to reset a control to its default value. Press Ctrl+U / Command+U for Auto Tone and Ctrl+Shift+U / Command+Shift+U for Auto White Balance. Press V to toggle between Grayscale and Color treatment. Press W to pick up and release the White Balance tool.*

Note: For this image we will not use the Vibrance or Saturation controls. The Saturation control alters the intensity of color from washed-out and gray to very vivid and intense. A slight increase in color saturation can create a very pleasing effect but over-saturating makes colors look artificial and color detail will be lost. The Vibrance slider alters the saturation in a non-linear manner—boosting the less saturated colors in a photo and having less effect on the bolder areas, while avoiding over-saturating skin colors.

> *If you intend to convert an image to black and white, boosting the saturation before the conversion can result in a more dramatic effect in the final image.*

Adjusting contrast using the tone curve

Working with the Tone Curve enables you to adjust contrast in different parts of the tonal range selectively. Tone curve corrections should not be applied until after the imaged has been processed as necessary with the controls in the Basic panel. The tone curve maps the distribution of tonal values in the input image along the x-axis to a new distribution of tonal values in the output image along the y-axis. The dark end of the range is at the lower left and the light at the upper right.

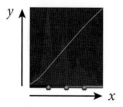

A linear tone curve at a 45° incline from the lower left corner to the upper right corner has no effect on the image; each tone value in the input image is mapped to the identical tone value in the output image. Raising the tone curve above this line maps tone values to a lighter value; lowering it darkens the tonal values.

A tone curve section that is flatter than 45° compresses a range of tone values from the input image to a narrower range in the output image. Some tone values which were distinguishable in the input image become indistinguishable in the output image and image detail is lost. A tone curve section that is steeper than 45° expands tone values; the differences between tone values becomes more noticeable and the image contrast is increased.

In Lightroom, the tone curve is constrained so that the curve is always ascending—so if you increase the incline of one section of the curve you'll end up with a decreased incline somewhere else. You'll have to make a compromise. When using the tone curve, the trick is to increase the contrast in the range where you have the most tonal information; recognizable by a peak in the histogram. At the same time, try to place the flatter parts of the tone curve in ranges where there is less information in the image (troughs in the histogram) or where a lack of contrast is not as disturbing or noticeable. A typical tone curve intended to increase mid-range contrast starts flat in the lower left corner (less contrast in the shadows), is steep in the center (more contrast in the mid-tones), and ends flat in the upper right corner (less contrast in the highlights).

For the image at hand we'll customize the tone curve to selectively increase the contrast in the well-lit wall area of the church, which is the focus of attention in the photo. For this substantial enhancement it will be worthwhile sacrificing a little of the contrast in the shadowed area at the lower left and in the sky.

1   If necessary, expand the Tone Curve panel in the right panel group. In the Navigator, set the Loupe view zoom level to Fit.

2   From the Point Curve menu at the bottom of the Tone Curve panel, choose Linear, Medium Contrast, and Strong Contrast in turn and notice the effect each setting has on the image. You can use any of these tone curve presets as a starting point for your adjustments. For this image, Medium Contrast works best.

Note: The choice of point curve preset also constrains the amount of play in the adjustment controls.

3   In the tone curve display, note the silhouette of the histogram plotted in the background. This gives you an indication of the tonal ranges where an increase in contrast might be most effective.

4   Position the pointer over the tone curve. As you move from left to right you'll notice the names of the ranges you're moving over displayed at the bottom of the tone curve grid.

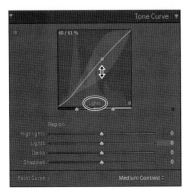

Whether you use the sliders, enter numeric values, or drag directly in the tone curve grid, the tone curve controls raise or lower the curve by moving the center points of these four ranges: Shadows, Darks, Lights, and Highlights. The overall shape of the tone curve changes to accommodate your adjustments, becoming flatter in one place and steeper in another. The extent to which you can adjust each section of the tone curve is indicated by the gray area that appears when you position the pointer over that section.

💡 *By default, the four tonal ranges are of equal width. You can change their width by dragging the controls below the tone curve to reposition the dividing lines between adjacent tonal ranges.*

5   To see which areas in the image correspond to the different tonal ranges, click the Target tool button in the top left corner of the Tone Curve panel and move the pointer over the image in the Loupe view. As you move the pointer over the shadowed area in the lower left of the image you can see that these tones account for much of the first peak in the histogram around the 25% mark. Most of the tonal values in the blue sky are represented in the second peak in the histogram just below the 50% input level. The tones in the well-lit church wall are mostly spread between input levels of 60% to 90%.

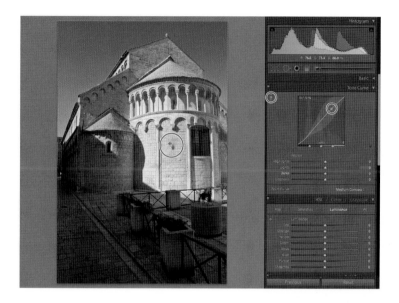

Lowering the Lights value in the tone curve should produce the effect we're after: increasing the contrast in the well-lit church wall by steepening the curve for the input values above 60%. The compromise is a flattening of the curve for lower input values; reducing contrast in the sky and shadow areas where a loss of detail is less noticeable.

6   Watch the tone curve as you move the target cursor over the well-lit church wall. When you see that the Lights adjustment control is selected on the Tone Curve, click and drag downwards in the image. Release the mouse button when the Lights value is adjusted to −40. Remember: you can only adjust the tone curve by dragging directly in the image when you are using the Tone Curve Target mode.

7   Click the Target button in the top left corner of the Tone Curve panel again to turn off target mode.

8   To compare your image with and without the tone curve adjustment, switch the tone curve adjustment off and on by clicking the On/Off switch icon at the left side of the Tone Curve panel header. Review the effect in a few different areas of the image at 100% zoom level. You can see how effectively your adjustment enhanced the image detail in the stone wall of the church.

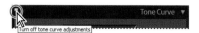

Note: The image was also darkened as a whole because the tone curve was pushed below the diagonal. This works quite well for the image at hand. In another case, you could lessen the effect by raising the Shadows value in the Tone Curve or by readjusting the levels using the controls in the Basic panel.

9   When you're done, set the zoom level to Fit and make sure the tone curve adjustment is turned on.

The image now looks quite acceptable. To improve it even further you can apply additional sharpening and reduce some of the noise that's visible in the sky area.

Sharpening detail and reducing noise

The Detail panel contains controls for sharpening image detail, reducing noise, and correcting chromatic aberrations. Sharpening helps make edges more pronounced and gives the image a crisper look. A slight amount of sharpening is applied to your Raw images by default, so apply additional sharpening with caution. Noise is most noticeable in images shot under low-lighting conditions or at a high ISO setting. The image for this exercise was shot at an ISO setting of 800 and contains a slight amount of noise, mostly noticeable the sky area. Chromatic aberrations, or color fringes, are more noticeable with lower quality lenses or near the edges of an image shot with a wide-angle lens; in both cases the lens has been unable to focus the different wavelengths of incoming light correctly on the sensor. There are no chromatic aberrations noticeable in the image used for this exercise.

1   In the right panel group, scroll down or collapse other panels if necessary, and then expand the Detail panel. In the Navigator panel, set the zoom level for the Loupe view to 1:1 (100%).

Note: Image sharpening and noise reduction are always best executed at 100% magnification.

2   For this image, the sharpening amount is already set to 25%. To compare the image with and without this default sharpening, switch the Detail controls off and on by clicking the On/Off switch icon at the left side of the Detail panel header. Review the effect in a few different areas of the image at 100% magnification. When you're done, make sure you've turned the Detail settings back on.

The default sharpening has already done a good job of emphasizing the edges in this image. You can still improve the crispness of the photo but first you need to create a mask to restrict the effect of your adjustment to areas with edge detail. In the case of our lesson image, this will enable you to sharpen architectural detail but avoid accentuating the noise in the sky area where it will be easily noticeable.

3   Position the photo in the Loupe view so that you can see some of the sky and part of the church wall at the same time. Hold down the Alt / Option key and drag the Masking slider to the right. The mask is displayed in the Detail panel preview and in the Loupe view when the zoom level is set to 1:1 or higher. Release the pointer when most of the sky area is masked (black) but the edge detail on the church wall is still unmasked (white). We used a value of 50.

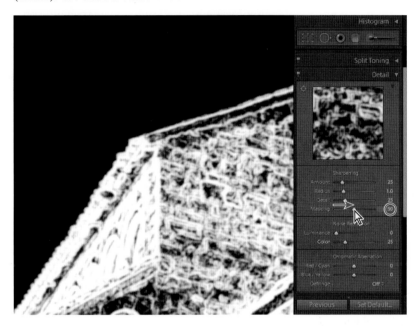

4   To sharpen the image further, drag the Amount slider to the right. With the extensive mask in place, you can afford to increase the sharpening by a relatively large amount. We raised the setting to 100.

5   Compare the image with and without sharpening once again by clicking the On/Off switch icon at the left side of the Detail panel header. Review the effect in several areas of the image at 100% magnification.

6   By way of comparison, make sure the detail controls are turned on and drag the Masking slider all the way back to its default setting of 0. Then Undo and Redo to see the effect of applying sharpening with and without the mask. Pay particular attention to the sky area where unmasked sharpening accentuates noise.

7   When you're done, return the Masking setting to 50.

Most of the noise in this image is *luminance noise*—variations in the brightness of pixels which should be equally bright. Luminance noise looks similar to film grain and is in general less of a problem than color noise, or *chrominance noise*—bright blue, red and purple spots in an area that should be a uniform hue.

To reduce color noise, use the Color slider under Noise Reduction in the Detail panel. You should use the Color slider with caution; color noise reduction is achieved by blurring the image's blue channel which can result in blurring of some of the image detail. The Luminance noise slider should also be used judiciously to avoid softening detail in the image.

8   Position the photo in the Loupe view so that you can some of the sky and part of the church wall at the same time, as shown in the illustration below. Drag the Luminance slider all the way to the right to a value of 100. You can see that the luminance noise in the sky has now disappeared. However, you'll also notice a marked blurring of the detail in the church wall. You'll need to find a compromise between reducing noise and maintaining the sharpness of the image. Drag the Luminance slider back to 0, and then slowly to the right until you notice the first improvements in the sky area but before the details on the church wall become blurred. We used a value of 30.

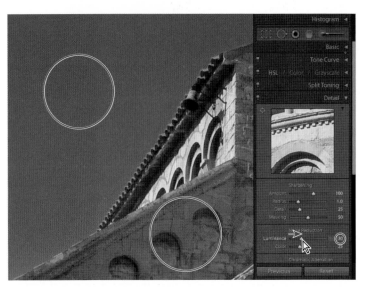

Removing or adding vignettes

Lens vignetting is a phenomenon that results in reduced brightness or saturation of color towards the edges of an image. A vignette is usually an accidental effect caused by a combination of the focal length, type of lens, and filters used. The Lens Correction controls in the Vignettes panel enable you to correct undesired vignetting. On the other hand, the effect can also be used creatively to draw the attention to the center of the image. You can use the Post-Crop controls to apply creative vignetting effects to an image.

1   Set the zoom level to Fit. You'll notice that the sky is slightly darker towards the corners of the image. The same edge darkening is also present, though less noticeable, in the shadowed areas in the lower corners of the image.

2   In the right panel group, scroll down or collapse other panels if necessary and expand the Vignettes panel.

3   Under Lens Correction, drag the Amount slider to the right until the lens vignetting in the corners of the image appears to be corrected. We used a value of +20.

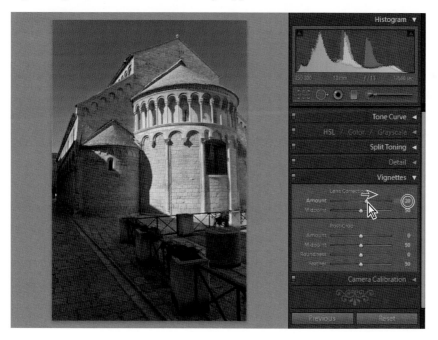

You'll now add a post-crop vignette, a creative effect that can be used to draw the viewer's attention to the center of an image or to *frame* the image as you'll do in the following exercise.

4   In the Post-Crop controls, set the Amount to −80, Midpoint to 0, Roundness
to −100, and Feather to 20.

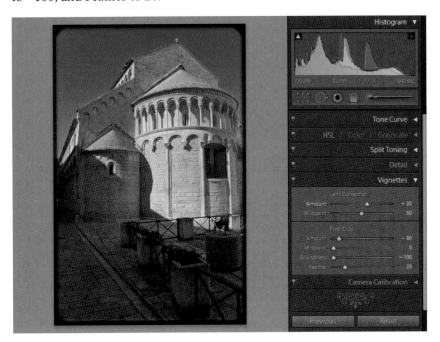

5   (Optional) If you prefer a lighter frame, try setting the Amount to +60.

*Note: This example takes the Post-Crop vignetting feature to the extreme. For your own
images, start by experimenting with slight deviations from the default values to discover
effects that might enhance your images.*

6   For the remainder of this lesson, remove the Post-Crop vignette by double-clicking
the word Post-Crop in the Vignettes palette. This resets the Post-Crop control to its
default setting without affecting the Lens Correction settings.

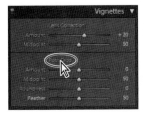

Making discrete color adjustments

You can adjust discrete shades of color in your image using the controls in the HSL / Color / Grayscale panel. You can change the hue, saturation, or luminance for specific color ranges independently. When converting an image to grayscale you can fine-tune the way that each color in the image will contribute to the grayscale mix. Use the Split Toning panel to apply creative duotone effects to a grayscale image.

Understanding hue, saturation, and luminance

The color of each pixel in your image can be expressed either as a set of RGB values or as a combination of hue, saturation, and luminance values. You can calculate hue, saturation, and luminance values from RGB values, and vice versa.

Once you understand hue, saturation, and luminance, describing color in these terms seems far more natural than using RGB values, especially when it comes to describing changes in color. For example, darkening the blue colors in your image can be done by reducing the luminance value for the blue color component. Expressed in RGB values, a light blue might be composed of R: 42, G: 45, and B: 63, while a darker blue uses R: 35, G: 38, and B: 56; certainly not a very intuitive model for describing color adjustments.

When you describe a color by its name—red, yellow, green—you're referring to the color's hue. Saturation is the boldness or intensity of a hue, ranging from neutral and grayed to vivid and un-muted. Luminance is a measure of how much light is emitted by a color on a scale from black to white; luminance can be described as a measure of brightness.

The full range of hues can be displayed as a color wheel. Adjusting the hue moves a given color around the color wheel in one direction or the other.

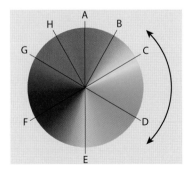

*Selected hues: **A.** Red. **B.** Orange. **C.** Yellow. **D.** Green. **E.** Aqua. **F.** Blue. **G.** Purple. **H.** Magenta.*

Saturation can be visualized on a color wheel with fully saturated colors around the edge of the circle and less saturated colors closer to the center. As the saturation of a color is increased it moves from a neutral gray in the center of the wheel to a pure, vivid hue on the rim.

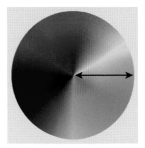

Luminance is the measure of brightness of a color, ranging from the minimum value for black to the maximum value for white. Luminance can be represented on the color wheel model by adding a third dimension, with a completely underexposed—or black—wheel at the bottom and a completely overexposed—or white—wheel at the top. Decreasing luminance makes a given hue darker, increasing luminance makes it lighter.

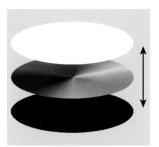

The terms tint, shade, and tone can all be expressed with reference to hue, saturation, and luminance. A *tint* is a pure hue mixed with white; a hue with increased luminance and a reduced saturation. In our three-dimensional color wheel model the tints of a hue are found along the line from the pure hue on the rim of the wheel in the middle to the center point of the white wheel at the top. A *shade* is a pure hue mixed with black; a hue with decreased luminance and saturation, located along a line from the pure hue on the rim of the wheel in the middle to the center point of the black wheel at the bottom. A *tone* is a pure hue mixed with a neutral gray, located along a line from the pure hue on the rim of the wheel in the middle to the respective gray on the central axis.

Adjusting colors selectively

In the next exercise you'll darken the blue of the sky in the photo. You can do this by reducing the luminance of the blue color range while leaving the hue and saturation unchanged.

1　Set the zoom level to Fit.

2　In the right panel group, scroll up or collapse other panels, if necessary, and expand the HSL / Color / Grayscale panel. If not already selected, click HSL (Hue, Saturation, Luminance) in the panel header, and then click the Luminance tab.

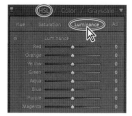

3　Click the Target tool button in the upper left corner of the Luminance pane. In the Loupe view, click in the sky area and drag the pointer downwards to reduce the luminance of the color range under the pointer. Release the mouse button when the Luminance value for Blue reaches −20. You can see from the Luminance sliders that Lightroom also found some purple in the sky and has therefore made a slight adjustment to the luminance value for purple as well.

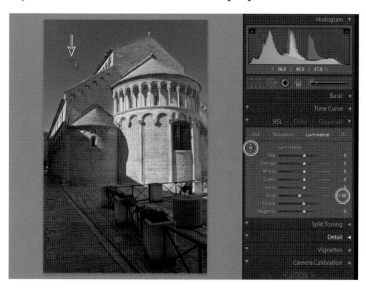

4   Click the Target button again to disable target mode.

5   To compare the image with and without the luminance adjustment applied, switch the HSL / Color / Grayscale adjustment off and on by clicking the On/Off switch icon at the left side of the panel header. Note that the adjustment has not affected the gradient from lighter blue near the horizon to darker blue at the top. It is important to understand that the luminance adjustment is not restricted to one discrete hue value but is applied across a range of colors to either side of the target hue. When you're finished reviewing the effect, make sure HSL / Color / Grayscale adjustment is turned on.

You can adjust the hue or saturation in the same way. Select the Hue or Saturation tab, then use the Target tool to adjust the color in a specific area in the image. You could also use the respective slider controls. Click the All tab for access to all the sliders for Hue, Saturation, and Luminance at the same time. In the Color tab the sliders are grouped by color rather than by hue, saturation, and luminance. Click the All tab to see the sliders for all colors at the same time.

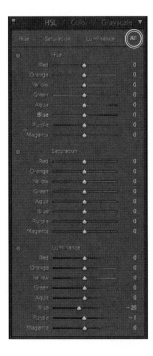
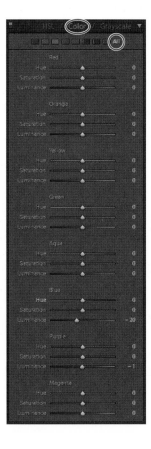

Converting an image to grayscale

When Lightroom converts a photo to grayscale, each color in the image is mapped to a tone of gray according to a default mix. To change the look of the resultant image you can adjust the predominance of each color in the mix. In other words, you can change the extent to which each color contributes to the grayscale information.

1 Click Grayscale in the header of the HSL / Color / Grayscale panel. You can see the result of the default grayscale mix in the Loupe view.

2 To adjust the grayscale mix selectively in different areas of the image click the Target tool button in the upper left of the Grayscale Mix pane. In the Loupe view, click the area you wish to adjust and drag upwards or downwards to lighten or darken that part of the image. Click in the sky area and drag upwards to increase the value of Blue in the mix to about +30; then click the bright church wall and drag downwards to reduce the value for Orange to about −20.

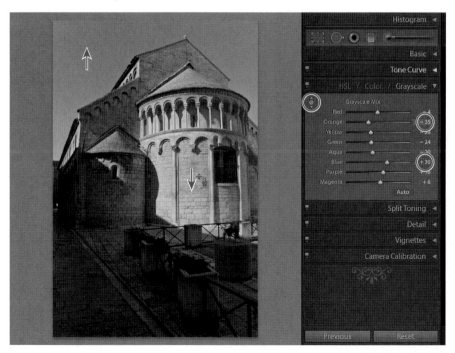

3 Click the Target button again to turn target mode off.

4 To compare the image before and after your adjustments to the grayscale mix, switch the Grayscale mix adjustment off and on by clicking the On/Off switch icon at the left side of the HSL / Color / Grayscale panel header. When you're done, make sure the Grayscale Mix control is turned on.

Split toning

A split toning effect replaces the darker tones (shadows) in an grayscale image with shades of one color and the lighter tones (highlights) with tints of another. The effect can be quite subtle and restrained or very striking and unusual depending on your choice of colors and your intention.

1　In the right panel group, expand the Split Toning panel. If possible, keep the HSL / Color / Grayscale panel open so you can see the settings for the grayscale mix at the same time.

2　Right-click / Control-click the image in the Loupe view, and then choose Settings > Creative - Antique Grayscale from the context menu. Note the changes in the Split Toning panel. The Antique Grayscale effect uses a sepia tone for the highlights and a less saturated and slightly warmer color for the shadows. By checking the other panels in the right panel group you can see that the Antique Grayscale preset has changed the grayscale mix and also the settings in the Basic, Tone Curve, Detail, and Vignettes panels.

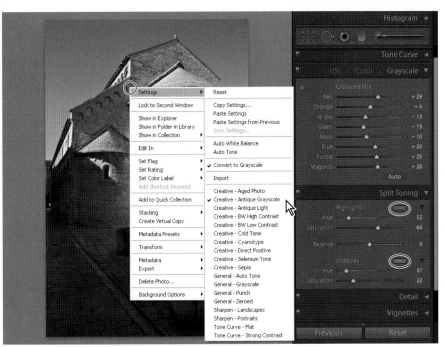

If you wish to apply some of the settings from a preset (or another image) and not others, you can copy just the settings you want. In this case, you'll copy the color settings from the Split Toning panel.

3   Right-click / Control-click the antique grayscale image in the Loupe view, and then choose Settings > Copy Settings from the context menu.

4   In the Copy Settings dialog box, first click the Check None button, and then activate only the Split Toning option. Click Copy.

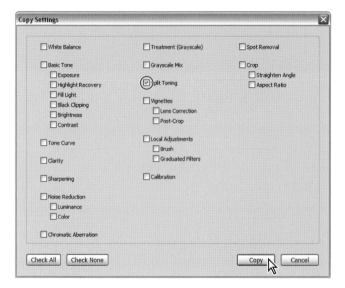

5   Choose Edit > Undo Preset: Creative - Antique Grayscale to return to the grayscale image with all your customized settings.

6   Right-click / Control-click the image in the Loupe view and choose Settings > Paste Settings from the context menu. By checking the panels in the right panel group, you can see that this time only the settings in the Split Toning panel have been altered.

Synchronizing settings

To copy, or *synchronize*, settings from one image to a multiple selection of images, use the Synchronize Settings command.

1   Select all three images in the Filmstrip. If necessary, click the image of the church so it's the active (the most selected) image. Synchronizing the selected images will copy settings from the active image to all the other images in the selection.

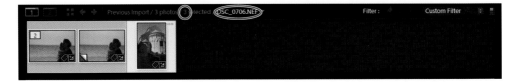

2   Click the Sync button below the right panel group or choose Settings > Sync Settings.

3   In the Synchronize Settings dialog box (note the similarity to the Copy Settings dialog box), click the Check None button and activate both the Treatment (Grayscale) and Split Toning options. Click Synchronize.

All three images are converted to grayscale and have the duo-tone effect applied.

> 💡 *The Synchronize Settings command in the Develop module copies absolute values from one image to the others. To apply relative changes to a selection of images—such as increasing exposure by 1/3 step independent of the current exposure settings in the destination images—you can use the Quick Development panel in the Library module.*

Local corrections

All the adjustments you've made in this lesson so far have been applied globally—across the entire image. For example, increasing Fill Light affects all the shadowed areas in a photo; you can't lighten one area selectively or some areas more than others. With the local correction tools, you can do both.

Using the Graduated Filter tool

With the Graduated Filter tool you can created a gradient mask through which you can apply an adjustment so that the effect is stronger in one area and fades off across the rest of the image.

1 In the Filmstrip, select only the church image. Click the Graduated Filter button just below the Histogram panel, or press M. You'll notice that additional controls appear below the tool buttons. If the controls look different than in the illustration below, click the Show Effects Slider button near the top right corner of the pane.

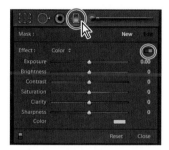

2 In the Graduated Filter controls pane, make sure New is selected as the Mask setting. Adjust the Exposure setting to a value of 0.36.

3 With the Graduated Filter tool, drag from a point near the lower left corner of the image to the upper right, as shown in the illustration below, and then release the pointer. You have just created a basic gradient mask, which you will go on to fine-tune in the following steps of this exercise.

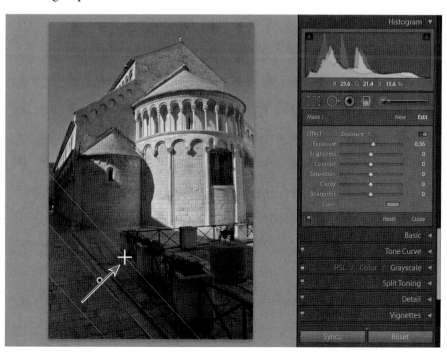

4   You can see the effect on the image at a glance; the exposure is gradually increased towards the lower left corner. In the Graduated Filter pane, the Mask setting has changed to Edit. You can still change the settings for the adjustment and reposition, rotate, resize, and fine-tune the gradient mask.

5   Increase the Exposure setting to 1.00. Then adjust the gradient mask as shown in the illustration below. Drag the pin to reposition the center of the gradient, drag the center line to rotate the mask, and drag either of the outer lines to increase or reduce the steepness of the gradient; the narrower the band, the more abruptly the adjustment is faded into the image. Hold down the Alt / Option key while dragging one of the outer lines to keep the center line fixed at its current position. The outer lines represent the boundaries beyond which the adjustment is applied at 100% of the specified value on one side and 0% on the other. Press the H key to hide or show the adjustment pin.

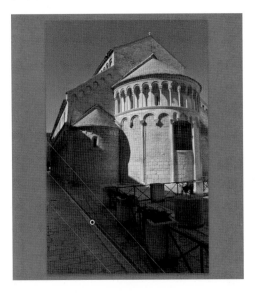

6   To evaluate the image with and without the graduated filter adjustment, click the On/Off switch icon in the lower left corner of the mask pane. When you're done, make sure the graduated filter adjustment is activated.

7   Click the Graduated Filter button again to disable it.

💡 *You can use more than one graduated filter in a single image, each with its own position, direction, size, and adjustment settings.*

Using the Adjustment Brush tool

You can use the Adjustment Brush tool to paint adjustments directly onto different areas of the image selectively.

1   Click the Adjustment Brush button below the Histogram panel, or press K. The Adjustment Brush tool settings appear below the tool buttons.

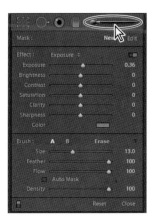

In addition to the adjustment sliders, which were also available for the Graduated Filter tool, the Adjustment Brush tool settings also contain controls for setting up brushes. You can set a different size, softness, flow, and density for each of three brushes: two for applying the adjustment or effect and one to erase it.

For this exercise, you'll use the Adjustment Brush tool to apply a local adjustment to the sky area.

2   Make sure New is selected beside Mask in the Adjustment Brush tool controls pane.

3   Set Exposure to 0. Click the color box to choose a color to tint the effect. We choose a saturated red.

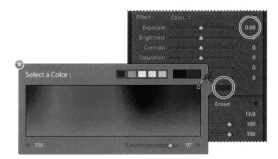

4   Click brush A and activate the Auto Mask option. When you begin painting an area with the Adjustment Brush, the Auto Mask option will detect the edges of the area based on similar color values and mask the image outside those edges.

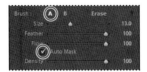

5   Paint over the entire sky area. Even though the auto mask feature does a good job of detecting the edges of the sky, you should still avoid painting outside the area. Hold down the Alt key / Option key while dragging to erase areas you've brushed over accidentally.

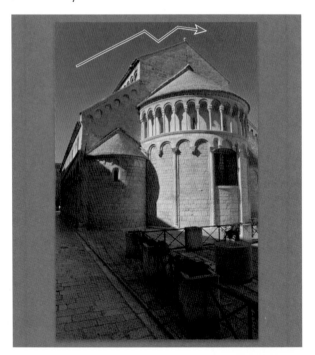

6   Click the Adjustment Brush tool again to disable it.

💡 *You can use the Adjustment Brush to create more than one adjustment area in a single image, each with its own settings. To delete an adjustment area, select its pin, and then press delete.*

Working with and external image editor

To do further pixel-based editing, you can open your image in an external editor such as Photoshop or Photoshop Elements—from within the Lightroom workspace.

> 💡 *You can select your preferred external editor and set file format preferences in the External Editing tab of the Preferences dialog box.*

Select the photo you wish to edit with the external editor. Then select your preferred image editing application from the Photo > Edit In menu.

If you have the latest version of Photoshop CS3 (version 10.0.1 or later) installed on your computer, you have additional options for processing multiple photos, such as creating a panorama, merging to HDR (High Dynamic Range), or combining them in a single Photoshop document with each photo on its own layer. Right-click / Control-click a multiple selection of images in the Filmstrip or the Grid view, and then choose any of the Edit In options from the context menu.

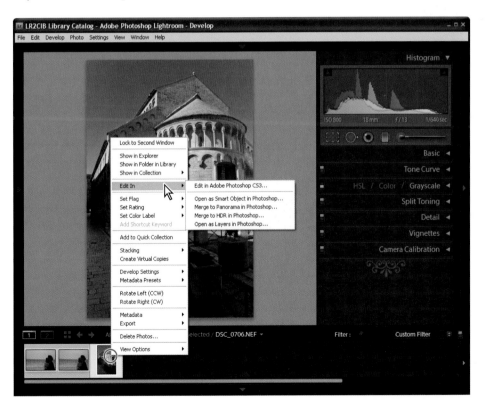

Lightroom will render your Raw images into a pixel-based image file format—or ask the Photoshop Camera Raw plug-in to perform the conversion—and open the resulting images in your external editor. When you've finished editing your photos in the external editor, save your changes and return to Lightroom.

Note: Don't rename the exported files or Lightroom will not be able to locate the edited versions in order to import them into the library. When saving from Photoshop or Photoshop Elements, make sure to activate the Maximize Compatibility option.

The edited versions of your images will automatically be added to your library. The original image files will remain unchanged.

For more information, please refer to "Editing in other applications" in Lightroom Help.

You are now familiar with a wide variety of basic skills as well as some specialized techniques for more sophisticated image editing tasks. Experiment with the tools, settings, and options on your own to discover more of the depth and power of the Develop module.

Remember: all your edits are non-destructive—so enjoy!

Review

▶ **Review questions**

1   How do you undo changes or return quickly to a previous develop state?

2   What is white balance?

3   What does a tone curve represent and what is it used for?

4   What are the two kinds of noise you might encounter in a digital image and what can you do about them?

5   Which tools are used to perform local corrections?

▶ **Review answers**

1   You can undo one modification at a time using the Undo command. You can jump back multiple steps at once in the History panel. You can create snapshots of important develop states so that you can return to them quickly.

2   An image's white balance reflects the composition of the red, green, and blue components in the light source when the picture was taken. It is used as a calibration benchmark to correctly interpret and render the color information recorded by the camera's sensors.

3   A tone curve adjusts the distribution of the tonal ranges in an image. The curve represents the way tonal information from the original image will be mapped to the adjusted image. It can be used to increase or decrease the contrast in specific tonal ranges.

4   Digital images may contain two kinds of noise: luminance noise, which is a result of variation in the brightness of pixels which should be of the same luminance, and color (chrominance) noise: bright blue, red and purple spots in an area that should be a uniform hue. Each kind of noise can be reduced using the appropriate noise reduction slider in the Detail panel.

5   You can restrict adjustments to selected areas of your image with the Graduated Filter tool and the Adjustment Brush tool.

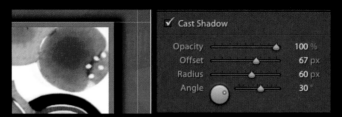

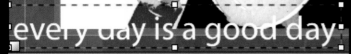

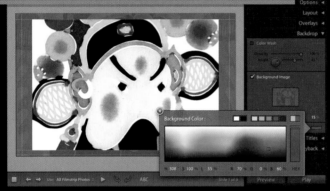

In the Slideshow module you can quickly put together an impressive on-screen presentation complete with stylish graphic effects, transitions, text overlays, and even music.

7 | Creating Slideshows

Now that you know how to import, review, organize, and enhance your photos, it's time to learn how Lightroom can help you to share them with friends and family or present them to a client.

Lightroom makes it easy: the Slideshow module offers a range of basic slide templates and provides all the tools you'll need to make them your own. Choose a template as a starting point; then customize the layout, color scheme, and timing. Add borders, shadows, backdrops, and overlays to create a slideshow that will complement your work and captivate your audience.

In this lesson, you'll create your own slideshow by following these easy steps:

- Grouping the images for your slideshow as a collection.
- Viewing an impromptu slideshow.
- Choosing a slideshow template.
- Adjusting the slide layout.
- Changing the background color and adding a backdrop image.
- Adding a text overlay.
- Adjusting the playback settings.
- Saving your customized template.
- Previewing and playing your slideshow.
- Exporting your presentation.

Getting started

This lesson assumes that you are already familiar with the Lightroom workspace and with moving between the different modules. If you find that you need more background information as you go, refer to Lightroom Help, or the previous lessons in this book.

Before you begin, make sure that you have correctly copied the Lessons folder from the CD in the back of this book onto your computer's hard disk and created the LR2CIB Library Catalog file. See "Copying the Classroom in a Book files" and "Creating a catalog file for working with this book" on page 3.

1   Start Lightroom.

2   In the Adobe Photoshop Lightroom - Select Catalog dialog box, make sure the file LR2CIB Library Catalog.lrcat is selected under Catalog Location, and then click Continue.

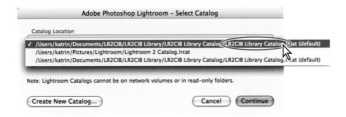

3   If the Back Up Catalog dialog box appears, click Skip Now.

4   Lightroom will open in the screen mode and workspace module that were active when you last quit. If necessary, click Library in the Module Picker to switch to the Library module.

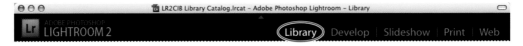

Importing images into the library

The first step is to import the images for your slideshow into the Lightroom library.

1   If you're not already in the Library module, switch to it now.

2   Choose File > Import Photos From Disk.

3   In the Import Photos Or Lightroom Catalog dialog box, navigate to the Lessons folder you've already copied into the LR2CIB folder on your hard disk. Select the Lesson 7 folder, and then click Import All Photos In Selected Folder / Choose. Lightroom will import only the image files, not the sound file Temple of the Moon.mp3.

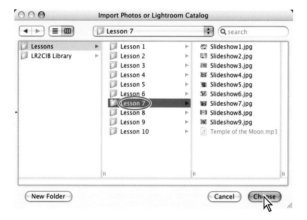

4   In the Import Photos dialog box, make sure the Show Preview option in the lower left corner of the dialog box is activated so that you can see thumbnail images of the photos you're about to import. For this exercise, leave all nine photos selected.

5   Choose Add Photos To Catalog Without Moving from the File Handling menu. Choose None from both the Develop Settings menu and the Metadata menu. Type **Lesson 7** in the Keywords text box, and choose Minimal from the Initial Previews menu. Make sure your settings are exactly as shown in the illustration on the next page, and then click Import.

The images, featuring details of Chinese papercuts, appear in the Grid view of the Library module and in the Filmstrip.

Playing an impromptu slideshow

Even before you leave the Library module you can play an impromptu slideshow, which is a convenient way to see a full-screen preview of the photos you've just imported. The Impromptu Slideshow can be launched from any of the Lightroom modules. The slide layout, timing, and transitions reflect the current settings in the Slideshow module.

1   In the Grid view of the Library module, choose View > Sort > File Name and View > Sort > Ascending.

2   Press Ctrl+A / Command+A or choose Edit > Select All to select all of the images you have just imported.

3   Press Ctrl+Enter / Command+Return to start the impromptu slideshow. The slideshow will cycle through the images until you press the Esc key or click the screen to stop playback.

Note: You can also start the impromptu slideshow in any module by choosing Window > Impromptu Slideshow or—in the Library and Develop modules—by clicking the Impromptu Slideshow button in the Toolbar.

💡 *While the impromptu slideshow is playing, press the Right Arrow key to advance to the next slide or the Left Arrow key to return to the previous slide. Press the spacebar to pause and resume playback.*

Setting up a slideshow

It's a good idea to group the images for your slideshow as a collection so that you can easily retrieve them when you want to work on your presentation, even though they may actually be stored in different folders on your hard disk. For example, you might assemble a collection of images featuring national monuments that includes a photo of the Statue of Liberty from your New York folder and a photo of the Golden Gate Bridge from your San Francisco folder. Once you have grouped the images as a collection you can call up the same selection at a single click. Grouping your images in a collection also has other advantages: you can make consistent adjustments across all the images, rearrange their display order, and easily add or remove images without deleting them from the catalog.

Creating a new collection

1   Check that all nine images for this lesson are still selected. If not, press Ctrl+A / Command+A or choose Edit > Select All.

2   In the left panel group, click the New Collection button (+) in the header of the Collections panel, and choose Create Collection from the menu.

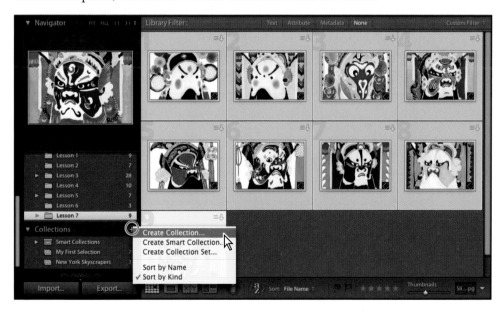

Note: To delete a collection, right-click / Control-click its name in the Collections panel, and choose Delete from the context menu.

3   In the Create Collection dialog box, type **My Slideshow** in the Name box and choose None from the Set menu. Under Collection Options, activate Include Selected Photos and disable Make New Virtual Copies; then click Create.

4   If not already selected, click your new collection in the Collections panel.

5   Activate the menu options View > Sort > File Name and View > Sort > Ascending.

6   Switch to the Slideshow module by clicking Slideshow in the Module Picker or pressing Ctrl+Alt+3 / Option+Command+3.

> *A collection is a grouping of images within the Lightroom catalog. Once you have saved a group of photos as a collection, you can rearrange their order in the Grid view or the Filmstrip. The new display order will be saved with the collection together with any settings you apply in the Slideshow, Print, or Web modules.*

The Lightroom Slideshow module

In the Slideshow module, the work area shows the Slide Editor view where you can see how your images look in the current layout template and preview your slideshow. Choose a slideshow template from the Template Browser in the left panel group and the Slide Editor view is updated to display the new layout (the illustration below shows the Crop To Fill template). In the Preview panel above the Template Browser you can preview the templates by moving the pointer over the list. The Toolbar below the Slide Editor view contains controls for navigating through the images in your collection, playing a preview of your slideshow, and adding text to your slides. You can use the controls in the right panel group to customize the slideshow template by tweaking the layout, adding borders, shadows, and overlays, changing the backdrop, adding title screens, and adjusting the playback settings.

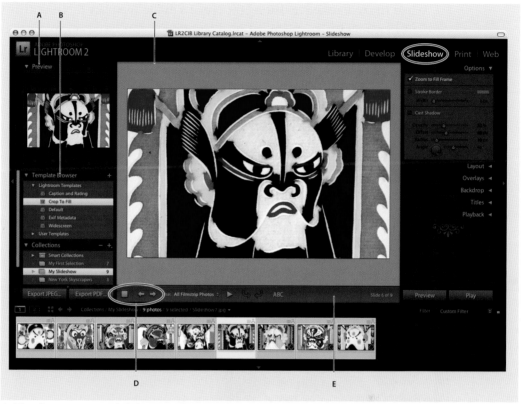

*A. Template preview. **B.** Slideshow templates. **C.** Slide Editor view. **D.** Playback controls. **E.** Toolbar.*

Choosing a slideshow template

The Lightroom slideshow templates provide a convenient starting-point for creating your own presentation.

1   In the Template Browser panel, move the pointer over the list of slideshow templates in the Lightroom Templates folder. The Preview panel shows you how the selected image looks in each template layout. Select a different image in the Filmstrip and preview the templates again.

2   When you've finished reviewing the options in the Template Browser, click the Widescreen template.

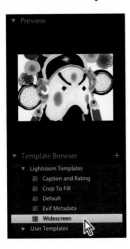

3   Select the first image, Slideshow1.jpg, by clicking it in the Filmstrip. From the Use menu in the Toolbar, choose All Filmstrip Photos.

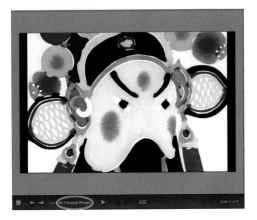

4   Click the Preview button at the bottom of the right panel group to preview your presentation in the Slide Editor view. When you're done, click in the Slide Editor view to stop the preview.

💡 *Click the Play button at the bottom of the right panel group to play your slideshow in full-screen mode.*

Template options for slideshows

As a convenient starting-point for creating your own slideshow, you can choose from these customizable Lightroom templates:

• **Caption And Rating**
This template centers the images on a grey background and displays the star rating and caption metadata for each photo.

• **Crop To Fill**
Your photos fill the screen and may be cropped to fit the screen's aspect ratio, so this is probably not a good option for images in portrait format.

• **Default**
This template is similar to the first, except that it incorporates your identity plate and displays the image file name rather than metadata information.

• **EXIF Metadata**
The slides are centered on a black background and include star-ratings, EXIF (Exchangeable Image Format) information, and your identity plate.

• **Widescreen**
Your images are centered and sized to fit the screen without being cropped: any empty space outside the image is filled with black.

Remember, you can always change the order of the images in a collection by dragging the thumbnails in the Filmstrip or Grid view. The rearranged order will be saved with the collection. Before dragging, make sure you have selected only the image or images you want to move. To remove an image from the collection, simply right-click / Control-click the image and choose Remove From Collection from the context menu.

Customizing your slideshow template

For the purposes of this lesson, you won't be adding an identity plate or metadata information to your slides, so the Widescreen template will serve as a good starting-point. You'll customize the template by modifying the layout, changing the background color, and overlaying text, and then liven up the show by adding a soundtrack. The controls in the right panel group enable you do all this and more. Let's start with the layout.

Adjusting the layout

Once you've chosen a slide template you can use the control panels in whatever order you wish to customize the settings. For this exercise you'll start with the Layout and

Backdrop panels, first modifying the layout and then changing the background color. In this way you'll get an idea of the overall look of the design before you make decisions about the style and color of borders and overlaid text. The Layout panel enables you to change the size and position of the photo in the slide layout by setting the margins that define the image cell.

1　If the Layout panel in the right panel group is currently collapsed, expand it by clicking the triangle beside its name. Make sure that the Show Guides and Link All options are activated, as shown in the illustration below.

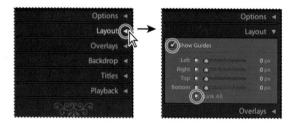

2　Position the pointer over the lower edge of the image inside the Slide Editor view. The pointer changes to a vertical double-arrow (↕) / vertical double-arrow with bar (⬍).

3　Drag the edge of the image upwards. You'll notice that grey layout guide lines appear against the black background around the scaled-down image. All four guides move at the same time because the Link All option is activated in the Layout panel. As you drag, watch the linked sliders and numerical values change in the Layout panel and release the mouse button when the values reach 50 px (pixels).

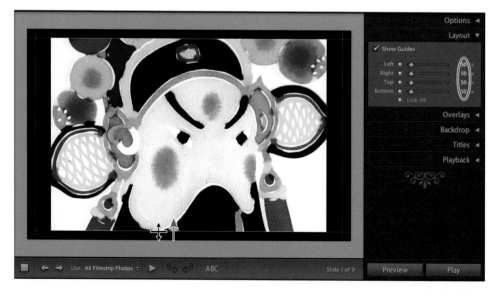

💡 *To adjust the image size, you could also drag the sliders in the Layout panel or click the pixel values at the right and type **50**. In this case you would only need to drag one slider or enter one value because the settings are linked.*

4   Collapse the Layout panel.

Setting the slide background

In the Backdrop panel set a background color for your slides, apply a color wash, or place a backdrop image. When all of the background options are disabled, the slide background is black. While a simple background can often be the most effective stage for your images, let's have fun with this exercise and try the full range of possibilities— just because we can!

1   Expand the Backdrop panel in the right panel group.

2   Choose Edit > Select None.

3   In the Backdrop panel, activate the Background Image option, and then drag the image Slideshow7.jpg from the Filmstrip into the Background Image box.

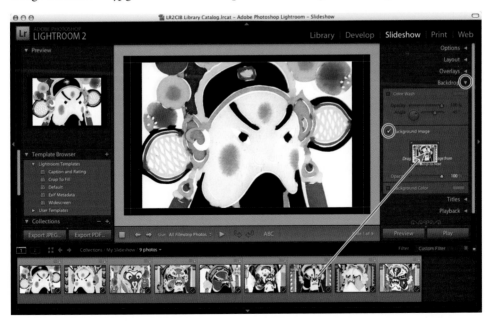

4 Drag the Opacity slider to the left until the value drops to 15%, or click the number beside the slider and type **15**. You'll see the change in the Slide Editor view.

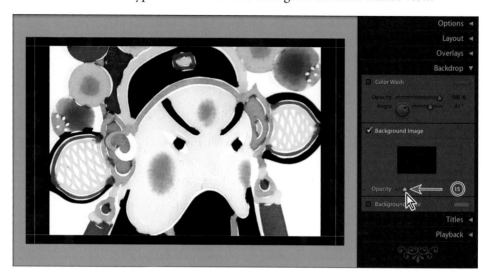

5 Activate the Background Color option, and then click the color swatch beside it. The Color Picker appears.

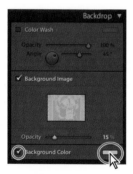

6 Drag the slider at the right of the Color Picker almost to the top, and then click a bright pink in the large color field on the left. We chose a color with the RGB values: R: 70%, G: 0%, B: 60%. You can enter these values directly by clicking each number and typing the new value in the box. If you see a hexadecimal value displayed in the lower right corner of the Color Picker rather than RGB values, click RGB below the color slider. The color you specified appears in the color box at the top right of the Color Picker, in the Background Color control, and in the Background Image preview. The

slide is now framed with a captivating pattern that, because it is taken from one of the papercut images, fits well with the rest of the series.

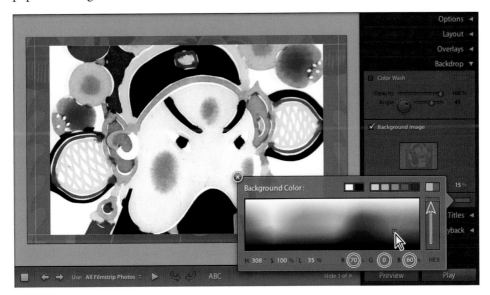

Note: A background image can be an effective device to set an overall theme for your slideshow, especially when it's applied at less than full opacity and perhaps overlaid with text.

7   Click the Close button in the upper left corner of the Color Picker to close it.

8   Activate the Color Wash option. The background color becomes an angled gradient from pink at the lower left to grey at the upper right. The effect looks faded: subtler and with more depth than the original, more vibrant pink. Experiment a little with the color wash controls. Try changing the angle, opacity, and color of the wash.

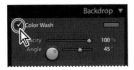

9   Disable the Color Wash option, and then collapse the Backdrop panel.

Adjusting stroke borders and casting shadows

Now that you've established the overall layout and color scheme, you can make the image stand out more against the background by adding a stroke border or a drop shadow.

1   In the right panel group, expand the Options panel.

2   Activate the Stroke Border option, and then click the color swatch beside it. The Color Picker appears.

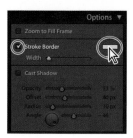

3   We'll stay within the same color scheme, so that the background doesn't become too busy and compete with our images. Drag the slider at the right of the Color Picker to the top, and click a bright pink in the large color field on the left. We choose a color with the RGB values: R: 100%, G: 0%, B: 100%. You can enter these values directly by clicking each number and typing the new value in the box. Click outside the Color Picker to close it.

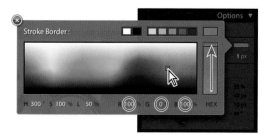

4   Change the stroke width by dragging the Width slider to set a value of 10 pixels or type **10** in the box beside the slider.

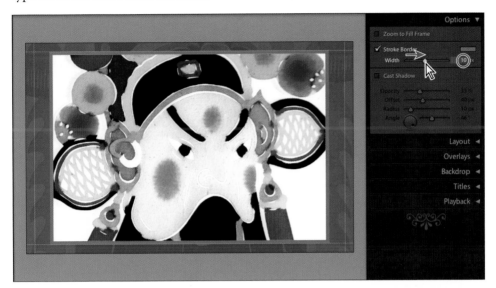

5   Now activate the Cast Shadow option in the Options panel and experiment with the controls. You can adjust the opacity of the shadow, the distance that the shadow is offset from the image, the angle at which the shadow is cast, and the Radius setting, which affects the softness of the shadow's edge.

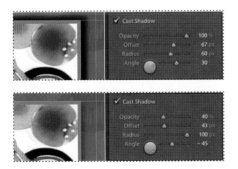

6   When you're finished experimenting, disable the Cast Shadow option; this extra effect doesn't add much to these very graphic images.

7   Collapse the Options panel.

Adding a text overlay

In the Overlays panel you can add text or an identity plate to your slides and have Lightroom display the rating stars you've assigned to your images or the captions that you've added to their metadata.

Note: In this exercise, you won't incorporate an identity plate in your slideshow. For more information on identity plates please refer to Lesson 2, Lesson 9, or the Lightroom Help topic "Add your identity plate to a slideshow."

The text—a Chinese proverb—will be overlaid on every slide, becoming part of the imagery so that its role is atmospheric and decorative rather than informative.

1   Expand the Overlays panel and activate the Text Overlays option.

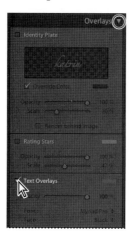

2   If the Toolbar is not visible below the Slide Editor view, press the T key. In the Toolbar, click the Add Text To Slide button (ABC); the Custom Text box appears in the Toolbar.

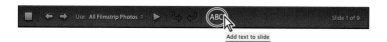

3   Type the Chinese proverb **every day is a good day** in the Custom Text box.

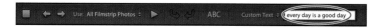

Using the Text Template Editor

In the Slideshow module, you can use the Text Template Editor to access and edit the information that is stored as metadata in your images and to specify which elements of that information you would like to display as text overlays on each slide.

You can add titles that differ from the original file names, or display captions, capture dates, image sizes, or any of numerous other options. You can save your choices as a text template preset and create presets with different sets of information for different types of presentation.

In the Slideshow module, click the Add Text To Slide button (ABC) in the Toolbar. Type anything at all in the Custom Text box and press Enter / Return. The text appears as an overlay in the Slide Editor. Make sure the text overlay is selected; then click the double triangle beside the Custom Text box in the Toolbar and choose Edit from the menu.

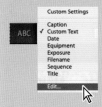

The Text Template Editor appears. In the Example text box, you will see a Custom Text *token*.

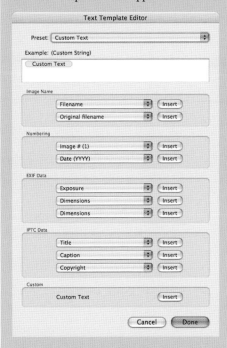

(Continued on next page.)

Using the Text Template Editor (cont.)

A token is a placeholder for whatever custom text you wish to specify. If you did not specify any other content for the token in the Text Template Editor the token would represent whatever custom text you already entered in the Toolbar. Click the token to select it and type anything at all in the example box. Click Done and the new custom text replaces the original in the Slide Editor view.

Open the Text Template Editor again by clicking the double triangle beside the Custom Text box in the Toolbar and choosing Edit from the menu. This time you will replace the custom text with another token chosen from the options in the Text Template Editor. Select the custom text in the Example box and delete it. In the Image Name options, click the top Insert button. A Filename token appears in the Example box. Click Done and the file name appears in the Slide Editor view.

Drag the file name overlay to the upper left corner of the slide and click outside the bounding box to deselect it. Click the Add Text To Slide button (ABC) in the Toolbar; then click the double triangle beside the Custom Text box and choose Edit from the menu. The text <empty> appears on the slide as a new text overlay. In the Text Template Editor, select the new Custom Text token in the Example box and choose Image # (01) from the upper menu in the Numbering options. Click Done and the image number (in two-digit format) replaces the text <empty> on the slide in the Slide Editor view.

In this way you can create as many text overlays as you wish and each text overlay can contain more than one token. Change the font, color and other options for your overlays using the Text Overlays controls in the Overlays panel. Resize the text by dragging the handles of the bounding box. Explore the options in the Text Template Editor

Preset menu: Apply, save, delete, or rename presets, which are saved sets of information tokens customized for different presentation purposes.

Image Name: Specify a text string containing the filename, folder name, or a custom name.

Numbering: Number the slideshow images and display image capture dates in various formats.

EXIF Data: Choose from Exchangeable Image Format data including image dimensions, exposure, flash settings and numerous other options.

IPTC Data: Choose from International Press Telecommunications Council data including copyright and creator details and numerous other options.

Custom: Add a custom text string.

For more details on using the Text Template Editor refer to Lightroom Help.

4   Press Enter / Return. The text appears in the lower left corner of the Slide Editor view and in the Overlays panel, the Text Overlays settings are updated in the Overlays panel to show the font details (Myriad Web Pro is selected in the illustration below).

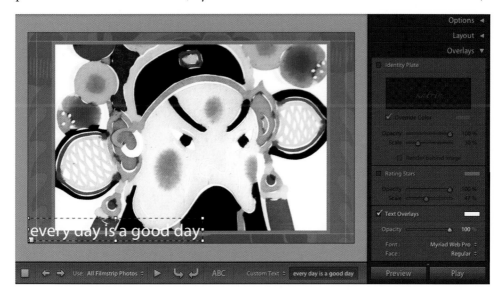

5   To change the font, click the double triangle beside the font name and choose a script font from the menu. We chose Zapfino, a calligraphic typeface—but any other calligraphic or script font such as Monotype Corsiva will suit our design. Zapfino is available only in Regular, so there are no other options available in the Face menu.

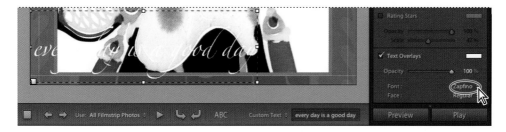

6 Adjust the size of the text by dragging the upper right handle of the bounding box to the right border of the slide. Release the mouse button when the text is the same width as the image.

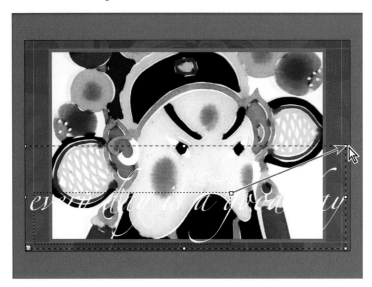

To achieve the desired effect of ambience and subtlety, we'll choose a color in the same range of pinks as the background and border.

7 Click the Text Overlays color box. The Color Picker appears.

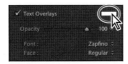

8 In the Color Picker, drag the color slide on the right to the top, and then click a pink in the large color field on the left. We used a color with the RGB values: R: 100%, G: 50%, B: 99%. Click outside the Color Picker to close it.

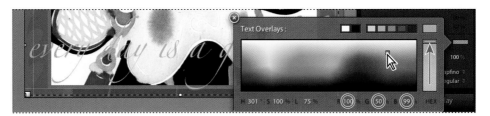

9   Drag the text box to align the base line of the text with the border of the image as shown in the illustration below.

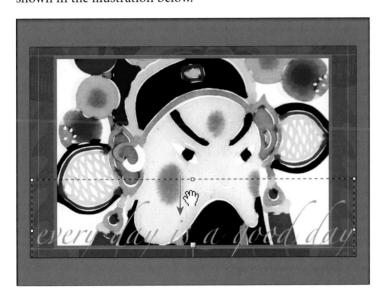

Note: *As you move the text, Lightroom tethers the bounding box either to the nearest of various reference points around the edge of the slide, or to a point on the border of the image itself. To see this in operation, drag the text around the slide, both inside and outside of the image, and watch the white tether-line jump from point to point. When you're done, return the text to its original position. Throughout a slideshow, the text will maintain the same position either relative to the slide as a whole or to the border of each image regardless of its size or orientation. You can use this feature to ensure that a caption, for instance, will always appear just below the left corner of each image no matter what its orientation while a title that applies to the presentation as a whole will remain in a constant position on the screen.*

For the purposes of this exercise, you won't need to pay attention to this issue as there is no variation in the size or orientation of the images.

10   To integrate the text into the image even more effectively, drag the Opacity slider to 50, or enter **50** in the Opacity box.

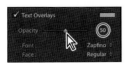

As a finishing touch you'll place a shadow behind the type to add depth and create the impression that the letters themselves are cut from paper.

Note: The Shadow option is only available on Mac OS.

11 On Mac OS, activate the Shadow option at the bottom of the Overlays panel. Drag the sliders or enter these values: Opacity: **64**, Offset: **20**, Radius: **8**, and Angle: **0**. Collapse the Overlays panel and deselect the text box in the Slideshow Editor view.

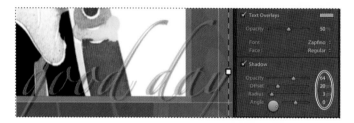

12 Select the first slide in the Filmstrip and click the Preview button at the bottom of the right panel group to preview your slideshow in the Slideshow Editor view. When you're done, press Esc to stop playback.

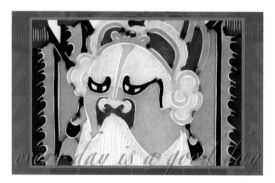

Adjusting the playback settings

In the Playback panel you can add a soundtrack to your presentation, set the duration for slides and transitions, or set the slideshow to display your images in random order. Adding a soundtrack can make your slideshow much more dynamic and compelling, so let's start with that.

You'll find a sound file named *Temple of the Moon.mp3* in your Lesson 7 folder. This piece of music will underline the Asian feel of the slideshow. However, feel free to choose any other file from your music library that you'd like to audition.

In order to play music with the slideshow, the sound file has to be placed into a playlist folder (Windows) or your Apple iTunes music library (Mac OS). Before continuing with this exercise, you'll need to do one of the following:

• (Windows) Place the music file in a folder on your hard disk. If you wished to use several files for a longer presentation, you would need to name the files so that they would play in the desired order.

• (Mac OS) Create an iTunes playlist containing the file (or files) for your soundtrack. See the iTunes documentation for information on creating a playlist.

Once you have placed the file correctly you can play it in your slideshow.

1 Expand the Playback panel in the right panel group, and activate the Soundtrack option.

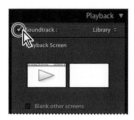

💡 *If you have more than one screen attached to your computer you'll see the Playback Screen pane in the Playback panel, as shown in the illustration above. You can choose which screen will be used for the full-screen slideshow and whether to blank the other screens during playback.*

2 To select the folder or playlist containing your music file (or files), do one of the following:

• (Windows) Click the text Click Here To Choose A Music Folder below the Soundtrack option checkbox. *(See illustration below.)* In the Browse For Folder dialog box that appears, navigate to and select a folder on your hard disk containing music files of your choice—for this exercise you can select the Lesson 7 folder, containing the music file *Temple of the Moon.mp3*.

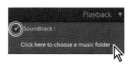

- (Mac OS) Choose the iTunes playlist containing Temple of the Moon.mp3 or other music files of your choice from the Library menu. If you don't see your playlist in the menu, choose Refresh Playlist From iTunes.

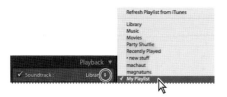

3   Click the Preview button at the bottom of the right panel group to preview the slideshow in the Slideshow Editor view. The music adds atmosphere to the slideshow. When you're done, press Esc to stop playback.

The next step is to fine-tune the timing of the slideshow by setting the duration of slides and fades.

4   Activate the Slide Duration option. Set the values to 3.5 seconds for Slides and 2 seconds for Fades, either by dragging the sliders or typing **3.5** and **2.0** in the respective boxes. This is quite a slow pace with long transitions, which fits well with the music and the character of the images.

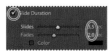

5   Deselect both the Random Order and the Repeat options, and then click the Play button at the bottom of the right panel group to see the slideshow in full-screen mode.

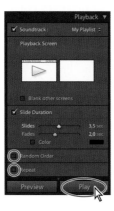

Seeing your slideshow in full-screen mode adds yet another dimension!

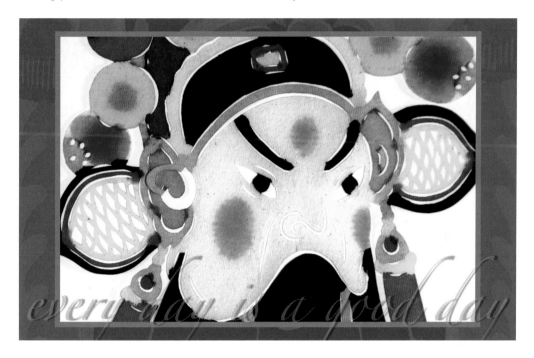

With the slideshow playing in full-screen mode, none of the menus are available. This is where keyboard shortcuts come in handy! Press the spacebar to pause and resume playback, the Right Arrow key to advance to the next slide, the Left Arrow key to return to the previous slide, or the Esc key to end the slideshow.

Saving the customized slideshow template

Having spent so much time customizing your slideshow template, you should now save it to become one more choice in the Template Browser menu.

Saving your customized slideshow template will save you a lot of time later should you wish to reuse this slideshow, extend it, or use the template as a starting-point to create another presentation. By default, your customized template will be listed with the User Templates in the Template Browser panel.

1   With your slideshow still open in the Slideshow module, click the Create New
Preset button (+) in the Template Browser panel header, or choose Slideshow > New
Template.

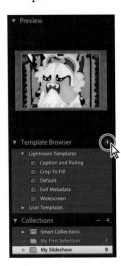

2   In the New Template dialog box, name your template **My Pink Slideshow**. Leave
the default User Templates folder selected in the Folder menu, and click Create.

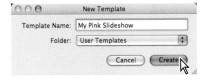

💡 *When saving a customized template it's a good idea to give it a descriptive name. This
will make it easier to find as you add more and more choices to the Template Browser
menu.*

3   Check that your customized template is now listed under User Templates in the
Template Browser panel.

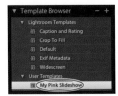

Exporting a slideshow

In order to send your slideshow to a friend or client or to play it on another computer, you can export it as a PDF file.

Note: PDF slideshow transitions work when viewed using the free Adobe Reader or Adobe Acrobat. Exported slideshows won't include music, randomized playback order, or your customized duration settings.

1 In the Slideshow module, click the Export PDF button at the bottom of the left panel group.

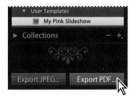

2 In the Export Slideshow To PDF dialog box, navigate to your Lesson 7 folder, and then name the slideshow **My Slideshow** in the File Name / Save As text box.

3 Drag the Quality slider to 100, or type **100** in the text box beside it.

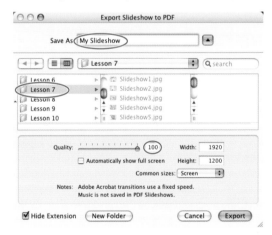

Note: You need to adjust the Quality settings to suit the purposes for which your exported presentation is intended. If you intend to share your slideshow on a CD ROM, you can export it for full-screen playback at the highest quality setting. Should you wish to attach your slideshow to an email, choose a lower quality setting and a smaller size.

4   Activate the option Automatically Show Full Screen to display the slideshow in full-screen mode when opened in Adobe Reader or Adobe Acrobat.

5   In the Common Sizes menu, accept the default size for your computer screen or choose whatever size you deem appropriate.

6   Click Export. My Slideshow.pdf will be saved to your Lesson 7 folder.

Modifying and Organizing User Templates

The Template Browser offers numerous options for organizing your templates and template folders:

• **Renaming a template or template folder**
You cannot rename the Lightroom Templates folder, any of the Lightroom templates, or the default User Templates folder. To rename any of the templates or template folders that you have created, right-click / Ctrl-click the template or folder in the Template Browser and choose Rename from the context menu.

• **Moving a template**
If you wish to move a template into another folder in the Template Browser, simply drag the template to that folder. If you wish to move a template into a new folder, right-click / Control-click the template and choose New Folder from the context menu. The selected template will be moved into the new folder as it is created. If you try to move one of the Lightroom templates, the template will me copied to the new folder but will still remain in the Lightroom Templates folder.

• **Updating a custom template's settings**
If you wish to modify one of your own custom templates select it in the Template Browser and make your changes using any of the controls in the right panel group. To save your changes, right-click / Control-click the template in the Template Browser and choose Update with Current Settings.

• **Creating a copy of a template**
You may wish to create a copy of a template so that you can safely make modifications without affecting the original. If you wish to create a copy of the currently selected template in an existing template folder, click the Create New Preset button (+) in the Template Browser panel header. In the New Template dialog box, type a name for the copy, choose the destination folder from the Folder menu, and click Create. If you wish to create a copy of the currently selected template in a new folder, click the Create New Preset button (+) in the Template Browser panel header. In the New Template dialog box, type a name for the copy and choose New Folder from the Folder menu. In the New Folder dialog box, type a name for the new folder and click Create. The new folder appears in the Template Browser. Click Create in the New Template dialog box to dismiss it. The copied template will be created in the new folder.

• **Exporting a custom template**
To export your custom slideshow template so that you can use it in Lightroom on another computer, right-click / Control-click the template name in the Template Browser menu and choose Export from the context menu.

(Continued on next page.)

Modifying and Organizing User Templates (cont.)

• **Importing a custom template**

To import a custom template that has been created in Lightroom on another computer, right-click / Control-click the User Templates header or any of the templates in the User Templates menu and choose Import from the context menu. In the Import Template dialog box, locate the template file and click Import.

• **Deleting a template**

To delete a custom template, right-click / Control-click the template name in the Template Browser and choose Delete from the context menu. You can also select the template and click the Remove button at the bottom of the right panel group. You cannot delete the templates in the Lightroom Templates folder.

• **Creating a new templates folder**

To create a new empty folder in the Templates Browser, right-click / Control-click the header of any other folder and choose New Folder from the context menu. You can drag templates into the new folder.

• **Deleting a templates folder**

To delete a template folder, you'll first need to delete all the templates within that folder—or drag them to another folder. Right-click / Control-click the empty folder, and choose Delete Folder from the context menu or simply select the empty folder and click the Remove button at the bottom of the right panel group.

Well done! You have successfully completed another Lightroom lesson. You learned how to view your image collection as an impromptu slideshow and then created your own stylish slideshow presentation. In the process, you've explored the Slideshow module and used the control panels to customize a slideshow template—refining the layout and playback settings and adding a backdrop, text, borders, and a soundtrack. In the next chapter you'll find out how to present your work in printed format. But first, review the questions and answers for this lesson on the next page.

Review

▶ **Review questions**

1   How do you view an Impromptu Slideshow?

2   Which Lightroom slideshow template would you pick if you wished to display metadata for your images?

3   What options do you have when customizing a slideshow template?

4   What are the four Cast Shadow controls and what are their effects?

▶ **Review answers**

1   To view an Impromptu Slideshow, press Ctrl+Enter / Command+Return. You can also choose Window > Impromptu Slideshow.

2   The EXIF Metadata template, which centers photos on a black background and displays star ratings and EXIF information for the images, as well as an identity plate.

3   In the right panel group you can modify the slide layout, add borders and text overlays, create shadow effects for images or text, change the background color or add a backdrop image, adjust the durations of slides and fades, and add a soundtrack.

4   The four Cast Shadow controls have the following effects:

• Opacity: Controls the opacity of the shadow ranging from 0% (invisible) to 100% (fully opaque).

• Offset: Affects the distance that the shadow is offset from the slide. As the offset is increased, more shadow becomes visible.

• Radius: Controls how sharp (lower settings) or soft (higher settings) the edges of the shadow appear.

• Angle: Sets the direction of the light source, which affects the angle at which the shadow is cast.

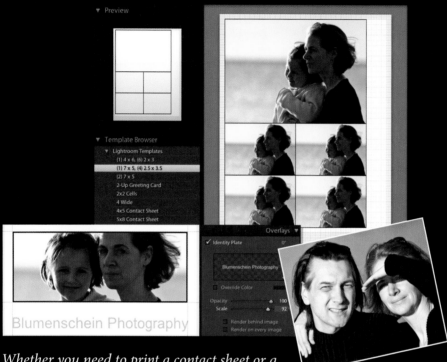

Whether you need to print a contact sheet or a fine art mat, Lightroom makes it easy to achieve professional results with a choice of highly customizable layout templates.

8 Printing Images

The Lightroom Print module offers all the tools you'll need to quickly prepare any selection of images from your library for printing.

You can print a photo singly or repeated at different sizes on the same sheet, or create an attractive layout for multiple images. Add borders, text, and graphics, and then adjust settings for print resolution, sharpening, paper type, and color management with just a few clicks.

In this lesson, you'll explore the Print module as you become accustomed to the steps in the printing workflow:

• Selecting and grouping your photos.

• Choosing a layout template.

• Creating a custom print template.

• Adding borders to your images.

• Adding an identity plate.

• Adding text.

• Adjusting print settings.

• Setting printer driver options.

• Saving print settings as an output preset.

Getting started

This lesson assumes that you are already familiar with the Lightroom workspace and with moving between the different modules. If you find that you need more background information as you go, refer to Lightroom Help or the previous lessons in this book.

Before you begin, make sure that you have correctly copied the Lessons folder from the CD in the back of this book onto your computer's hard disk and created the LR2CIB Library Catalog file. See "Copying the Classroom in a Book files" and "Creating a catalog file for working with this book" on page 3.

1   Start Lightroom.

2   In the Adobe Photoshop Lightroom - Select Catalog dialog box, make sure the file LR2CIB Library Catalog.lrcat is selected under Catalog Location, and then click Continue.

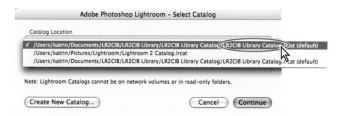

3   If the Back Up Catalog dialog box appears, click Skip Now.

4   Lightroom will open in the screen mode and workspace module that were active when you last quit. If necessary, click Library in the Module Picker to switch to the Library module.

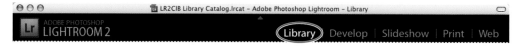

5   Choose File > Import Photos From Disk.

6   In the Import Photos Or Lightroom Catalog dialog box, navigate to the Lessons folder you've already copied into the LR2CIB folder on your hard disk. Select the Lesson 8 folder, and then click Import All Photos In Selected Folder / Choose.

7   In the Import Photos dialog box, choose Add Photos To Catalog Without Moving from the File Handling menu. Choose None from both the Develop Settings menu and the Metadata menu. Type **Lesson 8** in the Keywords text box, and choose Minimal from the Initial Previews menu. Make sure your settings are exactly as shown in the illustration below, and then click Import.

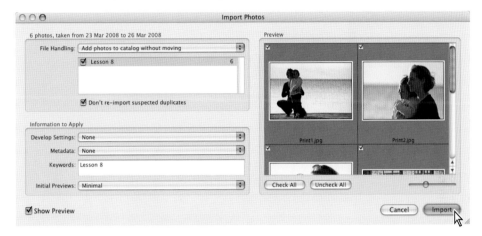

You have imported the photos into your library. You can see thumbnails of your images in the Grid view of the Library module and in the Filmstrip.

Creating a new collection

It's a good idea to group the images for your print job as a collection so that you can easily retrieve them even though they may actually be stored in different folders on your hard disk. Grouping your images in a collection has other advantages: you can make consistent adjustments across all the images, rearrange their display order, and add or remove images. You can use the temporary Quick Collection in the Catalog panel, or create a new collection that will appear in the Collections panel.

1   Select all six images for this lesson by pressing Ctrl+A / Command+A or choosing Edit > Select All.

2   In the left panel group, click the New Collection icon (+) in the header of the Collections panel and choose Create Collection from the menu.

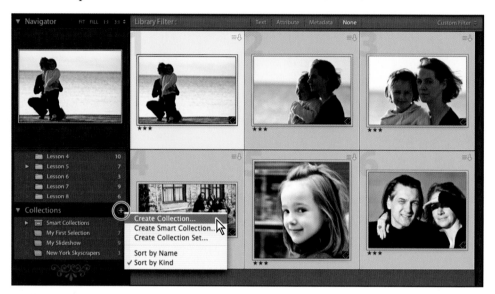

3   In the Create Collection dialog box, type **My Prints** in the Name box and choose None from the Set menu. Under Collection Options, activate Include Selected Photos and disable Make New Virtual Copies; then click Create.

Your new collection is now listed in the Collections panel.

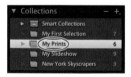

Note: To delete a collection, right-click / Control-click its name in the Collections panel and choose Delete from the context menu.

4   The images for this lesson are intended to be sorted by name. To arrange the photos into the intended order, choose View > Sort > File Name and View > Sort > Ascending.

5   Click Print in the Module Picker to switch to the Print Module.

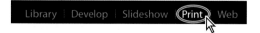

About the Lightroom Print module

In the Print module you'll find tools and controls for each step in the printing workflow. Organize your photos, choose a template and refine the layout, add borders, text, or graphics, and adjust the output settings; everything you need is at your fingertips.

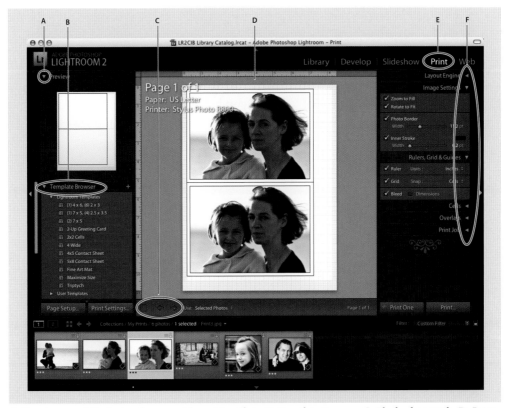

*A. Preview panel displaying the current layout template. **B.** Template Browser. **C.** Playback controls. **D.** Print Editor view. **E.** Print module selected in the Module Picker. **F.** Panels for setting layout and output options.*

In the Print module's left panel group are the Preview and Template Browser panels. By moving the pointer over the list of templates in the Template Browser you can see a thumbnail preview of each layout displayed in the Preview panel. Select your photos in the Filmstrip and choose a template from the list and the Print Editor view at the center of the workspace will be updated to show how your photos look in the new layout.

The Template Browser contains templates of two distinct types: Picture Package layouts and Contact Sheet / Grid layouts. The first three preset Lightroom templates in the list are Picture Package layouts, which repeat a single image at a variety of sizes on the same page. The other eight Lightroom templates are Contact Sheet / Grid layouts, which can be used to print multiple photos at the same size on a single sheet. As the name suggests, Contact Sheet / Grid layouts are based on a grid of image cells. They range from contact sheets with many cells to single-cell layouts such as the Fine Art Mat and Maximize Size templates. All of the preset templates can be customized and you can save your modified layouts as user-defined templates, which will be accessible from the menu in the Template Browser.

You'll use the controls in the right panel group to customize your layout template and to specify output settings. You'll see a slightly different suite of panels in this group depending on which type of template you have chosen. The Layout Engine panel at the top of the group indicates whether the template is a Contact Sheet / Grid or Picture Package layout.

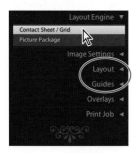 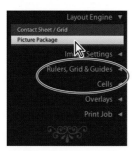

Use the controls in the Image Settings panel to specify the way in which your photos are fitted to their image cells and to add borders. For a Contact Sheet / Grid template, you can use the Layout panel to adjust the margins, cell size and spacing, and to change the number of rows and columns that make up the grid. Use the Guides panel to show or hide a selection of layout guides. For a Picture Package template, modify the layout with the Rulers, Grid & Guides panel and the Cells panel. For both types of template, you can use the Overlays panel to add text and graphics and the Print Job panel to set print resolution, print sharpening, paper type, and color management options.

The photos in your collection are displayed in the Filmstrip across the bottom of the workspace. In the Filmstrip, you can select which images you wish to print and drag their thumbnails to change the order in which they will appear in a multiple-image page layout.

Distinguishing the Lightroom print templates

The Template Browser offers a choice of eleven preset Lightroom print templates that differ not only in basic layout but may also include a variety of design features such as borders and overlaid text or graphics. Templates may also differ in their output settings: the print resolution setting for a contact sheet will be lower than the resolution set for a template designed for producing finished prints. You can save time and effort setting up your print job by starting with the template that most closely suits your purpose.

In this exercise you'll be introduced to the different types of template and learn how to use the panels in the right panel group to examine the characteristics of each layout.

1   In the left panel group, make sure that the Preview and Template Browser panels are expanded. If necessary, drag the top border of the Filmstrip down as far as possible so that you can see all of the Lightroom templates in the Template Browser. In the right panel group, expand the Layout Engine panel and collapse all the others.

2   Choose Edit > Select None, and then select just one of the images in the Filmstrip. The Print Editor view at the center of the workspace is updated to display the selected photo in the current layout.

3   If necessary, expand the Lightroom Templates folder inside the Template Browser panel. Move the pointer slowly over the list of preset templates to see a preview of each layout in the Preview panel.

4   Click the first template in the Template Browser: "(1) 4 × 6, (6) 2 × 3." The new template is applied to the image in the Print Editor view. Look at the Layout Engine panel in the right panel group. You'll see that the Layout Engine panel indicates that this template is a Picture Package layout. In the Template Browser, click the third Lightroom template "(2) 7 × 5." The Layout Engine panel indicates that this is also a Picture Package layout.

5   Now choose the fourth preset template in the Template Browser: "2-Up Greeting Card." The Layout Engine panel indicates that the template "2-Up Greeting Card" is a Contact Sheet / Grid layout, and the Print Editor view at the center of the workspace displays the new template.

6   In the Layout Engine panel, click Picture Package. The Print Editor view is updated to display the last selected Picture Package layout: "(2) 7 × 5." Click Contact Sheet / Grid in the Layout Engine panel and the Print Editor view returns to the last selected Contact Sheet / Grid layout: "2-Up Greeting Card."

About the Lightroom print templates

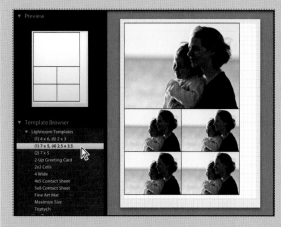

The Template Browser contains both Contact Sheet / Grid and Picture Package templates. Of the preset Lightroom templates, the first three are Picture Package layouts and the other eight are Contact Sheet / Grid layouts.

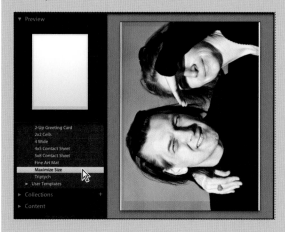

The Maximize Size template will rotate a landscape format image to fit the page.

As you move between the two layout engines you will notice that a different suite of control panels become available in the right panel group. Panels common to both layout engines may differ in content.

7 In the right panel group, expand the Image Settings panel. In the Layout Engine panel, change the layout engine and expand the Image Settings panel again. Toggle between the two layout engines and notice how the options available in the Image Settings panel change.

You can see that the selected photo fits to the image cell differently for each of the templates. In the Picture Package layout "(2) 7 × 5," the Zoom To Fill option is activated in the Image Settings panel and the photo is zoomed and cropped to fill the image cell. In the Contact Sheet / Grid layout "2-Up Greeting Card," the Zoom to Fill option is disabled and the photo is not cropped.

8   Select the Contact Sheet / Grid layout engine. Look at the page number box in the Toolbar: it reads "Page 1 of 1." Press Ctrl+A / Command+A or choose Edit > Select All to select all six images in the collection. The page number box in the Toolbar now reads "Page x of 6." The "2-Up Greeting Card" template is now applied to all six photos, resulting in a print job of six pages. Use the navigation buttons in the Toolbar to move between the pages and see the layout applied to each image in turn in the Print Editor view.

9   For the last step in this exercise, collapse the Image Settings panel and expand the Print Job panel. You will notice that in the Print Job panel, the Print Resolution for this template is set to 240 ppi. In the Template Browser, choose the "4×5 Contact Sheet" template. The Print Resolution option in the Print Job panel becomes disabled and the Draft Mode Printing option is activated. The Print Editor view now displays all the photos in the collection arranged in a contact sheet layout.

Navigating through your document

Many print jobs result in more than one page. The Toolbar below the Print Editor view shows the number of the page currently displayed and a total page count, and offers buttons for navigating through the pages of your print job. The square button to the left will take you to the first page of the document. Click the arrow buttons to return to the previous page or to advance to the next. Scrub back and forth on the page number indicator to quickly navigate your document or click to enter a page number to jump to.

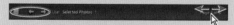

As an alternative to using the navigation buttons in the Toolbar, use the Home, End, Page Up, Page Down, and left and right arrow keys on your keyboard, or choose from the navigation commands in the Print menu.

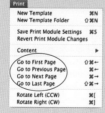

Selecting a print template

Now that you've explored the Template Browser, it's time to choose the template that you will customize in the next exercise.

1 Click the template "4 Wide." If you have customized your default identity plate, you may want to uncheck the Identity Plate option in the Overlays panel for now.

2 Choose Edit > Select None. In the Filmstrip, select the images Print1.jpg, Print2.jpg, and Print3.jpg. The Images will be arranged in the template in the same order in which they appear in the Filmstrip. Drag the images inside their grid cells to reposition them as shown in the illustration below.

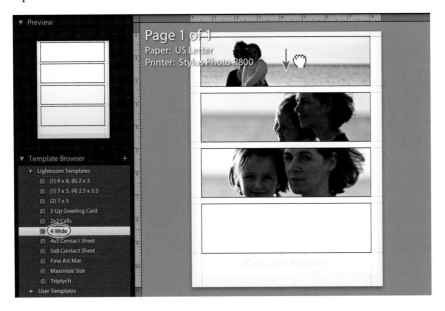

💡 *By default, each photo will be centered in its image cell. To expose a different portion of an image that is cropped by the boundaries of its cell, simply drag the photo to reposition it in the cell.*

Specifying the printer and paper size

Before you customize the template, you'll need to specify the paper size and page orientation for your print job. Doing this now may save you the time and effort of readjusting the layout later.

1   Choose File > Page Setup.

2   In the Print Setup / Page Setup dialog box, choose the desired printer from the Name / Format For menu.

3   From the Paper Size menu, choose Letter (8.5 x 11 In.) / US Letter. Choose the portrait format option as Orientation, and then click OK.

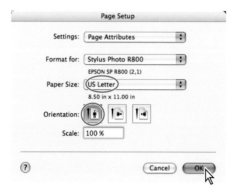

Note: Lightroom automatically scales your photos in the print layout template to fit the paper size you have specified. In the Print Setup / Page Setup dialog box, leave the scale setting at the default 100% and let Lightroom fit the template to the page—that way, what you see in the Print Editor view will be what you'll get from your printer.

Customizing print templates

Having established the overall layout, you can now use the controls in the Layout panel to fine-tune the template so that the images fit better to the page.

Changing the number of cells

For the purposes of this exercise, we need only three of the four image cells preset in the 4 Wide template.

1   If necessary, expand the Layout panel in the right panel group.

2   In the Page Grid controls, drag the Rows slider to the left or type **3** in the box at the right of the slider. *(See illustration on page 280.)*

Modifying the page layout of a print template

Layout controls for Contact Sheet / Grid and Picture Package templates

Depending on which type of print template you are working with, you'll find a slightly different suite of panels in the right panel group. The Image Settings, Overlays, and Print Job panels are available for both template types but the controls for modifying the page layout differ. If you have chosen a Contact Sheet / Grid template, you'll customize your layout using the *Layout* and *Guides* panels. For a Picture Package template, you'll use the *Rulers, Grids & Guides* panel and the *Cells* panel.

Picture Package templates are not grid-based so they are very flexible to work with; you can arrange the image cells on the page either by dragging them in the Print Editor view or by using the controls in the Cells panel. You can resize a cell using the width and height sliders or simply drag the handles of its bounding box. Add more photos to your layout with the Cells panel controls or Alt-drag / Option-drag a cell to duplicate it and resize it as you wish.

Lightroom provides a variety of guides to help you adjust your layout. Guides are not printed: they appear only in the Print Editor view. To show or hide the guides, activate Show Guides in the Guides panel, or choose View > Show Guides (Ctrl+Shift+H / Command+Shift+H). In the Guides panel you can specify which guides will be displayed in the Print Editor view.

Note: *The Margins and Gutters guides and Image Cells guides—available only in a Contact Sheet / Grid layout—are interactive; you can adjust your layout directly by dragging them in the Print Editor view. When you move these guides, the Margins, Cell Spacing and Cell Size sliders in the Layout panel will move with them.*

Using the Layout panel to modify a Contact Sheet / Grid layout

Ruler Units sets the units of measurement for most of the other controls in the Layouts panel and for the Rulers guide in the Guides panel. Click the Ruler Units setting and choose Inches, Centimeters, Millimeters, Points or Picas from the menu. The default setting is Inches.

Margins sets the boundaries for the grid of image cells in your layout. Most printers don't support borderless printing, so the minimum value for the margins is dependent on the capabilities of your printer. Even if your printer does support borderless printing, you may first need to activate this feature in the printer settings before you can set the margins to zero.

Page Grid specifies the number of rows and columns of image cells in the layout. The grid can contain anything from one image cell (Rows: 1, Columns: 1) to 225 image cells (Rows: 15, Columns: 15).

Cell Spacing and **Cell Size** settings are linked so that changes you make to one will affect the other. The Cell Spacing sliders set the vertical and horizontal spaces between the image cells in the grid; the Cell Size controls change the height and width of the cells. *Keep Square* links the height and width settings so that the image cells remain square.

(Continued on next page.)

Modifying the page layout of a print template (cont.)

Using the Guides panel to modify a Contact Sheet / Grid layout

Rulers are displayed across the top and at the left of the Print Editor view. If Show Guides is activated, you can also show the rulers by choosing View > Show Rulers (Ctrl+R / Command+R). To change the ruler units, click the setting in the Layout panel.

Page Bleed shades the non-printable edges of the page, as defined by your printer settings.

Margins and Gutters guides reflect the Margins settings in the Layout panel; in fact, dragging these guides in the Print Editor view will move the Margins, Cell Spacing, and Cell Size sliders in the Layout panel.

Image Cells shows a black border around each image cell. When the Margins and Gutters guides are not visible, dragging the Image Cells guides will change the Margins, Cell Spacing, and Cell Size settings.

Dimensions displays the measurements of each image cell in its top left corner, expressed in whatever units of measurement you have chosen for the Ruler Units.

Using the Rulers, Grids & Guides panel to modify a Picture Package layout

Rulers shows the rulers and lets you set the units of measurement just as you would in the Layout panel when you're working with a Contact Sheet / Grid template.

Grid displays a grid guide behind the image cells in the Print Editor view. As you drag the cells, you can have them snap to each other or to the grid (or turn the snap behavior off) by choosing Cells, Grid, or Off from the Snap menu options. The grid divisions are affected by your choice of ruler units.

Note: The snap behavior helps you to position the image cells accurately on the page. If you accidently overlap your photos, Lightroom will let you know by displaying a triangular yellow warning icon (!) in the top right corner of the page.

Bleeds and **Dimensions** are the Picture Package equivalents of the Page Bleed and Dimensions guides.

Using the Cells panel to modify a Picture Package layout

Add To Package offers six preset image cell sizes that can be placed in your layout at the click of a button. You can change which of the presets is assigned to each button by clicking its menu triangle. The default presets are standard photo sizes but you can edit them if you wish.

New Page adds a page to your layout, though Lightroom automatically adds pages if you use the Add to Package buttons to add more photos than fit on a page. To delete a page from your layout, click the red X in its upper left corner of the page in the Print Editor view.

Auto Layout optimizes the arrangement of the photos on the page for the fewest cuts.

Clear Layout removes all the image cells from the layout.

Adjust Selected Cell lets you change the height and width of an image cell using sliders or numerical input.

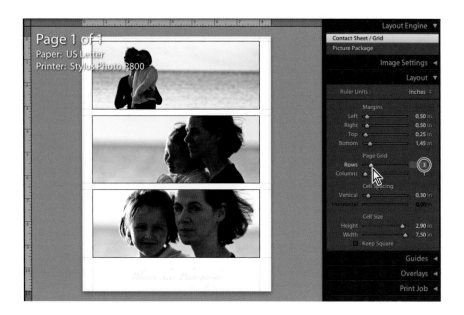

3   Experiment with the Margins, Cell Spacing, and Cell Size sliders—making sure to undo (Ctrl+Z / Command+Z) after each change. Activate the Keep Square option under the Cell Size sliders. The Cell Width and Cell Height sliders are locked together at the same value and the look of the layout has changed dramatically with a single click. When you're done, disable the Keep Square option.

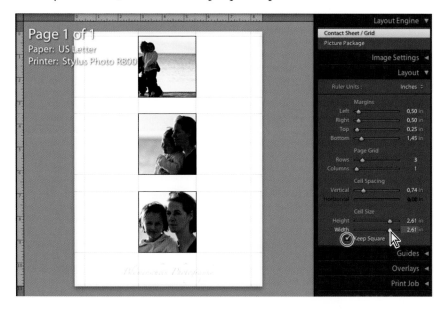

4 The black lines you might see around the photos are merely guides to show you image cell boundaries; they will not appear on your printed page. These guides are helpful while you are adjusting the cell size and spacing but they will be distracting when you are adding printable borders to your layout in the next exercise. If necessary, expand the Guides panel below the Layout panel and disable the Image Cells option.

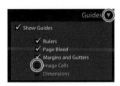

5 Collapse the Layout and Guides panels.

Creating a stroke border

The Image Settings panel offers options that affect the way your photos are fit to the image cells, and a control for adding stroke borders.

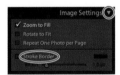

In the next exercise you'll add a border around each of the three images and adjust its width.

1 Expand the Image Settings panel. For the 4 Wide template, the Zoom To Fill option is activated. This means that our photos are cropped in height to fit the proportions of the image cells.

2 Click the Stroke Border checkbox and drag the Width slider to the right or type **2.0** in the box at the right of the slider. For your reference, 72 points (pt) are one inch.

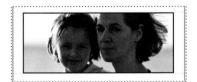 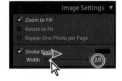

💡 *You can change the color of the border color by clicking the Stroke Border color swatch and choosing a color from the color picker.*

Using the Rotate To Fit option

By default, Lightroom will place photos so that they are upright within their image cells. The Rotate To Fit option in the Image Settings panel will override this behavior so that your photos are rotated to match the orientation of the image cells. For presentation layouts you would not wish to have images displayed in different orientations on the same page but in some situations this feature can be very helpful and save on expensive photo paper too!

The Rotate To Fit option is particularly useful when you wish to print photos in both portrait and landscape formats on the same sheet, as large as possible and without wasting paper, as shown in the illustration on the right.

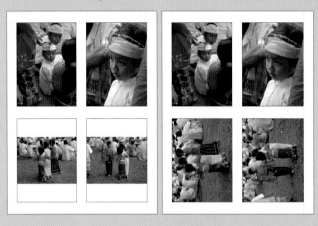

Another situation where you might choose to use the Rotate To Fit setting is when you are printing contact sheets. As you can see in the next illustration, Rotate To Fit enables you to see all the photos at the same size regardless of the image orientation.

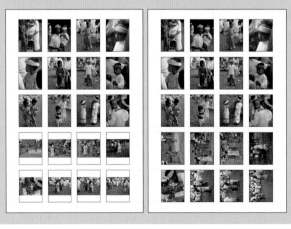

Note: For a Picture Package template such as the "(2) 7 x 5" layout show in the illustration below, the Image Settings panel contains two controls for borders. Use the Photo Border control to specify the width of a blank frame between the edge of each photo and the boundary of the image cell. The Inner Stroke control is the Picture Package equivalent of the Stroke Border control.

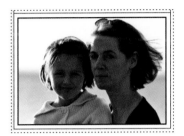
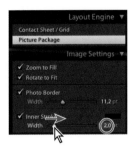

3   Collapse the Image Settings panel.

Customizing your identity plate

The options in the Overlays panel enable you add an identity plate or text to the layout. You can quickly edit your identity plate or add photo info, captions, page numbers, or crop marks to your prints. To begin with, you'll modify the identity plate to suit our sepia-toned images.

1   Expand the Overlays panel.

2   Activate the Identity Plate by clicking the checkbox. Then click the triangle in the lower right corner of the identity plate preview and choose Edit from the menu.

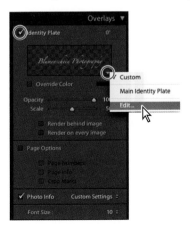

3 In the Identity Plate Editor dialog box, activate the Use A Styled Text Identity Plate option. Choose Arial, Regular, and 36 point from the font menus. At this point, you could also change the default color for the identity plate text by clicking the color box at the right of the font size menu; we choose a light gray. Then select the text in the text box and type **Blumenschein Photography** (or a name of your own choice). Click OK.

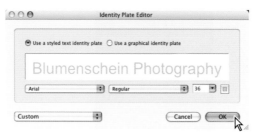

💡 *If your text is too long to be fully visible in the text box, resize the dialog box or reduce the font size until you've finished editing.*

4 In the Overlays panel, drag the Scale slider to the right until the identity plate text is the same width as the image. You can also scale the identity plate by clicking it in the Print Editor view and dragging the side or corner handles of its bounding box.

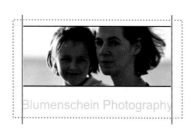
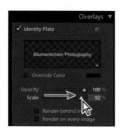

💡 *By default the identity plate will be oriented horizontally on the page. This setting (0°) is indicated at the top right of the Identity Plate pane in the Overlays panel. To change the orientation of the identity plate in your layout, click on the 0° indicator and choose 90°, 180°, or –90° from the menu. To move the identity plate to a different position in your layout, simply drag it in the Print Editor view.*

5 Now you'll change the color of the identity plate. Click the Override Color checkbox to set the color of the identity plate for this layout without affecting the settings defined for the identity plate.

6   Activate the Override Color options, and then click the Override Color swatch. In the Color Picker, enter the RGB values: R: **40**%, G: **35**%, B: **20**%, and then click outside the Color Picker to close it. The color of the identity plate overlay is now matched to the sepia tones of the photos.

Note: If you see a hexadecimal value displayed in the lower right corner of the Color Picker rather than RGB values, click RGB below the color slider.

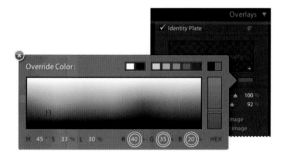

Note: Lightroom operates in the RGB color space. You don't need to choose color settings or color profiles until you are ready to output your photos. You will learn about color management options later in this lesson.

7   As a final step in this exercise, use the Opacity slider or type **90** in the text box beside it to set an opacity value of 90% for the identity plate. This feature can be particularly effective if you wish to position your identity plate over an image.

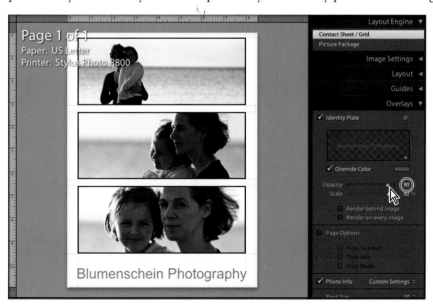

Adding captions and metadata information

In this exercise, you will add a caption and metadata information (in this case, sequence numbers for the images) to your layout using the Overlays panel and the Text Template Editor. You'll find more detailed information on the Text Template Editor in the section "Using the Text Template Editor" in Lesson 7, "Creating Slideshows."

1   In the Overlays panel, click the checkbox to activate the Photo Info overlay option. Choose Edit from the menu to the right.

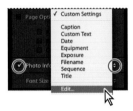

2   In the Text Template Editor, choose Sequence from the Preset menu.

3   Click to place an insertion cursor just before the first token in the Example text box and then type **Antique Grayscale** (the name of the Develop module preset that produced our sepia effect). Be sure to add a space between your text and the first token. Click Done to close the Text Template Editor. The images in the Print Editor view are now captioned and numbered.

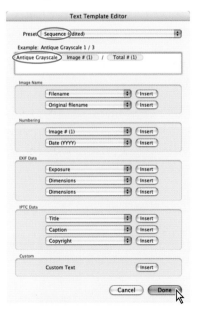

4   If not already selected, click the Font Size triangle in the lower right corner of the Overlays panel and choose 10 pt from the menu; then collapse the Overlays panel.

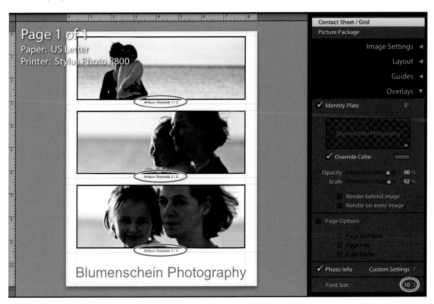

Saving your customized print template

Having started with a preset template, you've created your own page design by modifying the layout and adding borders, an identity plate, and captions to the images. You can now save your customized layout for future use.

1   Click the Create New Preset button (+) in the header of the Template Browser panel header, or choose Print > New Template.

2   In the New Template dialog box, type **My Wide Triptych** in the Template Name text box. By default, new templates are saved to the User Templates folder. For this exercise, accept the default User Templates as the destination folder and click Create.

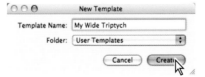

3   Your new template appears in the User Templates folder in the Template Browser panel where you can access it quickly for use with a new set of images in the future—as shown in the illustration below with the last three images in the Filmstrip selected.

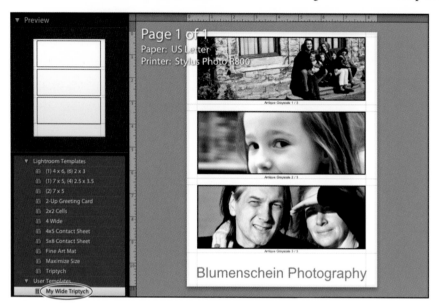

Configuring the output settings

The final step before you're ready to print your layout is to adjust the output settings in the Print Job panel.

1   Expand the Print Job panel in the right panel group.

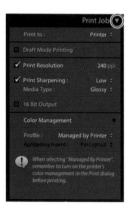

From the Print To menu at the top of the Print Job panel you can choose to send the job directly to your printer or generate a JPEG file, which you can print later or send out for professional printing. The controls in the Print Job panel vary slightly depending on which option is selected in the Print To menu.

2   Choose Printer from the Print To menu at the top of the Print Job panel.

Activating the Draft Mode Printing option disables the other options in the Print Job panel. Draft Mode Printing results in high speed output at a relatively low quality, which is an efficient option for printing contact sheets or for assessing your layout before you commit it to high quality photo paper. The 4x5 Contact Sheet and the 5x8 Contact Sheet templates are preset for Draft Mode Printing.

The Print Resolution setting that is appropriate for your print job depends on the intended print size, the resolution of your image files, the capabilities of your printer, and the quality of your paper stock. The default print resolution is 240 ppi, which generally produces good results. As a rule of thumb, use a higher resolution for smaller, high quality prints (around 360 ppi for letter size). You can use a lower resolution setting for larger prints (around 180 ppi for 16" x 20") without compromising too much on quality.

Note: The terms "print resolution" and "printer resolution" have different meanings. "Print resolution" refers to the number of printed pixels per inch (ppi); "printer resolution" refers to the capability of the printer, called dots per inch (dpi). A printed pixel of a particular color is created by patterns of tiny dots in the few colors available as ink.

3   The Print Resolution control has a range of 72 ppi to 480 ppi. For this exercise, type **200** in the Print Resolution text box.

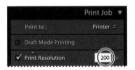

💡 *You should test different print resolution settings for a variety of image sizes on your intended paper stock. For a letter size print, a setting between 200 and 300 ppi might produce a satisfactory result.*

Images tend to look less sharp on paper than they do on screen. The Print Sharpening options can help to compensate for this by increasing the crispness of your printed output. You can choose between Low, Standard, and High Print Sharpening settings, and specify a Matte or Glossy Media Type. You won't notice the effects of these settings on screen so it's useful to experiment by printing at different settings to familiarize yourself with the results.

4   If not already selected, choose Low from the Print Sharpening menu.

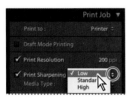

Note: The Sharpening feature in the Develop module compensates for blurriness in the original photo, while Print Sharpening improves the crispness of printed output on a particular paper type.

Working with 16 Bit Output on Mac OS 10.5

If you are running Mac OS 10.5 (Leopard) and are using a 16-bit printer, you can activate the 16 Bit Output setting. This will result in less image degradation and color artifacts in files that have been extensively edited. For further information on 16-bit output, consult the documentation for your printer or check with your output center.

Using color management

Printing your digital images can be challenging: what you see on screen is not always what you get on paper. Lightroom is able to handle a very large color space but your printer may operate within a much more limited gamut.

In the Print module, you can choose whether to have Lightroom handle color management or leave it up to your printer.

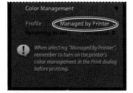

Color managed by your printer

The default Color Management setting in the Print Job panel is Managed by Printer. This can be the easiest option and, given the continuing improvement of printing technology, will generally produce satisfactory results.

Note: *For Draft Mode Printing, color management is automatically assigned to the printer.*

In the Print Setup / Print dialog box (File > Print Settings), you can specify the paper type, color handling, and other print settings.

Note: *The options available in the Print Setup / Print dialog box may vary depending on which printer you have selected.*

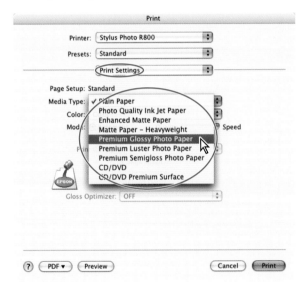

💡 *In Windows, click Properties in the Print Setup dialog box to access additional printer specific settings.*

If you choose Managed By Printer, make sure that you enable ICM Method for Image Color Management (Windows) or activate the ColorSync option in the Color Management settings (Mac OS) for the printer driver software so that the correct profile is applied before printing the image. Depending on the printer driver software, you can usually find the color management settings in the Print Document dialog box under Setup/Properties/Advanced (Windows), or in the pop-up menu below the Presets menu in the Print dialog box (Mac OS).

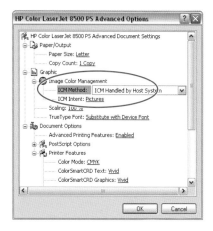

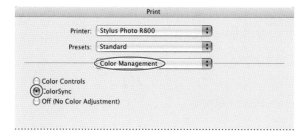

Note: *If you choose a custom printer color profile rather than Managed By Printer from the Profile menu in the Color Management panel, make sure color management is turned off in the printer driver software. Otherwise, your photos will be color managed twice, and the colors might not print as you expect them to.*

Color management controlled by Lightroom

Letting your printer manage color may be acceptable for general printing purposes but to achieve really high quality results it's best to have Lightroom do it. If you choose this option you can specify a printing profile tailored to a particular type of paper or custom inks.

1   From the Color Management Profile menu, choose Other.

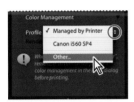

Note: Generally, you'll choose this option when the profile you want isn't listed in the Profile menu. Lightroom searches your computer for custom printer profiles, which are usually installed by the software that came with your printer. If Lightroom is unable to locate any profiles, choose Managed By Printer and let the printer driver handle the color management.

2   Depending on your printer and paper stock, choose one or more printer profiles. In the illustration below a profile for the Epson Stylus Pro R800 using glossy photo paper has been selected. Each profile you choose will be added to the Profile menu under Color Management in the Print Job panel for easy access.

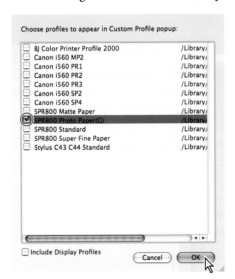

3 Once you have chosen a printer profile from the Profile menu, the Rendering Intent options are activated. The color space of an image is usually much larger than that within which most printers operate, which means that your printer may not be able to accurately reproduce the colors you see on screen. This may result in printing artifacts such as posterization or banding in color gradients as the printer attempts to deal with out-of-gamut colors. The Rendering Intent options will help to minimize these problems. You can choose between two Rendering Intent settings:

• **Perceptual** rendering aims at preserving the visual relationship between colors. The entire range of colors in the image will be re-mapped to fit within the color gamut your printer is able to reproduce. In this way, the relationships between all the colors are preserved but in the process even colors that were already in-gamut may be shifted as the out-of-gamut colors are moved into the printable range. This may mean that your printed image will be less vivid that it appeared on screen.

• **Relative** rendering prints all the in-gamut colors as they are and shifts out-of-gamut colors to the closest printable colors. Using this option means that more of the original color of the image is retained but some of the relationships between colors may be altered.

In most cases the differences between the two rendering methods are quite subtle. As a general rule, perceptual rendering is the best option for an image with many out-of-gamut colors and relative rendering works better for an image with only a few. However, unless you are very experienced it may be hard to tell which is which. The best policy is to do some testing with your printer. Print a very colorful, vivid photo at both settings and then do the same with a more muted image.

4 For the purposes of this exercise, choose Relative rendering as the muted tones of these antique grayscale images are very unlikely to be outside the printable range.

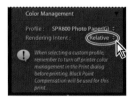

Saving your print settings as an output collection

Your layout is ready to print. You can now save your print settings as an output collection to use for another print job. That way you will be able to add photos to the collection later and the same output settings will be applied automatically.

An output collection is different from a normal photo collection. A photo collection is merely a grouping of images to which you can apply any template or output settings you wish. An output collection links a photo collection (or a selection of images from that collection) to a particular template and includes your output settings.

For the sake of clarity: an output collection also differs from a custom template. A template includes all your settings but no images; you can apply the template to any selection of images. An output collection links the template and all its settings to a particular selection of images.

1   Now that you have saved your customized layout as a user template, selected the images you wish it to contain and added print settings, click the Create New Collection button (+) in the Collections panel header and choose Create Print from the menu.

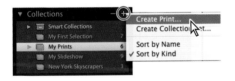

2   In the Create Print dialog box type a name for your print output collection. Activate Include Selected Photos and disable Make New Virtual Copies. Click Create.

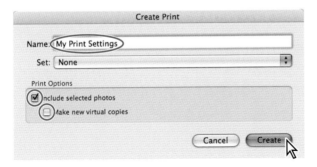

3   Your new output collection is now listed in the Collections panel. Note that your output collection has an icon representing a page layout, whereas an image collection is indicated by an icon representing a stack of photos.

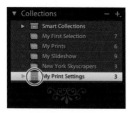

For more information, please refer to Lightroom Help under "Save print settings as an output collection."

Printing your job

1   Click the Print button at the bottom of the right panel group or choose File > Print.

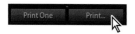

2   Verify the settings in the Print dialog box and click OK / Print to print your page, or click Cancel to close the Print dialog box without printing.

Click the Print One button to send your print job to the printer queue without opening the Print dialog box. This is useful if you print repeatedly using the same settings and don't need to confirm or change any settings in the Print dialog.

Note: *Calibrate and profile your monitor regularly, always verify that print settings are specified correctly, and use quality papers; all these measures will help you achieve better results when you print. However, there is no substitute for experience. Experiment with a variety of settings and options—and if at first you do succeed, consider yourself very lucky!*

Review

▶ Review questions

1   How can you quickly preview the preset print templates, and how can you see how your photos will look in each layout?

2   Which type of template would you choose to create a layout with a single photo repeated at various sizes on the same sheet, and how can you check which type of template you have chosen?

3   When you're working with the Print Setup / Page Setup dialog box, why is it better to leave the Scale setting at 100%?

4   For what purposes is Draft Mode Printing appropriate?

▶ Review answers

1   Move the pointer over the list of templates in the Template Browser to see a thumbnail preview of each layout displayed in the Preview panel. Select your images in the Filmstrip and choose a template from the list; the Print Editor view shows how your photos look in the new layout.

2   Picture Package layouts repeat a single image at a variety of sizes on the same page. The Layout Engine panel indicates whether a layout selected in the Template Browser is a Picture Package template or a Contact Sheet / Grid template.

3   Lightroom automatically scales your photos in the print layout template to fit the specified paper size. Changing the scale in the Print Setup / Page Setup dialog will result in the layout being scaled twice so your photos may not print at the desired size.

4   Draft Mode Printing results in high speed output at a relatively low quality, which is an efficient option for printing contact sheets or for assessing your layout before you commit it to high quality photo paper. The contact sheet templates are preset for Draft Mode Printing.

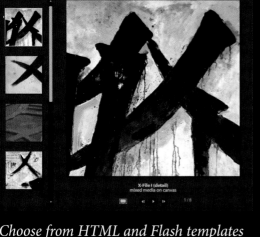

Choose from HTML and Flash templates
to quickly generate sophisticated interactive
web galleries for your photos, and then
upload your presentation directly to a web
server from within the Lightroom Web

9 Publishing your Photos on the Web

A web gallery is an excellent way to showcase your work on the web—whether you wish to share your portfolio with the world at large, let a client select images for proofing, or get feedback on work in progress from coworkers at a different location.

In Lightroom you can conveniently create web pages in either HTML or Flash format. The Web module provides a range of customizable gallery layout templates, and all the tools you need to build a striking website, preview it in a browser, and upload it to your web server.

In this lesson, the techniques and skills you need to build your own web gallery:

- Creating a Web Portfolio collection in your image library.
- Distinguishing between HTML and Flash gallery templates.
- Choosing a gallery template from the Template browser.
- Rearranging the order of the images in your gallery.
- Customizing the design of your gallery.
- Specifying the image quality and adding a copyright watermark.
- Previewing your web gallery.
- Saving your customized layout as a new template.
- Specifying settings for upload to a web server.

Getting started

This lesson assumes that you are already familiar with the Lightroom workspace, and with moving between the different modules. If you find that you need more background information as you go, refer to Lightroom Help, or the previous lessons in this book.

Before you begin, make sure that you have correctly copied the Lessons folder from the CD in the back of this book onto your computer's hard disk and created the LR2CIB Library Catalog file. See "Copying the Classroom in a Book files" and "Creating a catalog file for working with this book" on page 3.

1   Start Lightroom.

2   In the Adobe Photoshop Lightroom - Select Catalog dialog box, make sure the file LR2CIB Library Catalog.lrcat is selected under Catalog Location, and then click Continue.

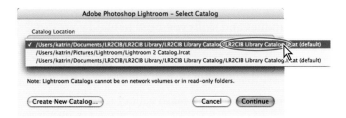

3   If the Back Up Catalog dialog box appears, click Skip Now.

4   Lightroom will open in the screen mode and workspace module that were active when you last quit. If necessary, click Library in the Module Picker to switch to the Library module.

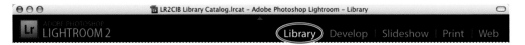

The Lightroom Web module

In the Web module you can build, preview, and even upload your own website to showcase your photos. Use the left panel group to preview the gallery layout templates in the Template Browser. Choose a template and the Gallery Editor view in the work area shows how your images look in the new gallery layout. In the Gallery Editor view, your gallery performs exactly as it will on the web. Use the panels in the right group to customize the gallery template. You can change the layout, the color scheme, or the background, and add text, borders, or effects. Preview your gallery in a web browser with a single click, or upload it to your web server from within Lightroom.

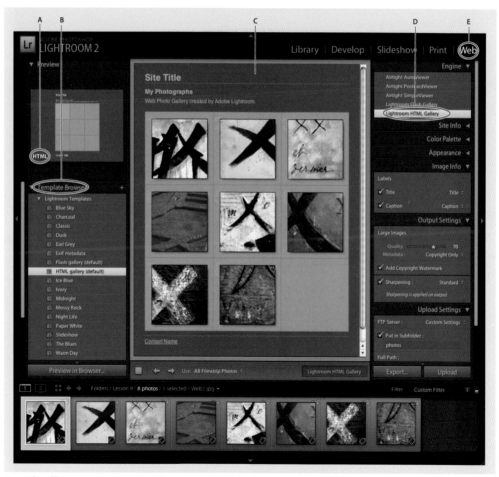

A. *Web gallery type.* **B.** *Template Browser panel.* **C.** *Gallery Editor view.* **D.** *Right panel group with the gallery type indicated in the Engine panel.* **E.** *Web module selected in Module Picker.*

Creating a basic web gallery

In this lesson you'll create a web portfolio based on a Flash template to showcase some photos of details from paintings.

Importing images to the library

First you need to import the images and group them into a collection that you'll create specifically for this project, making it easier to arrange the order in which the photos will appear on the website.

1   If you're not already in the Library module, switch to it now.

2   Choose File > Import Photos From Disk.

3   In the Import Photos Or Lightroom Catalog dialog box, navigate to the Lessons folder you've already copied into the LR2CIB folder on your hard disk. Select the Lesson 9 folder, and then click Import All Photos In Selected Folder / Choose. When importing, Lightroom will ignore image files in unsupported file formats, such as the file Web_Identityplate.png in PNG (Portable Network Graphics) file format, located in the Lesson 9 folder. You will use this file as identity plate later in the lesson.

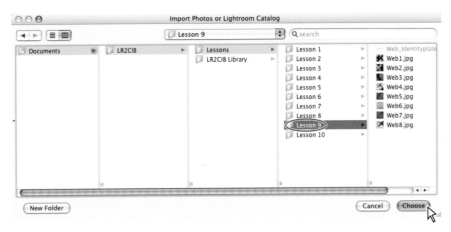

4   In the Import Photos dialog box, make sure the Show Preview option in the lower left corner of the dialog box is activated so you can see thumbnail images of the photos you're about to import. For this exercise, leave all eight photos selected.

5   Choose Add Photos To Catalog Without Moving from the File Handling menu. Choose None from both the Develop Settings menu and the Metadata menu. Type

Lesson 9 in the Keywords text box, and choose Minimal from the Initial Previews menu. Make sure your settings are exactly as shown in the illustration below, and then click Import.

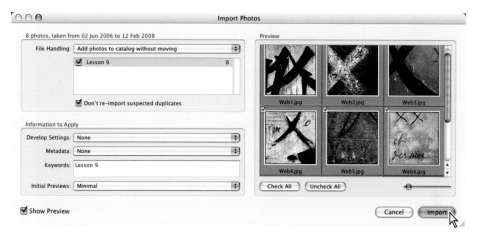

The eight images appear in the Grid view of the Library module, and in the Filmstrip.

Creating a new collection

It's a good idea to group the images for your web gallery as a collection, so that you can easily retrieve the same selection of images should you wish to re-work or extend your presentation. Creating a collection has other advantages: you can make consistent adjustments across all the images, rearrange their display order, and add or remove images. You can use the temporary Quick Collection in the Catalog panel, or create a new collection that will appear in the Collections panel.

> *Collections are groupings of images in the library catalog. A collection not only preserves the display order of the images it contains but also the settings applied in the Slideshow, Print, and Web modules.*

1   In the Library module, press Ctrl+A / Command+A to select all eight images.

2   Click the New Collection button (+) in the Collections panel, and choose Create Collection from the menu. *(See illustration on the next page.)*

Note: To delete a collection, right-click / Control-click its name in the Collections panel, and choose Delete from the context menu.

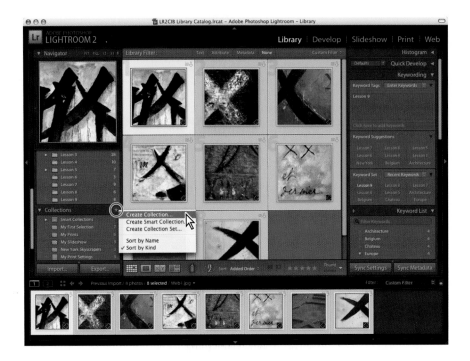

3 In the Create Collection dialog box, type **Web Portfolio** in the Name text box and choose None from the Set menu. Under Collection Options, activate Include Selected Photos and disable Make New Virtual Copies, then click Create.

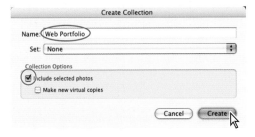

Your new collection appears in the Collections panel, containing the eight images from the Previous Import folder.

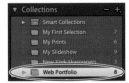

Distinguishing between HTML and Flash galleries

In the Template Browser you'll find both HTML and Flash galleries. As you move the pointer down the list, you'll see a preview of each template layout in the Preview panel. An icon in the lower left corner of the preview indicates the gallery type: HTML (HTML) or Flash ( ).

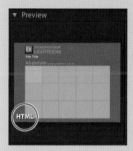
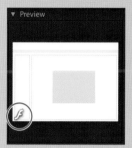

Both types of template can be customized to show your work in its best light. Add text and effects to your layout and change the color scheme, the background, and the image size.

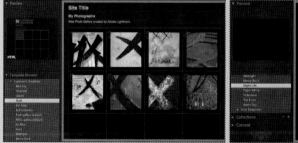
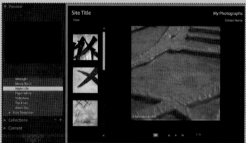

The HTML gallery templates enable you to produce simple web sites that are compatible with most browsers. The HTML pages generated can be customized further in an HTML editor.

Flash templates can produce more sophisticated web galleries, including animations, slideshows with smooth transitions, and other special effects. However, Flash galleries require that the viewer has the appropriate Adobe Flash Player plug-in. Should security settings be in place to block scripts and ActiveX controls, your audience may have to click through warning messages in the web browser before being able to see the gallery.

Choosing a template in the Web module

1 In the Collections panel, choose your Web Portfolio collection.

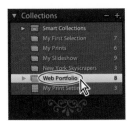

2 Switch to the Web module by clicking Web in the Module Picker. In the right panel group, expand the Engine panel. If it's not already selected, choose the Lightroom HTML Gallery from the list in the Engine panel. The Gallery Editor view in the work area shows how your images will look in the default HTML layout.

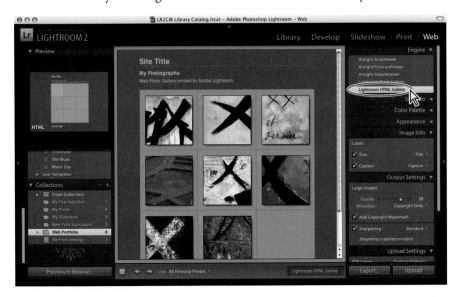

3 Arrange the panels in the left group and hide the Filmstrip, if necessary, so that you can see both the Preview panel and the list of templates in the Template Browser. Move the pointer down the list to preview the different template designs in the Lightroom Templates folder. The illustration on the next page shows a preview of the Dusk template. In this example, the HTML icon (HTML) in the lower left corner of the preview shows that this is an HTML gallery. Previews for Flash galleries show the Flash icon ($\mathcal{B}$).

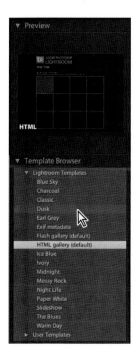

4 When you've finished previewing the gallery templates, click to select the template Flash Gallery (Default).

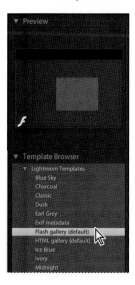

The Gallery Editor view in the work area shows your images in the new template layout.

5   In the Gallery Editor view you'll notice that the gallery has its own navigation controls below the large image. Click the Play button to view the gallery slideshow.

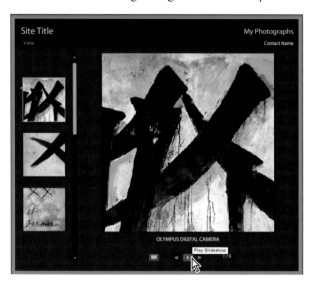

6   To stop the slideshow, press the spacebar.

Rearranging the order of your images

After seeing your slideshow in action, you may wish to change the order in which the images appear. In this exercise, you'll move the grey painting with the inscription *XX et dernier* to the end of the slideshow.

Note: The order of the images in the Grid view and the Filmstrip determines their display order in a Web gallery.

1   Click the Library Grid button (■) in the top left of the Filmstrip, or press G on your keyboard, to return to the Grid view in the Library module.

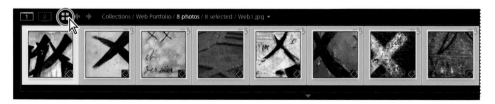

2 Before you continue, make sure your Web Portfolio collection is still selected in the Collections panel.

3 Choose Edit > Select None.

Note: Dragging an image that is part of a multiple selection will move all the selected images. If all images are selected you will not be able to rearrange their order.

4 Rearrange one or more images in the Grid view by simply dragging them to a new location. Release the pointer when a vertical black line appears to indicate the insertion point. As last step, drag the image Web6.jpg to the right edge of the last photo in the Grid view, as shown in the illustration below, and then release the pointer.

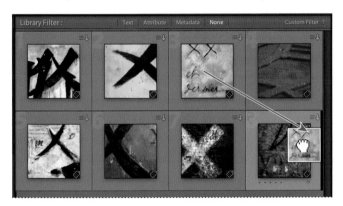

5 Click Web in the Module Picker and review the slideshow again in the Gallery Editor view. Notice that the image Web6.jpg now appears last. Press the spacebar to stop the slideshow.

💡 *You can also directly change the order of images in the Filmstrip in the Web module—without switching to the Grid view in the Library module first.*

6 (Optional) In the Web module, drag a thumbnail to a new position in the Filmstrip and release it when the vertical black line appears. If the Gallery Editor view in the work area is not updated automatically, choose Web > Reload. Switch to the Library module to confirm that the images in the Grid view are displayed in the same order as in the Filmstrip. Switch back to the Web module.

Note: It is only possible to rearrange the order of images in the Filmstrip or the Grid View if the images have been grouped as a collection.

Customizing your web gallery

You can save time by starting with the gallery template that is closest to the design you have in mind. Once you have made your choice, you can use the Site Info, Color Palette, Appearance, Image Info, and Output Settings panels in the right panel group to customize the template. You can add text, choose backgrounds and color schemes, and tweak the layout to change the look and feel of your gallery. In the following exercises, you will customize the text in your gallery template, adjust the layout, place a logo, and add a copyright watermark to the images.

Replacing text

In the Site Info panel you can add a website title, a collection description, contact information, and web or e-mail links. The information you enter in the Site Info panel will appear on your website.

1 If the Site Info panel is currently collapsed in the right panel group, click the triangle next to its name to expand it.

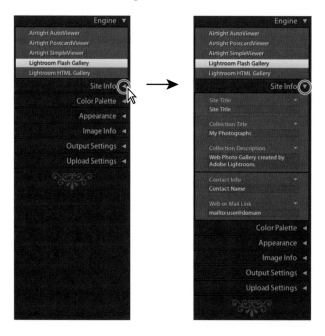

2 Click the default Site Title text in the Site Info panel and type a title for your site. Press Enter on your keyboard to update the title displayed in your layout in the Gallery

Editor view. In a web browser, the site title will also appear in the title bar of the browser window.

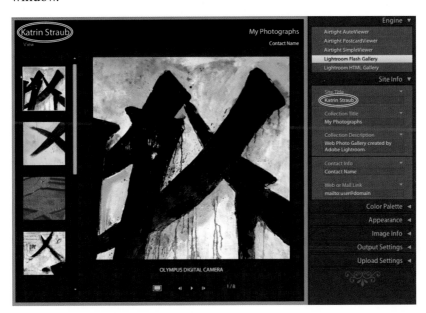

3 Click the triangle beside Site Title and note the entries in the Site Title menu. Lightroom keeps track of your entries for each of the text boxes in the Site Info panel. Instead of retyping information each time you create a new web gallery, you can choose previously entered details from this list.

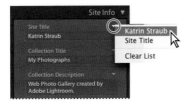

4 As an alternative to working with the Site Info panel, you can edit your titles directly in the Gallery Editor view in the work area. Click My Photographs (the Collection Title) in the top right corner of the Gallery Editor view and type a new title. Press Enter and both the gallery preview and the corresponding entry in the Site Info panel will be updated.

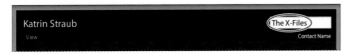

5   In the Site Info panel, delete the default text under Collection Description. If you wish to provide additional information about the images in your web gallery, you can enter it here. In this particular template, the viewer can see the information by clicking View below the site title and choosing About These Photos from the menu.

The last two items in the Site Info panel are Contact Info and Web Or Mail Link. Your web or email address will become an active link on your website, so the browser will either jump to the specified web page or launch your default e-mail application. Enter an e-mail address like this: *mailto:user@domain.com*, or a web address in the following format: *http://www.domain.com*.

💡 *As shown in the illustration below, you could create a link to a Home page where you can offer the viewer links to the other galleries you've created in Lightroom.*

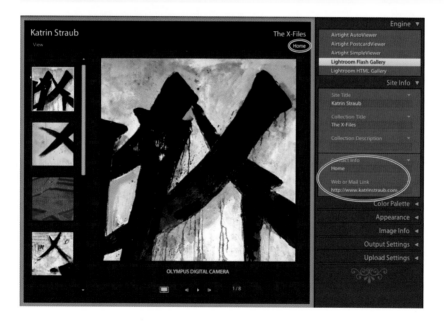

Changing colors

The controls in the Color Palette panel enable you to change the color scheme for your website. You can set the color for every element in your layout: background, borders, header, menu bar, and text. Choosing colors that work well together and look good on any system may seem a major challenge, but a few simple rules might help you to stay within a safe color palette:

- Use dark text on light backgrounds.

- Use light text on dark backgrounds.

- Don't rely on differences in color to convey essential information.

Color Palette differences for HTML and Flash galleries

The Color Palette panel shows different color options for HTML and Flash galleries. Refer to the following two illustrations to see which Color Palette option changes which element on the pages of an HTML gallery.

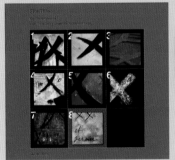

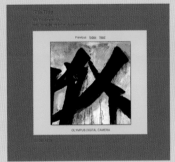

Refer to the following illustration to see which Color Palette option changes which element on the page of a Flash gallery.

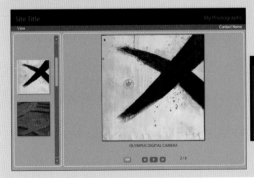

💡 *Neutral colors will compete less with your images. If you want to get serious about designing color schemes, kuler from the Adobe labs can be an invaluable tool (http://labs. adobe.com/technologies/kuler/).*

Appearance panel options for HTML galleries

The Appearance panel offers different options for Flash and HTML galleries. For example, in a HTML gallery you can specify the number of rows and columns used on the index page, which indirectly determines the size of the thumbnail images in the grid.

Change the number of rows and columns with the Grid Pages controls. The minimum grid is three by three—if your gallery contains more than nine images additional index pages will be generated.

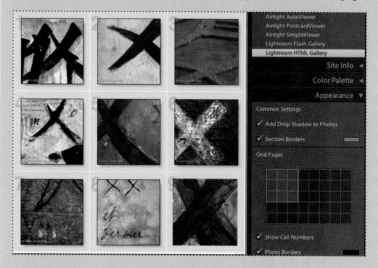

Among other options, you can add borders or drop shadows to your images and display an index number in the background of each image cell. These options give you great flexibility in customizing the look and feel of your HTML gallery. For a Flash gallery the options in the Appearance panel are more restricted.

In this exercise you'll change the color of the text for the site and collection titles.

1 Expand the Color Palette panel if necessary by clicking the triangle next to its name. You can collapse the Site Info panel to make more space.

💡 *To simplify working with the side panel groups, right-click / Control-click any panel header, and activate Solo Mode in the context menu. In solo mode, you can open only one panel in the group at a time.*

2 In the Color Palette, click the Header Text color swatch to open the Lightroom Color Picker.

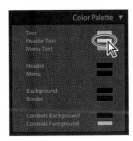

3 In the Color Picker, drag the slider at the right almost to the top, and click a bright red in the large color field on the left. We chose a color with RGB values of R: 90%, G: 10%, B: 15%. If you see a hexadecimal value displayed in the lower right corner of the Color Picker rather than RGB values, click RGB below the color slider. You can enter these RGB values directly by clicking the number and typing a new value. The color changes in the color swatch in the Color Palette panel and in the header text in the Gallery Editor view.

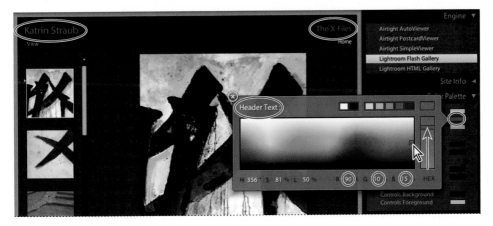

4 Close the Color Picker.

Next you'll adjust your layout using the Appearance panel. Note that the Appearance panel offers different options for Flash and HTML galleries.

Selecting a layout option for a Flash gallery

For a Lightroom Flash gallery template you have a choice of four layout options.

• **Scrolling**, with a scrollable row of index thumbnails beneath an enlarged image view.

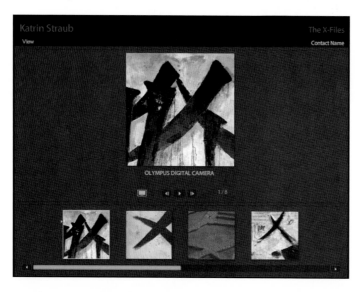

• **Paginated**, with thumbnails organized as an index beside an enlarged image view and navigation controls to access additional index pages.

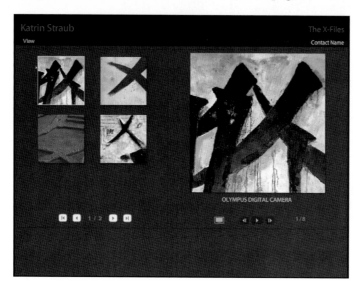

• **Left**, the layout of the Flash Gallery (Default) template, with a scrollable column of thumbnails on the left and an enlarged image view on the right.

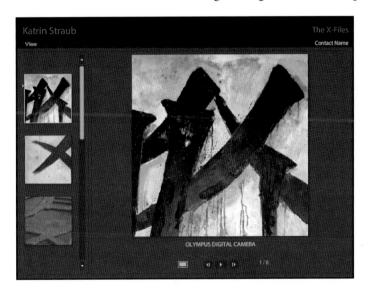

• **Slideshow Only**, displaying only the enlarged image view, with controls for navigating through the collection and playing a gallery slideshow.

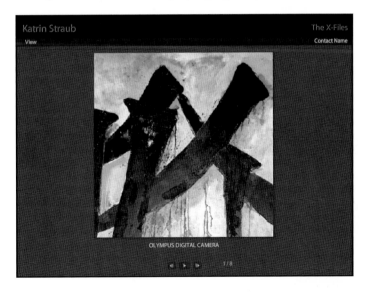

You can change the layout of your Flash gallery by using the controls in the Appearance panel.

1 If the Appearance panel in the right group is currently collapsed, click the triangle next to its name to expand it. You can collapse the Color Palette panel to make more space.

2 In the Appearance panel, click the double triangle beside Layout, and choose a new layout option from the Layout menu.

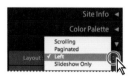

3 Notice the change in the layout of the gallery preview in the Gallery Editor view.

Note: In all but the Slideshow Only layout, the viewer can choose to view either a slideshow that will display only the large versions of the images or a gallery view with both the large images and the index thumbnails. To switch between the two views, click the View Slideshow button (▢) or the View Gallery button (▤) located beside the navigation controls under the enlarged image view.

4 In the Appearance panel, change the layout back to Left.

Personalizing your web gallery

Next, you'll personalize your web gallery by placing a logo in the header area.

1 In the Appearance panel, activate the Identity Plate option. Then click the Identity Plate preview, and choose Edit from the menu.

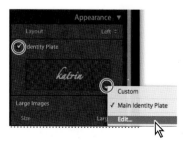

2   In the Identity Plate Editor dialog box, activate the option Use A Graphical Identity Plate, and then click the Locate File button.

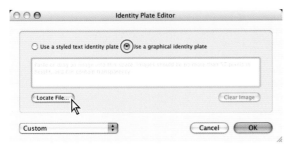

3   In the Locate File dialog box, navigate to the Lesson 9 folder, select the file Web_Identityplate.png, and then click Choose.

4   Click OK to close the Identity Plate Editor dialog box.

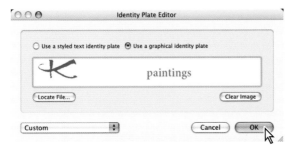

The new graphical identity plate appears in the top left corner of the gallery preview in the Gallery Editor view and in the Identity Plate preview in the Appearance panel.

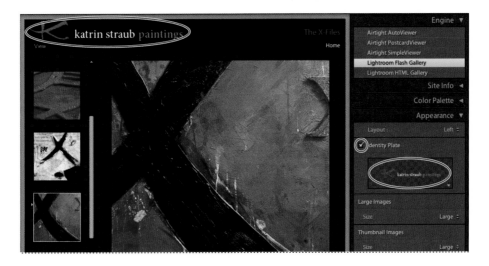

Note: For best results use an image that is no more than 60 pixels high so that it will not need to be scaled to fit your layout template. In this case we used an image with a height of 46 pixels.

Creating and modifying identity plates

You can personalize the Lightroom interface and your slideshows, Web presentations, and print layouts by adding your own identity plate.

A **Styled Text Identity Plate** will display the text you enter in the Identity Plate Editor dialog box. You can choose from the menus below the text box to specify the font characteristics.

A **Graphical Identity Plate** uses a graphic that is no more than 60 pixels high, in any of the following file formats: PDF, JPG, GIF, PNG, TIFF, or PSD (Windows) and JPG, GIF, PNG, TIFF, or PSD (Macintosh). The resolution of graphical identity plates may be too low for printed output. Choose Save As from the Enable Identity Plate menu, and give your identity plate a name.

To display your identity plate in the Lightroom workspace, choose Edit > Identity Plate Setup / Lightroom > Identity Plate Setup. In the Identity Plate Editor dialog box, activate the Enable Identity Plate option and choose one of your saved identity plates from the menu to the right.

Choose from the pop-up menus on the right side of the dialog box to change the font style, size and color for the Module Picker. The first color swatch sets the text color for the active module; the second swatch sets the text color for the others.

—From Lightroom Help

Note: The identity plate will replace the site title on your web page. However, when the gallery is viewed in a web browser, the text entered in the Site Title box in the Site Info panel will still be displayed in the title bar of the browser window.

Providing more information

You can display information about the images in your web gallery by choosing from a range of options in the Title and Caption menus in the Image Info panel. Display your images with no information at all, apply the same text to all the images at once, or show specific details retrieved from the metadata of each image. You can set up a text template that combines information drawn from different sources to compose titles and captions for your images automatically. In the next exercise, you'll add a title and caption to the first image.

1   Expand the Image Info panel in the right panel group. Make sure that both the Title and Caption options are activated. The title text will be displayed immediately below the

enlarged image view and the caption appears below the title in a smaller font size. Both can include whatever information you specify.

2 Click on the double triangle beside Title to see the list of available choices. The same choices are available in the Caption menu. Most of the options display information retrieved from the image's metadata.

Choose the Custom Text option to enter boilerplate text that will be displayed with every image.

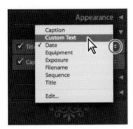

To provide specific information for each image, you'll use the metadata attached to it.

3 From the Title menu, choose Title. From the Caption menu, choose Caption.

Next, you'll need to enter the relevant information in the metadata for the images. You can do this in the Library module.

4 Press G to switch to the Grid view in the Library module.

5 In the Grid view, select the first image. If you arranged the images differently than shown in the illustration below, that's fine. Expand the Metadata panel in the right panel group. In the Title text box, type **X-File I (detail)** and for the Caption type **mixed media on canvas**. Then press Enter.

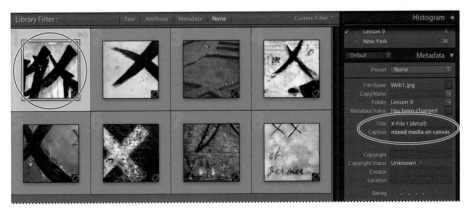

6 (Optional) Enter titles and captions for the other images.

7 Switch back to the Web module by pressing Ctrl+Alt+5 / Command+Option+5. Notice the additional information now displayed under the enlarged view of the first painting.

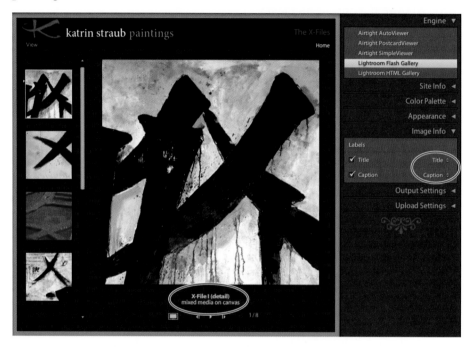

💡 *Choose Edit from the Title or Caption menus in the Image Info panel to open the Text Template Editor, where you can compose a text template drawing from many more options than are available in the Title and Caption menus. For more information on the Text Template Editor please refer to Lightroom Help.*

Specifying output settings

In the Output Settings panel you can control the image quality of the JPEG images generated for your web gallery. You'll need to find a compromise between image quality and file size. You can also choose to add a copyright watermark to the images—a minimal protection when making your work available to the public.

1 In the right panel group, collapse the Image Info panel and expand the Output Settings panel. Set the image quality to 70% with the Quality slider or click the value to the right, type **70** and press Enter. An image quality setting of 70% to 80% generally strikes a good balance between file size and image quality.

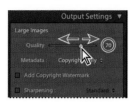

It's always a good idea to experiment with different quality settings. Depending on your images a lower setting might be sufficient, resulting in a website that loads faster.

2   At the bottom of the Output Settings panel, activate the Add Copyright Watermark option.

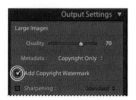

As for the Title and Caption settings in the previous exercise, the text to be added as a watermark will be retrieved from the image's metadata: the watermark will display whatever text is entered under Copyright in the Library module's Metadata panel.

3   Press G to jump to the Library module Grid view. Or, switch to the view last used in the Library module by pressing Ctrl+Alt+1 / Command+Option+1. Try to use the various keyboard shortcuts as often as possible—the more you get used to them the more efficiently you'll move between the Lightroom workspace modules and panels.

4   Select any image in the Grid view. You'll start by entering the copyright information for one image, and then apply it to all the others.

5   In the Metadata panel, type © **katrin straub 2008** in the Copyright text box and press Enter. Choose Copyrighted from the Copyright Status menu. *(See illustration and note on next page.)*

To enter the copyright character (©) in Windows, hold down the Alt key, type 0169 on your numeric keypad, and then release the Alt key. On Mac OS, press Option+g.

Note: If you don't see the Copyright text box or the Copyright Status menu in the Metadata panel, make sure you have Default selected from the Metadata Set menu in the panel header.

6   Select all the images in the Grid view by pressing Ctrl+A / Command+A. Then, click the Sync Metadata button below the right panel group or choose Metadata > Sync Metadata.

7   In the Synchronize Metadata dialog box, click the Check None button to make sure all checkboxes are cleared.

8   Activate just the checkboxes beside Copyright and Copyright Status under the IPTC Copyright heading. Don't click the Synchronize button yet.

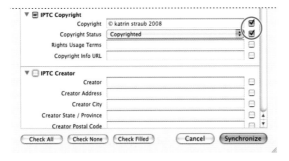

💡 *Should you have made a mistake entering the metadata in step 5, the Synchronize Metadata dialog box provides an opportunity to make corrections before applying the settings to all the images. You could also enter additional data at this stage.*

9 Click once in the Copyright text box. The copyright notice will be highlighted. Click a second time to clear the selection and a blinking text cursor will appear. If necessary, use the arrow keys to position the text cursor at the end of the text line. Change 2008 to 2009 by deleting the 8 and typing **9**. Don't press Enter—this would be equivalent to clicking Synchronize to dismiss the Synchronize Metadata dialog box, and we're not done yet. If you pressed Enter by mistake, choose Edit > Undo and click the Sync Metadata button to reopen the Synchronize Metadata dialog box.

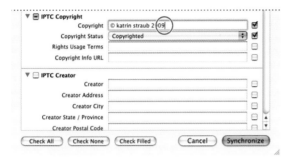

10 Use the scrollbar at the right of the Synchronize Metadata dialog box to scroll slowly down to the end of the list, making sure that none of the checkboxes are activated other than those for Copyright and Copyright Status. Then click Synchronize.

11 Choose Edit Presets from the Preset menu in the Metadata panel. In the Edit Metadata Presets dialog box, choose Save Current Settings As New Preset from the Preset menu. In the New Preset dialog box, name your new preset **copyright web**, and then click Create.

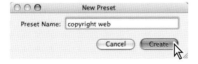

12 Click Done to close the Edit Metadata Presets dialog box. You've created a metadata preset that you can access quickly to apply the same data to other web galleries.

13 Switch back to the Web module. (Do you remember the keyboard shortcut?) You can see that the copyright notice is now displayed in the lower left corner of every image in the gallery, for the thumbnails as well as the enlarged views. *(See illustration on next page.)*

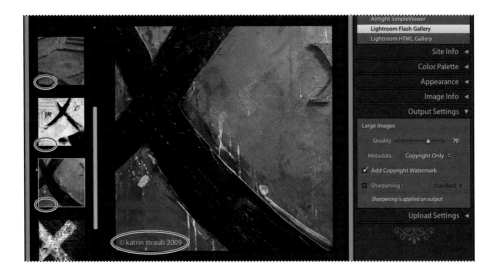

💡 *Using the Synchronize command, you can quickly update the copyright notice, for example. When it's time to change the date to 2010, select all the images in your web collection in the Library module, click Sync Metadata, edit the copyright message, and then click Synchronize.*

This concludes the section on customizing the look and feel of your web gallery. You've changed the site title text, added a link to your Home page, learned how to adjust the color scheme used throughout the gallery, modified the layout, personalized the web page by placing a graphic identity plate, and finally added titles, captions and a copyright watermark to the images. It's time to save all these modifications as a custom template that you can use as a starting point the next time you create a web gallery, but first let's preview your gallery in your web browser.

Previewing the gallery

To enable you to preview your web gallery in your system's web browser, Lightroom generates the web pages and the necessary image files in a temporary folder on your hard disk, and then opens the main page of the gallery in your web browser. You should always preview your gallery in this way before actually uploading it to your web site. Check that the navigation controls work as expected, examine the image quality of the pictures, and confirm that your photos appear in the correct order. Finally, you should resize the browser window to see how the gallery layout adapts to different display sizes.

1 To preview the gallery in your system's web browser, click the Preview In Browser button below the left panel group, or choose Web > Preview In Browser.

Note: Depending on the number of images in your web gallery, it may take a while for Lightroom to generate the necessary files. Watch the progress bar that appears in the upper left corner of the Lightroom workspace. You can cancel the Preview In Browser command at any time by clicking the small cross icon at the right end of the progress indicator—but for this exercise, let the process run its course.

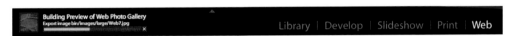

2 Once Lightroom has finished generating the necessary files, your web browser will open to the main page of your web gallery.

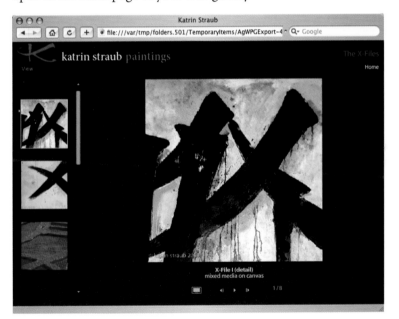

3 To see how the web gallery performs in your browser, run these simple tests:

• Click the Play button in the group of navigation controls below the large image to start the gallery slideshow.

• Click the Pause button or press the spacebar to stop playback.

• Use the scrollbar to scroll down the list of small thumbnail images on the left. Click a thumbnail to view the enlarged image on the right.

- Click the word View below the identity plate and choose Slideshow from the menu.

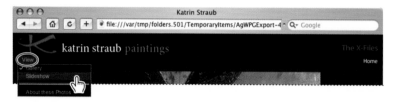

- Use the arrow keys on your keyboard to navigate from one image to the next.
- Click the View Gallery button at the left of the navigation controls below the large image to return to the gallery layout with the column of thumbnail images on the left.

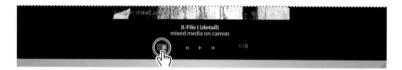

- Resize your browser window to see how the gallery layout works at different sizes.
- Examine the image quality of the pictures.
- Make sure the titles, captions, and copyright watermarks are displayed correctly.
- Click the Home button to see if it links correctly to your home page. (You'll need an active Internet connection.)

4   When you're done, close the browser window and return to Lightroom.

Saving your custom template

Having spent time and effort modifying the gallery layout, changing the color and text style, and adding titles, captions, an identity plate, and copyright watermarks—you should save your design as a custom web gallery template. The new template will be listed under User Templates in the Template Browser panel, where you can access it easily should you wish to rework or extend your web gallery or use your customized template as a starting point for creating a new layout. You can create additional folders in the Template Browser to help you manage your custom templates.

1   With your customized web gallery open in the Web module, click the Create New Preset button (+) in the header of the Template Browser panel or choose Web > New Template.

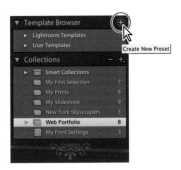

2   In the New Template dialog box, name your template **My Flash Copyright Gallery**.
Leave the default User Templates folder selected in the Folder menu, and then click
Create.

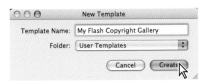

3   Your customized web gallery template is now listed under User Templates in the
Template Browser panel.

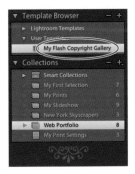

*Note: To create a new folder in the Template Browser, right-click / Control-click an existing
folder and choose New Folder from the context menu. To delete a folder, you'll first need
to delete all the templates it contains—or drag them into another folder. Select the empty
folder and click the Delete Selected Preset button (-) in the header of the Template Browser,
or right-click / Control-click the folder name, and choose Delete Folder from the context
menu. To delete a custom template, select the template and click the Delete Selected
Preset button (-) in the header of the Template Browser. You cannot delete the Lightroom
templates, the Lightroom Templates folder, or the default User Templates folder.*

Exporting your gallery

Now that you're happy with your gallery design and you've saved the template, you can export the web-site to your hard disk. You can run the exported website from your laptop if you need to present your work where there is no Internet connection and burn the exported files to a CD-ROM as a working backup or to send to a client or colleague.

1   Select My Flash Copyright Gallery from the User Templates folder in the Template Browser panel and click the Export button below the right panel group, or choose Web > Export Web Photo Gallery.

2   In the Save Web Gallery dialog box, navigate to your Lesson 9 folder. Type **My Web Gallery** in the File Name / Save As text box, and then click Save.

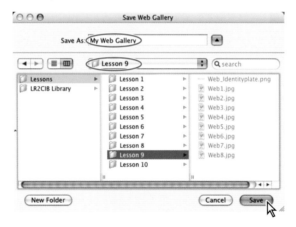

Lightroom will create a folder named My Web Gallery inside the Lesson 9 folder and generate all the necessary image files, web pages, subfolders and support files within that folder. Depending on the number of images in your gallery, this operation might take a while—the progress bar at the left of the top panel provides feedback as Lightroom completes the process.

3   When the export is complete, double-click the file index.html in the folder My Web Gallery inside your Lesson 9 folder. Your gallery opens in your default web browser.

4   When you're finished reviewing your gallery, close the web browser window and return to Lightroom.

> 💡 Before burning your web gallery to a CD-ROM for a client, create an alias of the index.html file, place it beside the folder containing the files for the website, and rename it **Start here**. This will make it easy for your client to launch your presentation.

Uploading your web gallery to a web server

In the last exercise of this lesson you will learn how to upload a web gallery to a server from within Lightroom. To do this, you will need to know your FTP server access information. You can obtain this information from your Internet service provider.

1   In the Web module, expand the Upload Settings panel in the right panel group.

2   From the FTP Server menu in the Upload Settings panel, choose Edit.

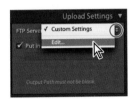

3   In the Configure FTP File Transfer dialog box, enter the server address, your username and password, and server path.

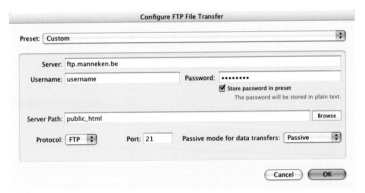

Note: For security reasons, don't activate the Store Password In Preset option unless you are the only person with access to the computer you're using.

4   From the Preset menu, choose Save Current Settings As New Preset.

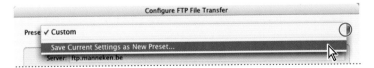

5   In the New Preset dialog box, enter a name for your FTP server preset, and then click Create.

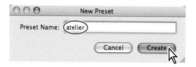

6   Click OK to close the Configure FTP File Transfer dialog box. You'll notice that the name of your new FTP server preset now appears in the Upload Settings panel.

7   To place the gallery inside a subfolder on your FTP server, activate the option Put In Subfolder and type a name for the subfolder that is relevant to the content of the web gallery. This subfolder name will become part of the URL of your web gallery. For example, we used **x_files** as subfolder name so the complete URL might look like this: http://www.katrinstraub.com/x_files.

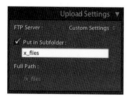

Note: To avoid possible compatibility problems with your web server, use only lowercase letters, the minus sign (-), and the underscore character (_) in the subfolder name. Avoid using spaces in the name.

8   Click the Upload button below the right panel group. If you didn't save your FTP server password in the Configure FTP File Transfer dialog box, you'll need to enter it now in the Enter Password dialog box, and then click Upload.

Uploading your web gallery to an FTP server generally takes much longer than exporting it to your local hard disk. You can watch the upload status in the progress bar at the left of the top panel.

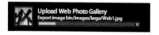

Once the upload is complete, you can enter the URL of your gallery in your web browser and admire your site live on the Internet. Don't send the URL to your client or friends before you've confirmed that everything works as expected!

Review

▶ **Review questions**

1   Why is it useful to create a collection to group the images that you intend to use for your web gallery?

2   What is the difference between HTML and Flash galleries?

3   Which panels would you use to customize the Lightroom web templates?

4   How do you add a copyright watermark to the images in your web gallery?

▶ **Review answers**

1   Grouping your images as a collection not only keeps them all in one place for easy reference—it will also make the process of updating and adjusting your web gallery much more efficient. Once a selection of images has been saved as a collection it is possible to rearrange the order in which they will appear in the gallery.

2   HTML gallery templates produce simple web sites that are compatible with most browsers. Flash templates can produce more sophisticated web galleries, including animations, slideshows with smooth transitions, and other special effects. However, Flash galleries require that the viewer has the appropriate Adobe Flash Player plug-in. Viewers may need to click through security messages in the web browser before being able to see the gallery.

3   The panels in the right panel group—the Site Info, Color Palette, Appearance, Image Info, Output Settings, and Upload Settings panels—contain controls for modifying the gallery layout templates available in the Template Browser.

4   In the Web module, activate the Add Copyright Watermark option in the Output Settings panel, and then enter a copyright notice for the images in the Library module's Metadata panel.

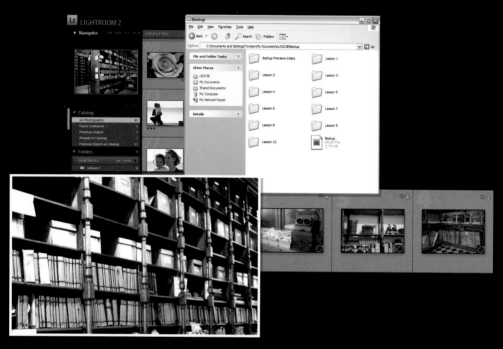

Saveguard your photoghraphs and develop settings against loss using Lightroom's build-in backup tools. Save just your catalog file, or your entire photo library—complete with develop settings and copies of your original image files.

Export photos in different file formats to be used in multimedia presentations, further processed in external image editors, burned to CD or DVD for archival purposes, or sent as an e-mail attachment.

10 Creating Backups and Exporting Photos

Lightroom offers a variety of options that make it easy to back up and export all the data connected with your image library. You can immediately create backup copies to an external storage device when importing images, have Lightroom automatically back up your catalog file at your preferred frequency, and perform full or incremental backups of your photos and develop settings. Lightroom supports a variety of file formats suitable to transfer your photo library to a different computer, to further process images in another appliaction, to archive your projects, and to optimize the file size of images exported for on-screen viewing.

In this lesson you'll learn a variety of techniques to help you to manage your image library, minimize the impact of accidental data loss, and streamline your workflow:

• Backing up your catalog file.

• Backing up the entire image library.

• Making incremental backups.

• Exporting metadata.

• Exporting photos for on-screen viewing.

• Exporting photos to be edited in another application.

• Exporting photos for archival purposes.

• Using export presets.

• Setting up automated post-export actions.

Getting started

Before you begin this lesson, make sure that you have correctly copied the Lessons folder from the CD in the back of this book onto your computer's hard disk and created the LR2CIB Library Catalog file. See "Copying the Classroom in a Book files" and "Creating a catalog file for working with this book" on page 3.

1   Start Lightroom.

2   In the Adobe Photoshop Lightroom - Select Catalog dialog box, make sure the file LR2CIB Library Catalog.lrcat is selected under Catalog Location, and then click Continue.

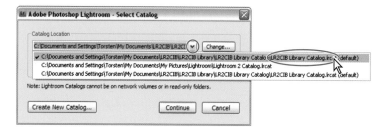

3   If the Back Up Catalog dialog box appears, click Skip Now.

4   Lightroom will open in the screen mode and workspace module that were active when you last quit. If necessary, click Library in the Module Picker to switch to the Library module.

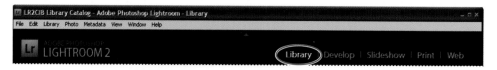

5   Choose File > Import Photos From Disk.

6   In the Import Photos Or Lightroom Catalog dialog box, navigate to the Lessons folder you've already copied into the LR2CIB folder on your hard disk. Select the Lesson 10 folder, and then click Import All Photos In Selected Folder (Windows) / Choose (Mac OS).

7   In the Import Photos dialog box, choose Add Photos To Catalog Without Moving from the File Handling menu. Choose None from both the Develop Settings menu and the Metadata menu. Type **Lesson 10** in the Keywords text box, and choose Minimal from the Initial Previews menu. Make sure your settings are exactly as shown in the illustration below, and then click Import.

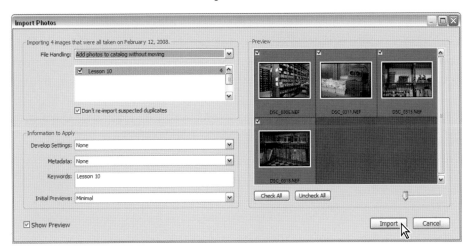

You have imported the images into your library; you can see thumbnails of your photos in the Grid view of the Library module and in the Filmstrip. You are now ready to start the exercises in this lesson.

Preventing data loss

The importance of a good backup strategy is often only understood too late. How much damage would be done if your computer was stolen right now? How many files would be irrecoverably lost if your hard disk failed today? How much work and money would that cost you? You can't prevent a disaster from happening but it is in your power to reduce the risks and the cost of recovery. Backing up regularly will reduce the impact of a catastrophe and save you time, effort, and money.

As for the rest of the files on your computer, you really should have your own backup strategy in place.

Backing up the catalog file

The Lightroom catalog file stores information for every image in your library: all the metadata including keyword tags, flags, labels, and ratings, as well as your developing and output settings. Every time you modify a photo in any way—from renaming the file during import to color correction, retouching, and cropping—all your work is saved to the library catalog file. It lists all your image collections and records the slideshow settings, web gallery designs, and print layouts associated with them as well as your customized templates and presets.

You may have copies of your original images stored safely on removable media, but in the event of a catastrophe such as a hard disk failure, accidental deletion, or a corrupted library file, you could still lose hundreds of hours of work if you haven't backed up your catalog. In the Catalog Settings dialog box, you can set Lightroom to initiate a regular backup of your catalog file automatically.

1   Choose Edit > Catalog Settings / Lightroom > Catalog Settings to open the Catalog Settings dialog box.

2   Click the General tab and choose your preferred backup frequency from the Back Up Catalog menu.

When a catalog backup is due, the Backup Catalog dialog box will appear when you launch Lightroom.

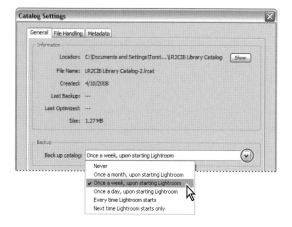

3   To initiate a catalog backup for this exercise, choose either Every Time Lightroom Starts or Next Time Lightroom Starts Only from the Back Up Catalog menu.

4   Click OK / the Close button (⊖) to close the Catalog Settings dialog box; then quit and relaunch Lightroom.

5   In the Adobe Photoshop Lightroom - Select Catalog dialog box, make sure the file LR2CIB Library Catalog.lrcat is selected under Catalog Location, and then click Continue.

The Back Up Catalog dialog box appears.

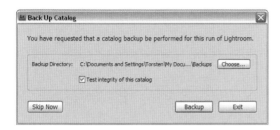

6   In the Backup Catalog dialog box, click the Choose button to change the folder where the backed up catalog will be stored. Ideally the backup should be located on a different disk than your original catalog file; for the purpose of this exercise you can select the LR2CIB folder on your hard disk. In the Browse For Folder / Choose Folder dialog box, select the LR2CIB folder as the backup directory and click OK / Choose.

7   Make sure the option Test Integrity Of This Catalog is activated. It's a good idea to keep this option activated whenever you back up your catalog; it would defy the purpose of making a backup if your original file was not in good working order. Click Backup.

Each time you back up your catalog, Lightroom will create a complete copy of the catalog file in the directory you specified and place it inside a new folder with a name composed from the date and time of the backup.

> 💡 *To save space on your backup drive, either delete the older backup files or compress them. Catalog files compress very effectively; you can expect a compressed catalog to be as small as 10% of the size of the original. Make sure to decompress the file before attempting to restore your catalog from the backup.*

Should your catalog be accidently deleted or become corrupted, you can now restore it either by copying the backup file to your catalog folder or by creating a new catalog and importing the contents of your backup file.

Note: To avoid inadvertently modifying your backup file, it's preferable not to open it directly from the Lightroom File menu.

8   Choose Edit > Catalog Settings / Lightroom > Catalog Settings.

9   In the Catalog Settings dialog box, click the General tab and reset your preferred backup frequency by choosing from the Back Up Catalog menu.

10 Click OK / the Close button (⊖) to close the Catalog Settings dialog box.

Note: Backing up the catalog file in this way does not make backup copies of the original image files or the preview images that Lightroom displays in the workspace. The previews will be regenerated as your catalog file is restored from the backup, but you'll need to back up your original image files separately.

Exporting metadata

Another way to reduce the impact of losing your catalog file is to export and distribute its content. The catalog is a central storage location for all the information associated with every image in your library. You can save a copy of the information relevant to each image in a separate file that will be stored alongside the original file. If you keep this exported information in sync with your catalog file—which can be done automatically— you have what is in effect a distributed backup of the metadata and develop settings for each of your photos.

1 Choose Edit > Catalog Settings / Lightroom > Catalog Settings. In the Catalog Settings dialog box, click the Metadata tab. In the Editing options, make sure that Automatically Write Changes Into XMP is disabled. Note the warning that changes made in Lightroom will not automatically be visible in other applications. Click OK / the Close button (⊖) to close the Catalog Settings dialog box.

2 Choose View > View Options. In the Library View Options dialog box, click the Grid View tab and activate Unsaved Metadata in the Cell Icons options. Then, click the Close button to close the Library View Options dialog box.

3 In the Grid view, you can see the Metadata File Needs To Be Updated icon (▤) in the image cells. If you don't see this icon it may be because Automatically Write Changes To XMP was activated when you imported the images and added keywords. Select any image in the Grid view and change the rating or apply a flag. The icon appears in the grid cell to indicate that the image now has unsaved changes in its metadata.

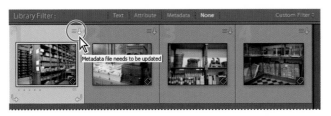

4 Right-click / Control-click the image and choose Metadata > Save Metadata To File from the context menu. After a short processing time, the Metadata File Needs To Be Updated icon will disappear.

5 Right-click / Control-click the image again and choose Show In Explorer / Show In Finder from the context menu. In the Explorer / Finder window, you'll notice another file with the same name as the selected image, followed by an .xmp file extension. This is what is called an *XMP sidecar file*, containing the exported metadata and develop settings associated with the image.

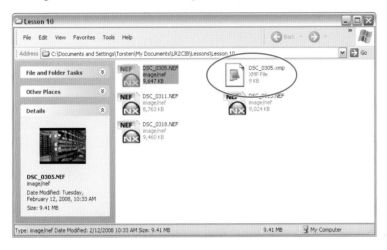

Note: *If you are working in Windows and you don't see the file name extensions, choose Tools > Folder Options in the Explorer window, click the View tab, and then disable Hide Extensions For Known File Types in the Advanced Settings for Files and Folders options.*

Lightroom creates a separate XMP sidecar file for each Raw file imported. Many camera manufactures use proprietary and undocumented formats for their Raw files and formats become outdated as new ones appear. Because of this, storing the metadata in a separate file is the safest approach, avoiding possible corruption of the Raw file or loss of the exported metadata.

For files in DNG, JPEG, TIFF, and PSD format, Lightroom writes the xmp data into the image file itself. These file formats have well-defined spaces within the file where XMP information can be stored without having any affect on the image data.

Applications such as Adobe Bridge and the Photoshop Camera Raw plug-in can read XMP metadata and will allow you to edit it. When you edit or add to an image's metadata in another application, Lightroom will show the Metadata Was Changed Externally icon (■) above the thumbnail in the Grid view. To accept the changes and update your catalog file accordingly, choose Metadata > Read Metadata From File. To reject the changed metadata and overwrite it with the information in your catalog file, choose Metadata > Save Metadata To File.

You can update the metadata for a batch of modified images—or even for the entire catalog with all its folders and collections—by selecting the images or folders to be updated and choosing Metadata > Save Metadata To File as you did with a single file in step 4. You can also configure Lightroom to export the metadata automatically whenever an image is modified. Although you might notice some slowing in performance as Lightroom writes information to the hard disk, the advantage is that you will always have an up-to-date copy of the metadata from your catalog stored either in the image files themselves or in their sidecar files.

6 In Lightroom, choose Edit > Catalog Settings / Lightroom > Catalog Settings. In the Catalog Settings dialog box, click the Metadata tab and activate Automatically Write Changes Into XMP in the Editing options. Click OK / the Close button (●) to close the Catalog Settings dialog box.

Note: XMP information exported in this way contains only the metadata that is relevant to the individual images: keywords, flags, labels, ratings, and develop settings. It does not include higher-level data that is relevant to the catalog as a whole such as information relating to stacks, virtual copies, and settings used in presentations.

Backing up the library

In the first exercise you backed up your catalog without the image files. In the second you updated your images files with just part of the catalog information. In this exercise you'll export your entire Lightroom library: images, catalog, stacks, collections—the works!

Exporting images as a catalog

When you export your photos as a catalog, Lightroom creates a copy of the catalog file and gives you the option to make copies of the master files and the image previews at the same time. You can choose to export the entire library, or just a selection of your images, as a catalog. Exporting images in this way is ideal for moving your photos together with all the associated Lightroom catalog information from one computer to another. You can use the same technique to restore your entire library from a backup after a data loss.

1   In the Catalog panel, click All Photographs. Then, choose File > Export As Catalog. You should save your backup files to a different hard disk than the one that stores your catalog and the master image files but for this exercise, you can save the backup files to the LR2CIB folder on your hard disk.

2   In the Export As Catalog dialog box, navigate to the LR2CIB folder you created on your hard disk. Type **Backup** in the File Name / Save As text box, disable Export Selected Photos Only and activate Export Negative Files and Include Available Previews. Click Save / Export Catalog.

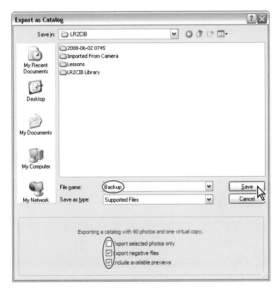

An initial progress bar is displayed while the new catalog is being created, which should only take a few seconds.

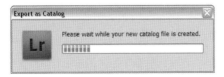

Lightroom then begins copying your image files to the new location as a background task.

3 Watch the progress bar on the left side of the top panel in the Lightroom workspace.

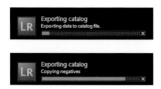

4 When the export process is complete, switch to Windows Explorer / the Finder and navigate to the LR2CIB folder. Open the new Backup folder.

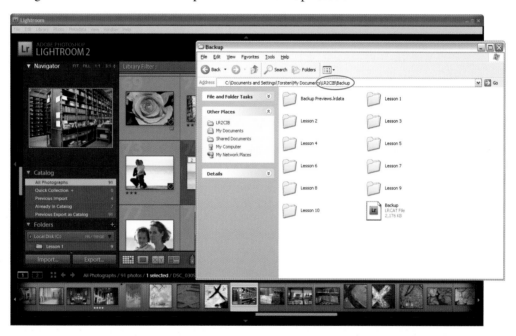

Note: You may see a different set of folders than you see in the illustration, depending on which lessons you've already completed.

5 You can see that the folder structure nested inside the Backup folder replicates the arrangement of folders you see in the Folders panel. All the master images in your Lightroom library have been copied into these new folders and the file Backup.lrcat is a fully functional copy of your original catalog.

6 In Lightroom, choose File > Open Catalog. In the Open Catalog / Open dialog box, navigate to the new Backup folder inside the LR2CIB folder. Select the file Backup.lrcat, and then click Open. If the Open Catalog dialog box appears, click Relaunch. Lightroom will open the backup catalog.

7   Other than the filename in the title bar of the workspace window, this catalog will be almost indistinguishable from your original. Only some minor status information has been lost. For example, you can see that the Previous Import folder in the Catalog panel is now empty.

8   Some of your preferences have been reset to default values which may differ from the choices you've made for your LR2CIB catalog: Choose Edit > Catalog Settings / Lightroom > Catalog Settings. In the Catalog Settings dialog box, click the General tab. The backup frequency has been reset to the default: Once A Week, Upon Starting Lightroom. Click Cancel / the Close button (●) to close the Catalog Settings dialog box.

9   To return to your original catalog, choose File > Open Recent > LR2CIB Library Catalog.lrcat. If the Open Catalog dialog box appears, click Relaunch.

10 If the Back Up Catalog dialog box appears, click Skip Now.

Doing incremental backups

In the usual course of events most of the images in your library will remain unchanged between backups. An incremental backup saves time by replacing only the backup copies and catalog entries of images that have been modified since the last backup.

Although Lightroom does not have an incremental backup command, you can achieve the same effect by regularly updating your existing backup with just those files in your main catalog that have been modified since the last backup.

1   In the Folders panel, select the Lesson 10 folder. Change the star rating for one of the images in the Grid view. This will be the incremental change to your library for the purposes of this exercise.

2   Choose File > Open Recent > Backup.lrcat to switch to the Backup catalog. If the Open Catalog dialog box appears, click Relaunch.

3   Choose File > Import From Catalog. In the Import From Lightroom Catalog dialog box, navigate to the LR2CIB folder. Drill down to the LR2CIB Library/LR2CIB Library Catalog folder. Inside that folder, select LR2CIB Library Catalog.lrcat, and then click Choose / Open.

4   In the Import From Catalog dialog box, choose Metadata And Develop Settings Only from the Replace menu in the Existing Photos section. Scroll down in the Preview panel to confirm that only the image you modified in step 1 is selected for import.

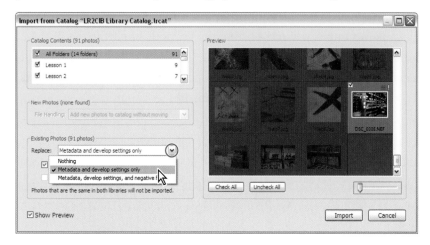

Note: When adding new images to your backup library, choose Copy New Photos To A New Location And Import from the File Handling menu. Then, click the Choose button to specify your current Backup folder as the destination for the copied files.

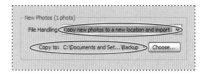

5   Click Import. You can see that the modified image has been updated with the rating you changed in the master catalog. You have just performed an incremental backup.

6   (Optional) In the Catalog panel, click All Photographs and choose Edit > Select All or press Ctrl+A / Command+A. Choose Metadata > Save Metadata To Files or press Ctrl+S / Command+S. This will export the metadata and develop settings for each photo in the backup library to the backup image file or its XMP sidecar, as an extra precaution against data loss.

7   To return to your original catalog, choose File > Open Recent > LR2CIB Library Catalog.lrcat. If the Open Catalog dialog box appears, click Relaunch.

8   If the Back Up Catalog dialog box appears, click Skip Now.

Exporting photos

The backup techniques we have discussed so far all produce backup files that can be read only by Lightroom or another application that is capable of reading and interpreting the exported XMP metadata. If you wish to send your work in a usable format to somebody who doesn't have Lightroom installed on his or her computer you'll first need to convert the images to an appropriate file format. This is comparable to saving a Word document as plain text or as a PDF document for distribution; some of the functionality is lost but at least the recipient can see what you're working on.

Your choice of file format for the exported photos will depend on the purpose for which the images are intended. To export an image for use as an e-mail attachment intended to be viewed on screen, use the JPEG file format and minimize the file size by reducing the resolution and dimensions of the image. To export an image to be edited in another application, use the PSD or TIFF file format at full size. For archival purposes you can export the images in their original file format or convert them to DNG.

Exporting JPEG files for on-screen viewing

For this exercise, you'll convert the images to grayscale before you export them so you'll be able to see at a glance that your develop settings have been applied to the images as they were exported.

1   In the Folders panel, select the Lesson 10 folder. Choose Edit > Select All, and then choose Photo > Develop Settings > Convert To Grayscale. If you prefer using keyboard shortcuts, press Ctrl+A / Command+A, and then press the V key.

2   With all four images still selected in the Grid view, choose File > Export.

3   In the Export Location area of the Export dialog box, choose Specific Folder from the Export To menu *(see illustration after step 4 on next page)* and click the Choose button below it to specify a destination folder. Navigate to your Lessons folder, select the Lesson 10 folder, and click OK / Choose.

4 Activate the Put In Subfolder option and type **Export** as the name for the new subfolder. Disable the option Add To This Catalog.

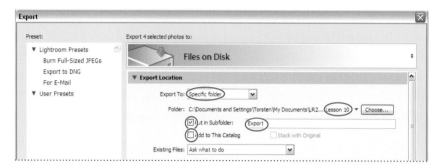

5 In the File Naming area of the Export dialog box, choose Filename from the Template menu.

6 In the File Settings options, choose JPEG from the Format menu and set a Quality value between 70% and 80% which generally makes an acceptable compromise between image quality and file size. From the Color Space menu choose sRGB: a good choice for images intended to be viewed on the web or in other circumstances where you are unsure what form of color management is used—if any at all.

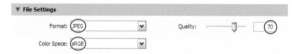

Note: You may need to scroll down in the Export dialog box to see the following settings.

7 In Image Sizing, activate the Resize To Fit option and choose Width & Height from the menu. Enter **600** for both width (W) and height (H) and choose Pixels from the units menu. This will proportionally scale each image so that its longest side is 600 pixels. Activate the Don't Enlarge option to avoid smaller images being upsampled. Set the Resolution at **72** Pixels Per Inch—although resolution settings are in general ignored for on-screen display. The reduction in file size is the result of reducing the total number of pixels that make up the image.

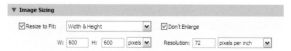

8   In the Output Sharpening settings, disable the Sharpen For option. Of the three Metadata options, activate only Minimize Embedded Metadata. From the After Export menu in the Post-Processing options, choose Show In Explorer / Show In Finder. Then, click Export.

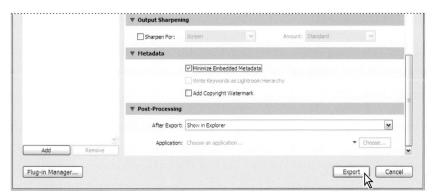

Using export plug-ins

You can use plug-ins to extend Lightroom's functionality. For example, you can download and install an iPhoto plug-in that extends the options in the Export dialog box. The Lightroom iPhoto plug-in enables you to export images in your preferred file format and then import them into iPhoto as an album. You can then take advantage of iPhoto's close integration with the Mac OS to browse your photos from within other applications or to transfer them to an iPod or iPhone.

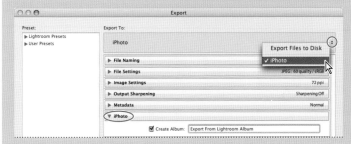

There are export plug-ins available to enable you upload photos directly from within Lightroom to your Flickr, SmugMug, Zenfolio, or Picasa Web accounts. Other export plug-ins let you create entire web galleries from the selected images and upload them to your FTP server. Worth mentioning are the plug-ins for PixelPost Photoblob, SlideShowPro, and IStockPhoto, to name just a few.

Search the Internet for Lightroom plug-ins or browse the Adobe Store (www.adobe.com/go/store) where you have access to thousands of plug-ins from third-party developers, either offering additional export functionality or helping you to automate tasks, customize workflows, create specialized professional effects, and more.

9   Watch the progress bar on the left side of the top panel in the Lightroom workspace. When the export process is complete, your Export folder inside the Lesson 10 folder will open in Windows Explorer / the Finder.

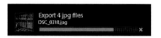

💡 *To have Lightroom notify you by playing a sound when the export process is complete, choose a sound from the menu under Completion Sounds in the General tab of the Preferences dialog box.*

10   In Windows Explorer, use the Filmstrip or Thumbnail view to see a preview of the images in the folder. In the Finder, select an image in Column view (or in Cover Flow in Leopard) to see its preview. You can see that the images are in black and white; your develop settings have been applied to the photos during the export process. The width of the images is 600 pixels and the file size is only about 100 kilobytes each.

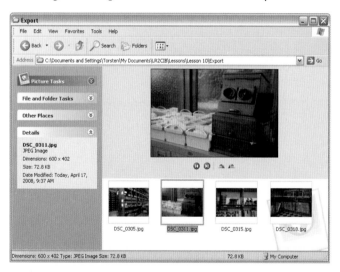

11   In Windows Explorer / the Finder, delete the four images in the Export folder, and then return to Lightroom.

Exporting as PSD or TIFF for further editing

1   In the Grid view, make sure all four images from the Lesson 10 folder are still selected.

2   Choose File > Export. In the Export dialog box, you'll notice that all your settings from the previous exercise are still in place.

> To export images using the same settings you used for the previous export (and without calling up the Export dialog box) choose File > Export With Previous.

3   In File Settings, choose PSD or TIFF from the Format menu. When saving in TIFF format, you have the option to apply ZIP data compression—a lossless compression—to reduce the resulting file size. Notice that AdobeRGB (1998) is automatically selected in the Color Space menu.

Note: If you intend to edit an image in an external application after exporting it, you should use the AdobeRGB (1998) color profile rather than the sRGB color profile. The AdobeRGB (1998) color profile has a larger color gamut, which results in fewer colors being clipped and the original appearance of your images being better preserved. The ProPhoto RGB color gamut is even larger, capable of representing any color from the original raw image. However, to correctly display images using the AdobeRGB (1998) or ProPhoto RGB color profiles on screen you need an image editing application capable of reading these color profiles. You'll also need to turn color management on and calibrate your computer display. Without taking these measures, your images will look bad on screen with the AdobeRGB (1998) color profile—and even worse with ProPhoto RGB.

4   Unless you have a particular need to output 16 bit files as part of your workflow, choose 8 Bits/Component from the Bit Depth menu. 8-bit files are smaller and compatible with more programs and plug-ins, but do not preserve fine tonal detail as well as 16-bit files. Lightroom actually operates in a 16 bit color space but by the time you're ready to export images you've usually already made any important corrections or adjustments that were necessary, so you won't loose much in terms of editing capability by converting the files to 8 bits for export.

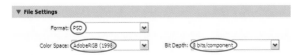

5   In Image Sizing, disable Resize To Fit to preserve all the information for every pixel in the original image.

> 💡 *Choose your preferred external editor, file format, color space, bit depth, compression settings, and file naming options in the External Editing tab of the Preferences dialog box. In the Lightroom workspace, choose Photo > Edit In and choose your preferred external image editing application from the menu. Lightroom will automatically export an image in the appropriate file format, open it in the external editor, and add the converted file to the Lightroom library.*

6   Leave the Output Sharpening and Metadata settings unchanged. If you have Adobe Photoshop CS2/CS3 installed on your computer, choose Open in Adobe Photoshop CS2/CS3 from the After Export menu in the Post-Processing options. Or, choose Open In Other Application, and then click Choose to select your preferred image editor. Click Export.

7   Wait until the export is complete and the images have opened in the external editor. You can see that the images are in black and white. They are 3872 by 2592 pixels in size—the same dimensions as the original Raw images.

8   Quit the external editor, delete the files from the Export folder in Windows Explorer / the Finder, and then return to Lightroom.

Exporting as Original or DNG for archiving

1   In the Grid view, choose Edit > Select None and then select only one of the images from the Lesson 10 folder. Choose File > Export.

2   In the Export dialog box, leave the Export Location and File Naming settings unchanged.

3   In File Settings, choose Original from the Format menu. Note that there are now no other File Settings, Image Settings, or Output Sharpening options available; Lightroom will export the original image data unaltered.

Note: *When you choose to export images in DNG file format you have additional options that affect the way the DNG files are created, but the original image data remains essentially unchanged.*

4   In the Post-Processing options, choose Show In Explorer / Show In Finder. Then click Export.

5   Wait until the export process completes and the Export folder inside the Lesson 10 folder opens in Windows Explorer / the Finder.

6   In Windows Explorer / the Finder, you'll notice that an XMP sidecar file has been saved together with the copy of the original RAW image. This XMP sidecar file contains the editing settings and any additional metadata, such as the rating you have applied to the image.

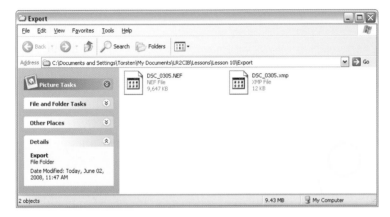

7   In Windows Explorer / the Finder, delete both files from the Export folder, and then return to Lightroom.

Using export presets

Lightroom provides presets for commonly performed export tasks. You can use a preset as is or as a starting point for creating your own. If you find yourself performing the same operations over and over again you should create your own presets to automate your workflow.

1   In the Grid view, select one of the images in the Lesson 10 folder and then choose File > Export.

2 In the list of presets on the left side of the Export dialog box, choose For E-Mail from the Lightroom Presets.

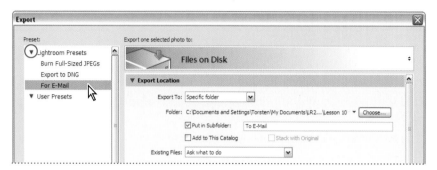

3 Note the export settings associated with this preset: Under Export Location, the subfolder name is To E-Mail. With the current File Settings, an exported file will be an sRGB JPEG file with a Quality setting of 50%. In the Image Sizing, the exported image is set to be resized so that its longest side will be scaled down to 640 pixels. In the Metadata options Minimize Embedded Metadata is activated, and under Post-Processing, Show In Explorer / Show In Finder is selected from the After Export menu. These are all reasonable settings if you intend your exported images to be viewed as email attachments. If you preferred different settings for any of the options, you could adjust them now.

4 Choose Burn Full-Sized JPEGs from the Lightroom Presets.

5 Note the changes in the export settings. Under Export Location, the subfolder name has changed to Lightroom Burned Exports. In File Settings, the JPEG Quality setting has been set to 100%. In Image Sizing, the Resize To Fit option is disabled. In the Metadata options, Minimize Embedded Metadata is disabled. Once again, you can adjust any of the settings in the preset.

Note: For this preset there are no Post-Processing actions to choose from. After exporting, Lightroom will automatically open the Choose Burner dialog box, where you can nominate your disk burner and specify the burn speed before clicking Burn to start the burn process.

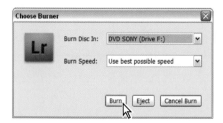

Setting up post-processing actions

You can streamline your export workflow by setting up an automated post-processing action. For example, when you export an image to be used as an e-mail attachment, you could have Lightroom automatically launch your e-mail application and prepare a new message with the exported image attached.

1 Choose For E-Mail from the Lightroom Presets and adjust the settings to your liking.

2 In the Post-Processing options, choose Go To Export Actions Folder Now from the After Export menu.

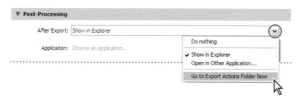

Lightroom opens a Windows Explorer / Finder window with the Export Actions folder already selected. You will place a shortcut or alias for your e-mail application into this folder.

3 Open a second Windows Explorer / Finder window and navigate to the folder containing your e-mail application. Right-click / Control-click the e-mail application icon and choose Create Shortcut / Make Alias from the context menu. Drag the shortcut or alias into the Export Actions folder.

4 Return to Lightroom. In Post-Processing, choose the new shortcut or alias to your e-mail application from the After Export menu.

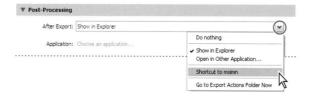

With the current settings you could export an image as a small JPEG file and Lightroom would automatically launch your e-mail application and open a new message with the image already attached. But first, there's one more step that can help automate the process even further.

Creating user presets

You can save your customized export settings as a new user preset. Export presets are always available from the File menu (File > Export With Preset) where you can start your export without having to open the Export dialog first.

1   Click the Add button in the lower left corner of the Export dialog box, just below the list of presets.

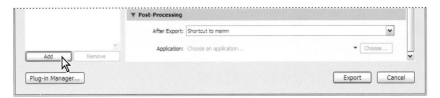

2   In the New Preset dialog box, type **For E-Mail And Attach** as the name for your new preset, choose User Presets from the Folder menu, and then click Create.

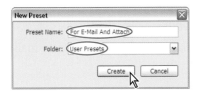

3   You can see that your new preset is now listed under User Presets.

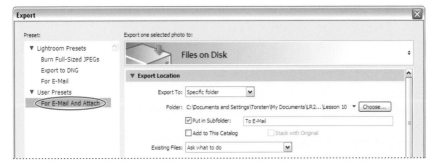

4   Click Cancel to close the Export dialog box without exporting any images.

5   Select one or more images in the Grid view and choose File > Export With Preset > For E-Mail And Attach.

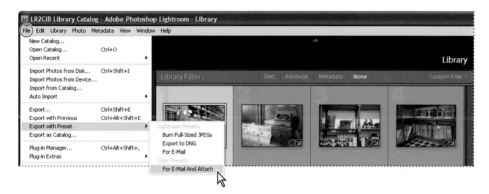

The export process will begin immediately. When exporting is complete, your e-mail application will be launched automatically and will open a new message with your exported photos already attached; all you need a to do is to enter the recipient's e-mail address and you're ready to send.

Review

▶ **Review questions**

1   What are the two basic components of your photo library that need to be backed up regularly?

2   How can you move a selection of images or your entire image library with all the associated catalog information from one computer to another?

3   How can you do an incremental backup of your photo library?

4   How would you choose between file formats for exporting your photos?

5   What is a post-processing action?

▶ **Review answers**

1   The two basic components of the image library are the original image files (or master files) and the library catalog file, which records all the metadata and the complete editing history for every image in the library as well as information about collections, user templates and presets, and settings for presentations and output.

2   On one computer, use the Export As Catalog command to create a catalog file together with copies of the original images and the available previews. On the other computer, use the Import From Catalog command.

3   Lightroom does not have an incremental backup command but once you have created a full backup of the library using Export As Catalog, you can switch to the backup catalog regularly and use the Import From Catalog command to update it. You can configure the import settings so only those images that have been modified since the last backup are imported from the main catalog. In this way, you can keep your existing backup catalog updated incrementally—avoiding the more time consuming process of making a full new backup.

4   The appropriate choice of a file format depends on the intended use of the exported images. To export images for on-screen viewing as e-mail attachments, you'd use the JPEG file format and minimize the file size. To export an image to an external image editing application you'd use PSD or TIFF and export the image

at full size. For archival purposes you can export the images in their original file format or convert them to DNG.

5   A post-processing action is a preset that can help to automate your workflow. You can choose a preset that will automatically burn your images to a CD or DVD after export, or one that will launch your e-mail application and attach your exported images to a new message. You can save your own action presets, which will be listed beside the Lightroom presets in the Export dialog box.

Index

Production Notes

The *Adobe Photoshop Lightroom 2 Classroom in a Book* was created electronically using Adobe InDesign CS2. Additional art was produced using Adobe Illustrator CS2, Adobe Photoshop CS2, and Adobe Photoshop Lightroom 2.

Team credits

The following individuals contributed to the development of this edition of the *Adobe Photoshop Lightroom Classroom in a Book*:

Project coordinators, technical writers: Torsten Buck & Katrin Straub

Production: Manneken Pis Productions (www.manneken.be)

Copyediting & Proofreading: John Evans

Designer: Katrin Straub

Special thanks to Christine Yarrow.

Typefaces used

Set in the Adobe Minion Pro and Adobe Myriad Pro OpenType families of typefaces. More information about OpenType and Adobe fonts is available at Adobe.com.

Photo Credits

Photographic images and illustrations supplied by Katrin Straub, Torsten Buck, John Evans, Klaus Wettermann, Han Buck, and Adobe Systems Incorporated. Photos are for use only with the lessons in the book.

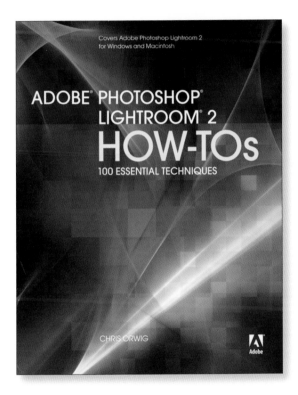
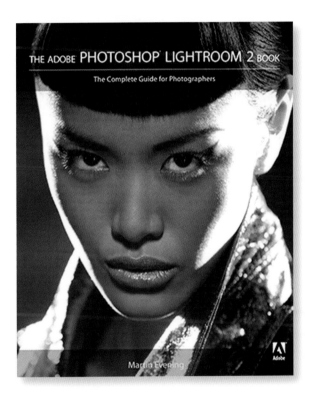

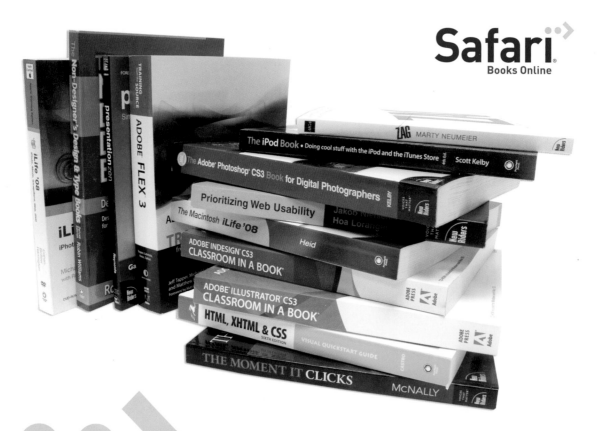